# Half
# Laughing
# Half
# Crying

# Half Laughing Half Crying

# Malcolm Boyd

ST. MARTIN'S PRESS • NEW YORK

*Design by Paolo Pepe*

Library of Congress Cataloging in Publication Data

Boyd, Malcolm, 1923–
Half laughing / half crying.

1. Boyd, Malcolm, 1923–  .  2. Episcopal Church—United States—Clergy—Biography.  3. Anglican Communion—United States—Clergy—Biography.  I. Title.
BX5995.B66A33  1986    283'.3 [B]    85-25194
ISBN 0-312-35663-3

First Edition
10 9 8 7 6 5 4 3 2 1

# To
## Mark Thompson

# Contents

## PART I: LIFE

Photo Album

## PART II: IMAGINATION

# Acknowledgments

Gratitude is expressed to Michael Denneny, my editor, for support, acumen, and sensitivity; Florence Feiler, my agent, for nurturing, wisdom, and perspicacity; and M. R. Ritley, who used her expertise with computerized composition systems, voluntarily and as an act of friendship, to prepare the manuscript for publication.

# Foreword

Malcolm Boyd is the irregular man, the informal man, but, anything but an alienated man, he always prefers to do his work and have his say *within* the peripheries of whatever establishment he is inhabiting.

What Malcolm seems to know mainly by instinct is that his mission is altogether in the American grain. It harks back to the days of Emerson and Theodore Parker and Orestes Brownson, to those restive ministers who found that their church had gone dry, that it was rationalistic and comfortable and far removed from human urgencies, and who, in their attempt to restore vitality to the religious life, expanded their ministerial activities into the whole range of human experience.

Emerson, more of a radical than Malcolm Boyd, eventually "signed off" from his church, but his definition of the role of the minister is close to Malcolm's. It is a question of bringing the church much more closely to bear upon immediate life, of mediating between the religious vision with which one has been entrusted and the common aspirations of common people.

And this involves new forms and idioms of prayer, new rituals of worship, new assumptions of priestly responsibility, new areas—sometimes, literally, new *places*—in which to exercise the religious energy. A new form of the sacramental life. Malcolm, to be sure, can on occasion be a good deal more antic than Emerson allowed himself to be; and though Emerson faced audiences all across the country, it is not easy to think of him performing, as Malcolm has done, in a California nightclub. But I dare say Emerson would have understood the impulse. He understood Whitman and *Leaves of Grass* at once:

> Unscrew the locks from the doors!
> Unscrew the doors themselves from their jambs!
>
> Whoever degrades another degrades me. . . .
>
> Through me many long dumb voices . . .
> Voices of the diseas'd and despairing, and of thieves and
> dwarfs . . . by me clarified and transfigured.

Malcolm's first mature experience was in the most secular field that even this secular culture has to offer: Hollywood and the television industry. Then, after divinity school and postordination study, came the peace marches, the parochial work among the poor, and the victimized ("the diseas'd and despairing"); the startling success of his books of prayers, and the evolution of a new style of religious expression; the campus attachments. Somehow the order of things in this educational process was exactly right.

Amid the general appreciation and enjoyment of his writing, probably not enough attention has been paid to what Malcolm means by "prayer." It is clear what he does *not* mean—he is not presenting us with a series of whining requests to be rescued by abrupt divine intervention from some unholy mess one has gotten oneself into.

Malcolm Boyd is, I would suggest, working within a distinct American rhetorical tradition (a tradition, to be sure, that has very ancient roots). The kind of prayer we encounter in Malcolm's writing was best defined by Emerson in *Nature*, nearly a century and a half ago. "In the uttermost meaning of the words," Emerson said, "thought is devout, and devotion is thought." He went on to ask rhetorically: "Is not prayer a study of truth—a sally of the soul into the unfound infinite."

So understood, a prayer is an *action*—a positive thrust into the circumstances of one's environment—racial, physical, sexual, political, *human*, in a concentrated attempt to gain a fresh fragment of knowledge. It is an adventure. It has, indeed, the same adventurous quality that Robert Frost ascribed to every good poem: it is "a figure of the will braving alien entanglements."

One could marshal other eminent American literary names to chart the tradition in which Malcolm writes his prayers. The point is that his prayers belong to a definite literary genre. And it is very opportune that they should do so. The impulse to pray is surely fundamental to human nature; all of us at times want to think devoutly, to borrow Emerson's formula, and we obviously have a lot to pray about (that is, to confront, penetrate, understand) at the present moment. Malcolm Boyd provides us with a form of expression in which we can take that action in a manner both contemporary and traditional.

*—R. W. B. Lewis*
*Yale University*

# Half Laughing Half Crying

# Introduction

Assembling the material for this book sharpened my perception of how I've lived not just one life, but several. At times the links between them have seemed obscure, even contradictory.

Always, I've been a writer. This caused me at the outset to interview artists and writers for the newspaper in my junior high school. Later, I wrote poems, prayers, numberless reviews and articles, and twenty books.

From the start I have been gay, although I didn't understand for a long time what this meant. How could I "be myself" as a gay boy and man? This question grew more complicated when, in my early thirties, I became a priest. My innermost identity seemed under a harsh judgment closely tied to that *other* part of myself. What was I supposed to do with seemingly inimical pieces of my life?

Working in Hollywood, it was my fortune to see fabled success and world celebrity at close range. To my astonishment, they often came to resemble abject failure. Underneath expensive wrappings I found loneliness, selfishness, spiritual decay, and egomania out of sync with human caring and a sense of mutuality.

My Hollywood life had seemed dilettantish, glitzy, very close to the surface. The next phase occurred inside a theological seminary. I decided that I wanted to help other people; wished my life to stand for more than "making it." I wasn't self-righteous so much as hurting; didn't there have to be more to one's brief life than glitter and taking? Where could I find peace and fulfillment?

Could I delve deeper, follow pursuits of serious thought and culture, even exercise the unused muscle of my soul?

I would try. During the ensuing six years—which included study at Berkeley, Oxford, the Ecumenical Institute in Switzerland, and Union Theological Seminary in New York—my Humpty Dumpty indeed fell off the wall. The pieces were scattered, then reassembled. One day I looked over my shoulder and realized I'd become a vastly different person.

However, this was only the beginning of a growth process that awaited me. Beyond caring for the needy, and harboring a vulnerable sensitivity, I had virtually no social consciousness. Events outside my life, coupled with the experience of working in a midwestern slum parish and later a college chaplaincy, soon led me into nearly full-time participation in the civil rights movement.

I watched incredulously as I seemed to become someone else, again. A privileged Establishment white person, long ensconced within boundaries of my own career or within cloistered walls, I now found myself walking through extreme danger in situations that took the lives of some of my friends. Working for civil rights was demanding, unsafe, plotted to change society. Participation in the peace movement followed; twice I was arrested inside the Pentagon in antiwar peace masses.

Ironically, critics who did not like me as a social activist suddenly smiled upon the same activist when he wrote a best-selling book.

When I came out of the closet in 1976 and told the world I am gay, I moved closer to wholeness as a person. One part of myself was finally reconciled to the rest of me. However, the mother of a friend of mine reacted angrily by burning my books in her backyard; a number of associates in organized religion vanished from my view as quickly as if they had melted on a summer's day.

Yet an open, dynamic, highly creative church invited me to climb aboard and become a vital part of its community. For the past several years I have functioned as writer-priest-in-residence at St. Augustine by-the-Sea Episcopal Church in Santa Monica, California. My activities have also included being president of the Los Angeles Center of PEN and a member of the AIDS Task Force of the City and County of Los Angeles.

My life thrusts forward, and I realize that the year 2000 is curiously within my reach. But, even as I stress living in the present, it is salutary to look backward. Need I say: this book is an exercise in integrating parts to the whole. Why did I choose *these* particular selections for inclusion in this book? Because they represent the major themes, ideas, commitments, and thrusts of my life up to now, in the form of my experience and my response to it. These range from Hollywood to the priesthood, civil rights to working as a performer at San Francisco's hungry i, writing in Israel to being a gay man in America. A major part of this material has never appeared in print before.

—*Malcolm Boyd*
*Santa Monica, California*
*June 1985*

# PART I:
# LIFE

*Following is what can be described as a montage. A reader will discover counterpoint in the storytelling; a balance between objective and subjective, linear and poetic, the expository and reflective, experience in the world and experience of the world within.*

# Hollywood

I packed my suitcase with very few things—wouldn't life be a simple matter now?—and on an early September morning in 1951, got into my car and started the drive from Hollywood to the theological seminary in Berkeley, California, where I would spend the next three years of my life.

What did I feel? The elation of expectation and enough hope to cover my fear. I was actively setting out, on that September morning, upon a pilgrimage inside as well as outside myself. On the morning I began driving toward the seminary, "God" was as hidden from me as my "brother" or "sister." Although I felt quite alone, I knew for certain that I was commencing a complex journey, a journey on which I would meet strangers.

When it was announced in the press that I was leaving Hollywood to enter a seminary, the story shared space with reports of a leading film idol's tragic, unexpected death and a suicide attempt by a prominent actress. All three stories were headlined in identical shocking boldface type.

At the going-away party for me (it was at the old Ciro's on Sunset Strip), even the bartenders stood and bowed their heads when the Lord's Prayer was said. Many people wept openly. They seemed to see the whole thing almost as a funeral—certainly not a joyful new beginning in life.

I sat on a dais, flanked by several Hollywood stars and a priest. After we ate, people stood up one by one to eulogize me. The mood was terribly sad. To them, religion obviously meant an area closed off from real life. Here I sat, a lively, enthusiastic young man with whom everybody in the room had enjoyed some kind of human relationship—and I was about to walk inside the forbidden ghetto of religion and close the door behind me. Some songs were offered. The priest prayed. Finally, I got up to say a few words. I nearly broke down. If the truth was faced—and everybody present was facing it—I was throwing out an irrevocable good-by to life *here* and *now*. Inside the religious stockade, would my head be shaved? Could I receive mail in the cell where I would be engaged in meditation all day? "Can I write to you?"

•    •    •

Candles flicker on a high altar.
   I am a young boy kneeling inside a great cathedral
      during the Holy Eucharist.
   I hear a priest's voice saying the words.
   Then a shuffling of feet as people go up to the
      altar.
I am praying
   For my mother
   For my father
   For my grandmother
   For my dead grandfather
   For my schoolwork
God is listening
   God is inside this holy place
   Be quiet in his presence
   Think holy thoughts.

•    •    •

Seven years earlier, one of the half-dozen largest advertising agencies in the country had hired me for its Hollywood office. I was to learn the business from the inside. I was soon producing my own radio show, a fifteen-minute, five-times-a-week, "live" network program, featuring a philosopher, a home economist, and Buddy Cole, who played a combination organ-celeste-piano.

In addition, I was agency contact man for both a Sunday-evening high-rated newscast and a daily network soap opera.

I smelled clean. I had the antiseptic, remote look of success. My suit was a paragon among suits, my shoes carried the aroma of fresh leather, my ties had an avant-garde relationship with my shirts. My barber had a celebrity clientele on an appointment basis. I dined on an expense account, and the martini before lunch became a sacrament. I dated very beautiful young starlets. My deodorant, after-shave, and cologne made me a walking collection of tasteful smells. Chatting with stars, writers, producers, and others who were then making the Hollywood scene, I was seething inside with macabre visions of success, while outwardly learning how to cultivate cool. I wanted more success. The people with whom I worked had already achieved it.

My real interest was in writing scripts. Night after night I returned to my office to spend hours at the typewriter. I had a friend who, like me, was an ambitious young man working in communications. We sat up together many nights, fashioning a script idea that nobody wanted. We considered ourselves sorry failures. I was delighted to find, several years later, that Bob Merrill had hit his stride in songwriting, probably best known as the writer of the lyrics for *Funny Girl*.

I wrote a script about an alchemist for a series called *The Count of Monte Cristo*. The setting was medieval; the plot laden with action and mystery. Time ran out at the end of the program so my writing credit had to be eliminated in the rush to get off the air—I was heartbroken. I did a lot of research for *Mainline*, a program about trains, for which the train sounds had to be accurately described in the script. The sound man was far more important than the actors. To my horror, just before the show I noticed that he had had a lot of drinks. I stood petrified inside the control booth, watching him do work that seemed as precise as that of a wood carver. He mixed train whistles and choo-choos with voices, faded locomotives in and passing trains out, raised a majestic train sound while increasing yet another train's speed to heighten the drama; it was thrilling to hear. All this without missing a cue or seeming to stop for breath, although he was sweating hard. When the show was over, we bought him black coffee.

I was "the kid" in the advertising agency. At the end of a long day, I joined the old-timers for drinks at their favorite bars. I learned agency politics and found out what gave ad men their ulcers. Along with the ribbing I got came a welcome to almost any events going on inside or outside the agency.

My first Hollywood office party was a complex affair. I was asked to mix drinks and to see that a particular guest—the mistress of a tycoon—received very, very stiff ones. This was ostensibly to test the legend of her wooden leg. Naturally, she drank everybody else under the table, showing none of the ravages of liquor or power politics. The latter she knew well: She had come to her present eminent position from lowly beginnings on the tycoon's switchboard, later moving into his public relations department. I learned afterward that she finally married him. When he died, she inherited his empire.

•      •      •

> My heart is turning to aluminum, my balls steel, my
>       liver silver, my soul gold.
>    To be totally functional would mean not to waste
>       work hours.
>    Laughter could be filed on old tapes. I might eliminate
>       pain, depression, and fear.
>    Credo: Do; don't be.
>    *How* not to turn into a machine?

•      •      •

The agency had a radio show starring a top musical personality who hit the bottle whenever his program was being taped for the network. Every week the ritual was repeated. The director and production crew gathered, waiting for the star, who was hosting a party next door at a prestigious restaurant. Finally—only after the musicians had gone on "golden hours" (overtime) and the budget had once again snapped—the star arrived to start taping. Even then the atmosphere was charged with temperament, missed cues, and infighting. I always attended these taping sessions, somewhat in awe of the combined glamour, power, and madness. One night the agency producer, after concluding the taping, evidently returned to his office and kicked a gaping hole in the door. We found it the next morning along with a cryptic note of resignation. The door was famous for a day; other agency people arrived to look at it, muttering suitably lugubrious remarks, casting glances heavenward, and gnashing their teeth (this life was rough for them, too). He never returned. I missed him.

As "the kid," I was not threatening to anybody. From my place in the circle I could see all but was seldom asked to speak. I spent some time in the downtown Los Angeles office of the agency. It was a block from Pershing Square, which used to be a palm-tree-lined square block where speakers harangued anyone who would listen, debates springing up at a moment's notice. It was like Hyde Park Corner in London.

I knew little about Pershing Square at that time. One afternoon, after an agency luncheon downtown, I decided to take my first walk through it. A sharp debate was going on. I stopped to listen for a few minutes. My blood pressure was stirred a bit, but not too seriously because I was thoroughly the junior executive in a major ad agency: my role was to be quiet, earnest, and dignified in a youthful way, as befitted someone being groomed for advancement in the club.

Moving on from that sharp debate, I came to yet another one. This time I became angered by what I heard, but kept my temper in check. However, just ahead a third man was delivering a raucously ideological message with which I found myself in violent disagreement. He was addressing a growing and spirited crowd. Shouting "Now, wait a minute!" I fought my way through to the speaker. Delighted to have an opponent, especially a junior executive type, he gave me a soapbox to stand on. We went at it furiously. The crowd seemed vastly entertained. After a while, looking out over the crowd, I was discomfited to see two of the top agency men standing on the sidelines, looking quizzically and with cool disdain on the scene. I was acting distinctly out of character—that is, out of my correct image. Without a word or a hint of recognition, they went executively on their way.

The show I had been producing was to move to San Francisco. It was at that time a place best suited for persons in the industry who were retired or independently wealthy. I was neither. I went job-hunting in Hollywood again. The large motion picture studios employed specialists to act in a liaison capacity with the then supremely important radio industry, representing both literary properties and film personalities to be utilized on radio programs. The purpose was nationwide publicity for new movie releases. I was hired as such a liaison man, as well as publicity unit-man on some movies. My salary leaped.

Here was the celebrity system, not as an abstraction or occasion for rhetoric, but in the flesh. Here was the motion picture, not as art but as pure commercial. This was exploitation straight-across-the-board. (My title was actually "director of radio exploitation.") Here was the curious tribal world: studio chiefs, mistresses receiving homage, forgotten wives who came out of retirement once a year to pour at stockholders' meetings, alcoholic old directors (some clutching their Oscars) and bright new ones on the make, writers who frankly considered themselves whores alongside others who felt they were Faulkners, friendly switchboard operators, and hard starlets lugging their mothers around with them.

Mildred Thornton, business associate of a top movie producer, who had company stock literally pasted on the soles of her shoes, sidled up to me. It was about eleven and the party was going full swing. An old-fashioned in hand, I was standing expectantly on the sidelines. I'd never had a good chance to become acquainted with Mildred Thornton and had just about decided to wipe out my error. She seemed to have the same idea.

I wondered what made her one of the most stunning women in the room and decided it was her bearing. Her slightly graying hair was piled on top of her head, and she was wearing a regal-looking white satin gown. The fact that she was weighted down with enough diamonds to sink the *Queen Elizabeth* was one of the few indications she was pushing fifty. I knew she'd been married once, a long time ago, and wondered who in hell she belonged to now.

"Who do you think is the most attractive woman here?" she asked me.

"I don't think you take second place," I told her, meaning what I said—if she could lose ten years.

"Come now," Mildred laughed in her tired, bored voice, which wasn't really either tired or bored. "Let's not stand on formality."

Two friends of mine were writers. They spent their days grinding out portions of scripts in the writers' building. What a factory it was. After a script had supposedly been completed, a second writer would invariably work on it, restructuring it and providing new dialogue. My writer friends went to studio sneak previews of their films. They were not invited, but got word via a grapevine as complex and foolproof as that of a medieval court. Sometimes I tagged along. Often the writers couldn't make sense of a film for which they had been given screen credit. They might not even be able to recognize several of the characters. The bewildered writers generally ended up getting loaded. It was all very funny and very destructive.

I was working in my Hollywood office on a Saturday morning, trying to catch up on paper work on a day when the switchboard would be closed and interruptions minimal. Loud voices outside my window distracted me. They continued, growing in intensity. I leaped from my desk and ran to the window. Two men stood, talking, on the pavement below. I would outshout them, ordering them to be more quiet and considerate. Just in time I noticed that one of the men was Samuel Goldwyn, the studio chief. The other was Howard Hughes. I retreated in silence from the window.

A production assignment once kept me working at a film studio for three nights in a row. I was tired and angry when the third night rolled around. A union regulation stipulated that personnel directly related to my project must be given a time break and fed at midnight. I decided management needed to be taught to respect workers' feelings. I contacted the most expensive catering service in Beverly Hills. Could they cater a sit-down dinner party at midnight? Yes?

At twelve o'clock, on an empty, dimly lighted, ghost-ridden soundstage in the studio, a curious, perhaps unprecedented affair began. I invited the night guards to join us; I compelled the cleaning women. Dinner was preceded by cocktails. Shrimp came before the steak entrees. There was wine. The desserts were lavish pastries. The cost was outrageous.

The next morning, I was called in by a studio executive. I was fired, he said. No, I replied, I quit. He looked disconcerted. Would I reconsider and stay, he asked. No, I definitely would not, I said. He begged me to stay. All right, I said, if I were given a raise. He consented. I departed his office with an anomalous new dignity within the studio.

I went to San Francisco on a vacation where I spent all my money. Returning to Hollywood, I found that I had been fired.

It had all seemed so important, and I had felt important because I was part of it. At least I had worked hard at it. I had quite sincerely *tried* (whatever that meant) but suddenly what I had accomplished on the job didn't mean very much. When I knew I was leaving I wasn't sure of anything any more—what I'd be taking with me, or what I'd be leaving behind.

Remembering how quickly others had been forgotten, on the very last day I took a penknife and carved my initials—very small —on the bottom part of the wooden desk in my office. It was absurd, of course, but I had left a mark. Even then, part of me realized that the only real way to leave a mark was to do something with my life, to use it in a way that would have meaning, but at the time I didn't think I could.

The next day I was gone, the hidden mark remained, and the telephone rang in my empty office.

Now, instead of job-hunting, I decided I wanted to write a novel. A friend provided an office for me to work in. I checked in every night at seven o'clock and wrote until dawn, interrupted only by the cheerful greeting of cleaning women. I started to make my novel a mystery but unfortunately ended up by trying to render a serious social commentary. I was represented by an excellent Beverly Hills literary agent who sent the completed manuscript to a New York colleague. She replied: "I have now read the manuscript and agree with you that Mr. Boyd has not written another 'Hucksters.' In fact, the whole novel, which has considerable merit, suffers from attempting to do a more serious job than it accomplished. As a matter of fact, when I first started it I thought it was going to be an extremely superior 'whodunit' and when I discovered it was not, it became pretty pretentious in my opinion. I still think it should be a murder story and in this category it would be outstanding. I don't suppose, though, that the author will agree to this. Thank you for the opportunity of letting me see this novel. I really do think there is a property here if the author is willing to revise."

The author was not.

Because of my previous contact with liaison work for the major movie studios, I decided that the independent movie producers, who were mushrooming all over Hollywood, needed their own liaison with radio. One fine New Year's Day in Southern California I opened up Mal Boyd & Associates, to represent a group of independent motion-picture producers.

As one of its first assignments, my office handled the radio exploitation for an insignificant film called *It Happened on Fifth Avenue*. The presence of Victor Moore in the cast was the only good thing about the picture. I was given a Fifth Avenue bus, which had been driven to the West Coast from New York by order of the producer. I worked out an arrangement with a women's daytime radio program on one of the major networks. I would take a busload of women from the studio audience for a sightseeing ride to the homes of various motion picture stars. A report of the trip would be made on a subsequent program; a motion-picture magazine would photograph the event.

One morning, after the show, network ushers in uniform escorted a group of selected women into the bus waiting at the curb outside the studio. Our strange pilgrimage got under way. Most of the women were excited about the idea but a few were actually tearful. They said good-bys to husbands and children, and were to return in late afternoon. Lunch on the bus was catered by Hugo, the Hot Dog King.

The first stop was the Beverly Hills mansion of Maria Montez and her husband, Jean-Pierre Aumont. Montez was at home in bed that day because the astrologer, whose advice she scrupulously followed, had warned of mishap if she left home. Outside, the women from the bus stomped in their high heels through the wet soil of a freshly planted garden. Then they walked into the mansion with its white wall-to-wall carpeting. Aumont graciously entertained. A cat vomited on the carpet stair off the den. It was a bad omen.

The next stop was Pickfair, the fabled estate of Mary Pickford, located up the hill from the mansion of Montez and Aumont. When the women, the members of my staff, and a half-dozen films stars who were accompanying us boarded the bus for the next excursion, we discovered that the bus could not manage the sharp incline. We asked several people to get off and await a second trip. But still the bus could not make it. It would start grinding up the hill, then come crashing back dangerously near the Montez-Aumont driveway. I decided that a fleet of cars should be summoned to take us, in relays, up the hill to Pickfair. Meanwhile, our schedule was wrecked.

After Pickfair, next on our agenda was the home of Jeanette MacDonald and her husband, Gene Raymond. The middle-aged women, crowding around the well-known couple in the garden, seemed momentarily almost overcome by this proximity to Hollywood holiness. They reached out with timid aggressiveness to touch MacDonald's gown. Tears came to the eyes of a few.

The Paul Henreid home at Malibu was on our list but had to be scratched. We were running very, very late. However, we managed to visit the home of Peter Lawford and his parents. It was near Pacific Palisades. When we got there, young Peter was out playing cricket or football somewhere, but Lady Lawford invited my staff to come inside for a quick libation that she sensed we badly needed. Due to the limitation of time, the women remained in the bus observing the facade of the Lawford residence.

When we emerged from the house a few minutes later, the bus had vanished.

It was a bad moment. Perhaps the occupants were lying in a ditch somewhere beneath an overturned bus that they had commandeered from the driver following a decision to mutiny. We soon learned that, fortunately, they had merely decided to use—immediately—the closest public restroom facilities they could find. Lady Lawford, who had driven with her maid to a nearby bus stop, came back to tell us that the occupants were queuing up outside the ladies' room of a gasoline station several blocks away. As soon as they returned, by unspoken assent we headed quickly back down Sunset Boulevard toward the heart of Hollywood. Light was rapidly diminishing. Husbands were no doubt worrying.

To bolster sagging morale, I led the occupants of the Fifth Avenue bus in song. We were in the middle of "Three Blind Mice" when the bus passed the Cock 'n' Bull bar and restaurant on Sunset Strip. At that moment the indefatigably sophisticated Monty Woolley emerged from the doorway. He caught one glimpse of the Fifth Avenue bus speeding by, heard the briefest strain of "Three Blind Mice," then urbanely turned back into the bar.

On another occasion my radio promotion featured a cow. The "Queen for a Day," on the now-defunct network radio program of that name, had received a cow as one of her gifts. It came from a leading dairy products firm. It was arranged that the queen, accompanied by her cow, would visit cowboy star Roy Rogers' famous horse, Trigger, at his farm. Photographers would be present to record the classic meeting. Roy Rogers' new movie would receive publicity on "Queen for a Day."

A fleet of black limousines bore the queen, a group of somber advertising men, the cow, and me out to the farm. The cow rode in the rear, in a trailer attached to the last car of the entourage. Liveried chauffeurs drove each of the five or six cars. The cow was extremely irritable; it needed to be milked, but nobody seemed to know how. As we drove along residential streets to reach the farm, children ran alongside the elegant open trailer bearing the discomfited cow.

At the farm the creature was led forth, along with the queen, to stand next to Trigger for photographs. Kids had by now gathered in a circle around us, gripped by a proper awe. I will never be sure what happened next. It seems that the queen, quite innocently, had tweaked the cow's ear. The beast was gone in a cloud of dust. The dead-serious ad men, in their shiny black shoes and expensive black suits, were soon lost in the cloud in hot pursuit. During the confusion, one huckster, who had decided not to take part in the hunt, sidled up to me. Would I, he asked, take special care with the photo captions. I said I would. They should stress, he continued, that the cow had been provided by the firm's canned milk division, not its fresh milk division. . . .

Soon the creature was captured and the tableau regrouped itself. Trigger, the queen, and the subdued cow were photographed for posterity. The queen good-naturedly wore a combination of her own clothes and gifts that had been showered on her. Over her housedress she gallantly sported a double silver-fox fur. On her head was a modish new hat; on her feet, her old flat shoes. Her fingers and arms fairly glittered with pieces of gift jewelry. I admired her good grace and sense of humor about it all. However, trouble lay ahead with the cow. That afternoon, the beast was manicured, feet and tail, by a leading cosmetics house. All went smoothly. But in the evening, while accompanying the queen to dinner, the cow had an unfortunate accident on the carpet of a nightclub.

HOLLYWOOD

The film colony was always impressed by a foreign accent, preferably British, and by journalistic credentials from London, Paris, Rome—or even Toronto. I gave a party for a visiting Canadian journalist in my modest bungalow in the hills of Hollywood. To my great surprise, a picture magazine suddenly decided to "cover" the party, and all the film studios in town were calling me to tell me which of their stars, accompanied by which press agents and photographers, were planning to attend.

The guests didn't trickle in—they arrived like a tidal wave. Almost immediately, people were queuing up for use of the single washroom, with its slow-running lavatory and quaint old hook on the door. Everybody moved, as if caught in a restless charade, round and round the modest rooms. Elizabeth Taylor remarked that the overcrowded party resembled the Black Hole of Calcutta. The mystery writer Craig Rice was seated on a couch pillow that slowly but steadily slipped backward until she was seated at a construction-crane tilt. She was nonchalantly continuing a conversation with a celebrated male star whose pillow had not been slipping; the contrast in angles was bizarre.

An important columnist became involved in an altercation with police officers. They were towing away his car. When he argued with them, he was taken to jail for the night and placed in the drunk tank. Ironically he had not been drinking but had merely stepped outside to his car to get his ulcer pills from the glove compartment. Some sixty cars were ticketed by the police.

The neighborhood was in an uproar. On one of the wettest nights of recent days, with rain cascading down the hills, no one could move or park a car within blocks due to the total jam created by my guests.

Photographers were flashing pictures, columnists and reporters taking notes. Celebrities moved in and out of the cottage with the abandon of children. While raking leaves in the yard the next day, trying to cope aggressively with a hangover, I discovered an expensive pair of eyeglasses, but never could locate the owner. I saw marks indicating how, instead of walking down my winding path, he had simply slid along a muddy knoll to the street below.

The night before, two prominent actors had engaged in a fistfight in front of the living room fireplace. One celebrated couple—both married to other people—had made love in my bedroom.

•     •     •

A rainy day in Hollywood.
    The movie studio is like a walled city
    It has a king
    It has a court
    The court gossip today is ingrown and fierce
    Everybody is talking about a mortal threat to a duke
    Blood is in men's eyes
    Studio walls, used to sun, are gray and wet
    The wet stucco smells
Let's have an extraordinary lunch!
    We'll use a studio limousine and driver
    We'll include a columnist so as to put everything on
        the expense account
    That posh new place on the Strip
    He makes the best martinis in town
    They have a roaring fire in a grate
    My God, we'll be warm
    Let's stay there all afternoon
    And plot some baroque scheme that will be fun, not
        power
    Tomorrow the sun will shine again.
    But oh the longing
    For a good plain resolve
    For a sturdy heart
    And a loaf of hot bread.

•     •     •

Undoubtedly, I was looking for a playwright, priest, or prophet who might present me with the accoutrements of my identity. I knew there had always been a form to my life, although I could not have defined it. The self: Malcolm. Who was he? At first, words had constituted my reality. Love. Success. Happiness. But I had never known what the words meant. Surely many sounds and images flowed into and through these words: I knew what it was to dream. My heart was still closed in upon itself. I could not comprehend either myself as a real person or the world as a real world.

It is hard for me now to feel a relationship with myself then. A great deal of what is called glamour touched my life, but only very lightly on the surface. I moved in the company of Stars and Other Successful People in a strange setting called Hollywood. I might rub elbows with Ava Gardner or Gary Cooper, Ingrid Bergman or Clark Gable. Dancing late at Mocambo's on a week night, I might find Lana Turner on the uncrowded dance floor. At a party or screening, Louella Parsons or Hedda Hopper, the royal chroniclers of the magic scene, might enter, transforming the so-so event into an *important* one.

One New Year's Eve I was driving, with Charles Chaplin, Jr., from one popular nightclub to another in a new black Cadillac his father had just given him. We had both been drinking. The accident occurred on Sunset Strip in front of the old Mocambo club. Charlie ran his car into another brand-new Cadillac—driven by my boss at Samuel Goldwyn Studios, where I was working on an assignment. The *cause célèbre* that ensued monopolized newspaper headlines for days. Charlie's father, the great comedian, was being pilloried by the media, and shortly afterward he left Hollywood for Europe.

Television had started; I became one of the first West Coast producers. I also appeared in an early Hollywood TV series. My function was to interview celebrity guests. Foolishly, I attempted to memorize a script rather than ad-lib. On my first show I was to walk through a door, make a few opening remarks, and introduce a guest. The door stuck. I had to kick it open. Then, with sweat pouring down my face, which was stiff with pancake make-up, I confronted the camera with a glazed smile, and parroted the lines I had learned by rote.

We had no money to pay guest stars in those days. Kirk Douglas, Ruth Roman, Charles Brackett, the producer, and James Wong Howe, the cinematographer, all appeared on one of my programs—without fee; Edgar Bergen and Charlie McCarthy made their TV debut on another. Two fledgling comics, Dean Martin and Jerry Lewis, did a routine one night. Gloria Swanson appeared on one of my shows just a week prior to beginning her screen comeback in *Sunset Boulevard.* A leading hat designer had provided a number of his millinery creations for the show and sent them to the studio in an armored car. He broke off further contact with us afterward because Miss Swanson, enthusiastically following the script, scattered several of the hats across the floor.

Those early days in television were fun. Of course, they were not without their seriousness, but it was seldom comprehended. Some of us were involved in a communications complex that was molding the thought and action patterns of millions of people. This did not, I think, tellingly break into our consciousness. Anyway, we had deadlines, budgets, ratings, guest stars, new formats, and audiences to worry about.

Yet a group of television producers, acting out of a sense of social responsibility, formed an association. I was elected president of the Television Producers Association of Hollywood. We organized a small committee to engage in drafting a self-censorship code. As a member of this committee, I considered it more important to criticize the dehumanizing caricature of a black person and the comic stereotype of a Chinese cook with long pigtails than to determine exactly how much of a woman's breast might be revealed on screen.

One of the independent producers for whom I acted as liaison with the radio industry was Triangle Productions. Its owners were Mary Pickford, Buddy Rogers, and Ralph Cohn. Miss Pickford and her husband were remote, legendary figures to me. Mary Pickford had been Hollywood's first major woman star. Her partners at United Artists had included Charlie Chaplin and Douglas Fairbanks; their triumvirate represented the industry's best-known personalities. Buddy Rogers had once topped all

Hollywood stars in fan mail, after the release of *Wings* in the late twenties, and had later become a noted bandleader. When Mary Pickford divorced Douglas Fairbanks, she married Buddy Rogers.

When I negotiated a network show for Buddy in New York, Miss Pickford closed her estate, Pickfair, to join her husband there. The three of us formed a packaging-production firm in New York called P.R.B., Inc., the initials representing our last names.

On the evening before I was to fly from Hollywood to New York to set up the machinery of our P.R.B. operation there, Mary gave a large reception at Pickfair for visiting journalists from various parts of the world. This was at the request of the U.S. State Department. An orchestra played on the lawn, Hollywood celebrities mingled with foreign reporters, and caviar by the tray was served along with champagne by the gallon.

Mary had, within this century, stirred millions of people in every corner of the world. Once, in a city square in Europe, thousands stood expressing adulation by moving their hands in a clapping motion—yet without making the noise of applause, for they had been told Miss Pickford felt ill.

I was able to see Mary in action with the public when, during my seminary days in Berkeley, California, she visited San Francisco as co-chair, with Mrs. Dwight D. Eisenhower, of a savings bond campaign. I stayed with her then. She won over any crowd at the drop of a hat. Television was new to her, yet she was candid and winning when she appeared on it.

A millionairess, Mary was frugal about small expenses. I dined with her one night in her suite at the Pierre in New York. She had ordered finnan haddie and boiled potatoes. She did not feel particularly hungry, she said. Might we not share a single order?

Once when I had been overworking and was dangerously tired, Mary suggested that I stay in the guest house at Pickfair, which was secluded and quiet. Queen Marie of Rumania had stayed there, so had the Mountbattens of England. The guest house possessed graceful elegance and pastiche; Mary's Academy Award Oscar was casually present in it. (During those years I helped to select the Oscar winners as a voting member of the Academy of Motion Picture Arts and Sciences.) I would spend my days at the pool, soothing my tired body and frayed nerves.

The first night, the butler turned down my bed, placed a pitcher of fresh water on the night table and early editions of the two morning newspapers on the bed, and told me that if burglars broke into the house during the night, seeking Mary's jewels, I should not be alarmed but merely punch a button that would quickly summon the Beverly Hills police. Thanks to this casual warning, I doubt that I slept a wink at night during my entire stay in the guest house, relying on sun and naps by the pool during the days to pull me through.

Mary drank, oh so sadly, during that time. The pressures of being the first great motion picture star, a business executive, and a living idol, were enormous. I've often thought that in a crazy way Mary was Marilyn Monroe, who lived all the long years to the end of the dream. I spent excruciatingly painful hours with Mary when she was drinking. At these times she seemed to have an uncanny, instinctively true insight into the dark midnight of her own soul. Finally, Mary withdrew from the world, living in a reclusive closet. Possibly, when she could no longer control life, she left it. Or, at least, narrowed it to a dimension of her power.

That power is exemplified in a visit Mary once made to San Simeon, William Randolph Hearst's estate. She flew up from Beverly Hills in a private plane. Arriving at San Simeon, Mary had a headache. She asked a butler for a glass of milk and a sandwich. He regretfully informed her that Mr. Hearst had issued a firm order that guests not be served food between meals. But, a glass of milk? To help assuage a headache? The butler said no. "Order my plane," replied Mary, who returned forthwith to Pickfair, where she presumably drank a glass of milk and ate a sandwich. She and Hearst remained friends, but she never visited San Simeon again.

One summer when I was a seminarian, Mary drove to Santa Barbara to visit me in a monastery where I was spending the summer. The prior invited her to tea.

He also asked a local socialite to prepare the accoutrements of a "proper tea." In awe of Mary's reputation as a world celebrity, the woman wished to make an impression. She overdressed, wore jewels, and brought along a silver service.

Mary wore a simple dress and no jewelry except her wedding ring. She had her chauffeur wait in town, and drove alone to the monastery nestled in the hills.

During the afternoon, Mary starred in a low-key drama. The brittle, gushing, bejeweled socialite name-dropped other movie stars, included Noel Coward, even the royal family in faraway Buckingham Palace. An orphan in a storm, Mary sought solace. She found it in the person of the white-robed prior. Caught by his steady gaze, warmed by his resonant voice, she engaged him in a discussion of metaphysics. Sipping clear tea, Mary declined sweets.

Mary deserved another Oscar for her performance as a beleaguered empress within a stark Byzantine drama in a monastery setting. Shades of Caesaro-papism. One sensed the presence of plotting courtiers lurking amid chapel shadows and tapestried corridors. Was poison concealed in an emerald ring? Did an army wait outside, ready to strike at an instant's notice?

The hinterland socialite talked ever more stridently of dukes and queens. Mary's voice grew eloquently still. Now, almost in a whisper, she spoke only of God.

# *Boy*

The soft light in the hallway seemed to flicker. There were footsteps on the stairs. My heart pounded. The footsteps were heavy —one, two, one, two. They came to the head of the stairs outside my room. It was the German woman who had been hired to stay with me while my parents went out to the theater.

I knew that she did not like me. She treated me kindly when my parents were with us, but showed a cold hostility when we were alone. What did she want? Now the footsteps ended. I must act as if I were asleep. I dared not move my eyelids or any part of my body. My back itched. My left leg felt as if it had a cramp.

The footsteps began again, creaking on the floor as they approached my bed. I wanted to cry out, leap from my sheets and blankets, and run toward the door. But she would catch me. She must be looking down at my body in the long silence. Was she going to lock me in a dark closet and tell me a large white rat would eat me? Even worse, would she cook me in a great stew? She would tell my father and mother, when they came home, that I had run away. They would believe her and the terrible injustice would stand. Don't let her do this to me! I heard her footsteps on the floor. She was going away, down the stairs.

I must have fallen asleep. Suddenly, as if they had just begun speaking, two voices broke into my hearing. They were angry. I listened harder. They belonged to my father and mother. I almost jumped out of my bed to run into their room. I was happy they had come home. I was safe again.

But the anger in their voices warned me. I lay still in my bed, listening. Then my mother said that she could not stand it any longer. My father swore at her. I heard a crash. What had happened? Was one of them hurt? I heard a door slam, and there was silence in the next room except for my mother's crying. The next morning I saw what had crashed. It was the glass covering a photograph of my father that always stood on their dresser.

All the next day the mood in the house was ominous. No one talked. I was treated as a child who did not know what had happened. That night my father and mother talked to me at the dinner table. They were going to separate, my mother said. That meant they would not live together anymore. My father took me up on his lap to hold me. He said they both wanted me to be happy. Would I decide which one of them I wanted to live with?

The next day, running at the beach, with the sand between my toes, in my eyes and mouth, I felt that my heart had closed in on itself.

How much can a child understand?

• • •

We were in search of a ghost.

It was a moonlit autumn night. We drove to the outskirts of the town to visit the haunted house of Count Arhyaz. No one knew if Count Arhyaz had ever actually existed, but according to local folklore his house turned into a ghost-packed castle at night. He was supposed to haunt the place.

My three friends and I—all of us students in the same high school—walked around the stone wall surrounding the house. Did a single light flicker in an upstairs window? The night was deathly quiet.

Shortly past midnight, we hoisted our bodies over the ivy-covered wall into a weed-filled remnant of a garden. The gaunt branches of a tree, heavy with dead leaves, reached ominously toward us. I bumped into a stone birdbath. The air was frigid, and our bodies grew cold as we ran from bush to bush, tree to tree, drawing closer to the house.

Legend had it that a gigantic hound dog ran wild in the garden at night. The maddened mastiff was supposed to tear to pieces anyone who entered the grounds. Did we hear the baying of the great dog under the half-moon?

Now we stood in the frozen air outside the back door of Count Arhyaz's castle. Suddenly a twig crackled underfoot. Afterward all of us remembered vividly Count Arhyaz's face, bloodless and whiter than snow. Didn't he stretch out his hand, start walking toward us? I would swear for years that he resembled Frankenstein's monster.

Propelling our bodies in manic high energy across dead leaves, we cried and shouted in desperate fear. Then we thrust ourselves over the wall, ran to our car, which had taken on the appearance of a hearse in the moonlight, and drove furiously away.

Over cups of hot chocolate at a diner in town, we did not talk to each other, but sat in a booth shivering from the cold and memories. Ghosts rattled around beneath our consciousness, refusing to come out and talk in the spacious and warm room where the electric lights blazed.

•    •    •

On the evening when Orson Welles produced his classic radio broadcast about an imaginary Martian invasion of earth, I attended a Sunday school supper at a Midwest cathedral. Bored, my high school friends and I concocted a plan to climb up inside the stone tower after everybody had departed. We would ring the bells of the cathedral after dark. It seemed to have the makings of a lark.

So, after supper, we separated ourselves from the rest of the people and patiently waited in a remote hall for them to go home. We decided not to go about our macabre business until we were locked snugly inside the cathedral. Finally, distant lights were turned off, doors bolted, voices drifted into the night.

The Orson Welles radio program had begun its fateful broadcast—which would shortly result in national terror—when the four of us, alone inside the Gothic structure, moved swiftly through its dark interior. The splendid stained-glass windows appeared to be mere leaded spaces. The gigantic sanctuary with its stone altar seemed a treacherous inky expanse where evil spirits lurked, ready to reach out with spiders' legs to pull us into a pit.

We found the door leading to the bell tower. The stairs were narrow and winding. We did not know what dead gargoyles or living church officials we might encounter face to face around the next turn of the stairs. Soon it became apparent we were being followed; I could hear the steady footsteps behind us. I told my companions to stop. We waited, holding our breath. The footsteps halted. We started again, tearing up the stairs, shouting at the top of our lungs to ward off evil spirits and confuse the demon in pursuit. We reached the bell tower, out of breath but ready to fight our pursuer. Only then did we realize the demon was our echo. We got down to the business of ringing the bells.

Unknown to us, the city was locked in deadly fear. To all intents and purposes, the Martians had landed. Switchboards of police stations, newspapers, and broadcasting companies were swamped with desperate calls. Some people were in the streets, others had started out in their cars toward safety in the hills beyond the city. Suddenly the bells of the cathedral boomed out their note of warning and possible death. Doom! Despair! Those who had held back in cynicism, rational behavior, or perhaps a growing edge of anxiety, leaped headlong (we learned afterward) into the cauldron of public discombobulation.

Alarm! Man the barricades! To the walls! Doors of private houses and apartments were thrust open as men, women, and children rushed into the night air. They looked toward the fortress of Almighty God, the Gothic stone pile of the cathedral, seeking reassurance or any sign of divine will. The cathedral presented the same face as always, betraying no evidence of God's intervention in human affairs except for the fact that its mighty bell tower shook—heaved!—with the growing splendor of the clashing night bells ringing out over humanity in disarray. Elderly women fell to their knees in prayer. Men crossed themselves. Rosaries were in evidence. Tears streamed down faces.

Soon word started reaching the people that there *were* no Martians. The best thing to do was go home and get to sleep. Breathless with excitement about our achievement of ringing the bells, the four of us were now making our way down the winding stairway when we heard the ominous sound of police sirens. We realized that they were coming for us. Wondering if ringing the bells had been a major civic offense, and totally without knowledge of what had transpired outside in the city that night, we raced into the cathedral sanctuary mere footsteps ahead of a small army of police.

As I crouched behind the bishop's throne in the shadows, it seemed to me that church and state were not adequately separated. When the police made their way up the stairway to the bell tower, we fled through a convenient herb garden toward our homes.

•    •    •

The train whistle blew.

I could feel its reverberations inside the old station and inside my flesh and bones. It seemed that I was being called to judgment.

The moment was a terrifying and hopeful one at the same time. I was going away to school. My trunk and two suitcases were already on the train. In a moment, after I said good-by once again, I would join them.

But what awaited me out there in the vast world? I did not know. Surely there would be new people, new situations, a new environment, new problems, and new definitions. I would grow up.

Now departure and judgment were biting at my heels, as I climbed the blackened steps of the already moving train. How little I knew of life that lay ahead.

# A Young Man

My face felt frozen in the icy wind.

I was a student walking along the wintry streets of the city. The pattern of falling snow hypnotically softened my vision. I felt no immediate connection with anyone or anything. The vast stone canyons were characterless. A light shining in a distant window mocked me.

A machine filled with people surged up the street, abruptly turned a corner. A body approached mine and, treading on ice, walked through a doorway. I had no route or destination, yet hurried. The city closed in upon me, its long street strangling me with the tenacity of a soiled scarf. I ran harder and harder to escape.

Must I wear this mask forever?

•　　　•　　　•

I drove the car faster.

My foot pushed the accelerator to the floor. I would obliterate an hour of the granite rock of time.

In the distance I could see a truck coming closer in the opposite lane. It was big and moving fast. Just then I got hemmed in by a slow sedan that had turned onto the highway directly in front of me from a dirt road.

My time was being hacked away. That time, holy and untouchable, was all I seemed to have in the world at that precise moment.

I gunned the motor, swerving my car out into the opposite lane. The big truck was just ahead and racing head-on toward me.

The sedan seemed to gain speed. I gambled on a few inches of distance and blew it all. The car wheel held in my hand was shaking.

When I passed the sedan and turned back into the right lane ahead of it, I felt my car almost brush the steel hulk of the leviathan truck.

Suddenly I was scared. Death had come close. It terrified me that I was running so fast. What was I running away from in terror and speed?

•          •          •

Two cars at night on a highway.

One car in the distance, just two lights, like very small bright eyes on the horizon, coming closer, closer, very close now, now they are here, now they are passed, now there is blackness. . . .

We will never know each other.

•          •          •

The sun burns the water. A rotating ball of fire has burned a black hole deep inside the cobweb layers of blue.

And, my passion burns me. Inside me it moves, pounds, gallops, dances, soars, flashes, whirls. I wish the strange fire might be still.

I see a river deep inside a jungle. The hot sun so close in the sky burns it. But why, but why must the sun inside me be *this* hot, *this* wild?

Perhaps it will temper me, grant me patience, claim a demanding peace.

•          •          •

Good-bys, I find, are hard.

There was a wonderful, old, very lived-in house that I loved. I had sat in front of its fireplace past midnight, looking at the last red coals in that old-fashioned hearth. I had stood, in the morning, outside in its garden, seeing the sky through the branches of its great trees. Finally, it was stripped, empty, cold. I stood for a moment in one of its rooms, to say good-by.

There was a tree at Oxford that had been alive when Charles I was king. The tree was a friend, and when I was leaving the university to return to America, I made a point of visiting it once more. Certainly, to say good-by. I wondered if we would meet again, and I was confident the great, friendly tree would outlive me on this earth.

Yet human good-bys are the hardest.

•     •     •

Where is the shade to let me hide? The sun is an angry god (god is not dead, despite the feverish ruminations of some neurotic seminarians; I feel his lash).

I think it would be cool to hide from the angry god. The ten commandments are harsh in the cloudless sky. The creed is a hot stone baking on the dusty ground.

Run! I must run from the angry god who is scorching the earth and burning my bare arms. What price will you extract from me, after you have drained all strength, all moisture?

A small green leaf on an old tree gives me sanctuary.

•     •     •

When my heart broke
    remember
    day, weather, faces
    time, sun, voices
    rain, decision, moon

Love me, love me
    called
    in hurt, fury
    to strangers
    clock didn't stop
    even when
    electricity turned off

Fear of failure
  desire to succeed
  issue press release
  announcing victory?
  nuclear weapons
  Star Spangled Banner
  deodorants
  Tanqueray, Chivas Regal, Courvoisier
  war
  poverty
  television
  politics-as-usual
  terrorism
  nationalism
  communism
  tourism
  orgasm

Symposium about life
  fifty years from now
  won't be here
  want to be here
  not fair

Want to be
  rock beside sloping road
  rocking chair shaded porch
  sea, roaring, churning
  windy day under sun
  voluminous Sunday newspaper
  on ice-cold newsstand
  picked up by anxious buyer
  carried into warm study
  guarded, studied, appreciated
  burned in great fireplace
  poem
  music
  myself

Create pattern
   out of emptiness
   mold life from nothingness
   alive
   find fragments
   put them together in

                    •     •     •

I feel detached from myself right now.

It seems there are maybe four parts of me, or twelve, or thirty. Am I a simple schizoid or a whole complex pattern?

Someone asked me how I live with loneliness. Lone-li-ness. It seemed to me the alternative would be to die with it.

In this moment I am here, and there, and over *there*, and back *here*. I am interestingly fragmented—in the present, the past, and the future. I am yellow and red and white and black and brown. I am Chinese in the thirteenth century, San Franciscan in the twenty-second, and Hun in the sixth. I am Babylonian. I am Assyrian. I am Chicagoan. I am Parisian. The human experience is splendid fun today.

                    •     •     •

I'm surprised how really hurt I am.

I thought I was too sophisticated to be. And, after all, it was merely a routine business matter.

So, suddenly, in an exceptionally bright moment of truth, I realized I was being treated as a thing, as a business commodity or a cog in an economic success story, rather than as a person.

The shades flew up, light was pouring in, and, in that moment of insight, I realized I had been fooling myself. I had thought that, underneath the dollars and brisk business talk, I was cared for as myself. But I was just being fattened for exhibition at the fair and, if a bidder could go high enough, the kill.

How to survive when impersonality jumps out from behind smiling masks and announces this is the way it is?

# The Golden Grape

In the late 1950s, after a brief and conventional parish assignment in Indianapolis, Father Boyd became a campus chaplain at Colorado State University, where he initiated free-wheeling coffee-house discussion of civil rights, poverty, war, sex—well, that's what's going on in the world, and why limit your ministry to doctrinaire religion? As the students gathered 'round and as the folk guitars strummed, wire services clattered out his name. Father Boyd was known as "the espresso priest" in those days when "espresso" had the sort of fuzzy connotation now reserved for pot and LSD—bananas, even. He was not that sort of a pusher, of course, but he was asked to change his style. Instead, Father Boyd quit and took a similar, and similarly colorful, position at Wayne State University in Detroit. While there, he was one of the first clergymen in the country to take part in civil rights demonstrations down south, and he was a familiar sight around local picket lines and poverty cores in Detroit.

Chicago *Tribune*, April 29, 1967

Boyd is a full time disturber of the peace, a jarring blend of Luther and Lenny Bruce, who is attempting to shock religion into being rele-

vant, to get back to what he calls "armpit theology."

London *Evening Standard*, March 22, 1967

On a winter night I can remember very well, I found myself
in a converted garage near Colorado State University, where I
was called from Indianapolis in 1959 to be the Episcopalian chaplain.

The lights were low; abstract designs were painted on the
walls. More than a hundred students sat on flat cushions on the
floor and drank espresso coffee or cold punch. We were listening
to folk singing and watching an interpretive dance. In a few
moments I would be speaking—seated on a high stool on the
small stage, lighted by a single bright spot.

I would read some lines of Tennessee Williams' *The Glass Me-
nagerie* and *Sweet Bird of Youth;* that part of Truman Capote's
*Breakfast at Tiffany's* where Holly Golightly leaves her cat behind in Spanish Harlem; some lines of dialogue from *The Sun Also
Rises* (but Hemingway doesn't seem to read well now, the sound
doesn't come off as one remembers it used to); a speech from
Camus' *The Plague;* Eliot's *The Hollow Men;* something of Ezra
Pound and Dylan Thomas. Then I would close by reading, without music, the lyrics of Cole Porter's "Love for Sale"—very immediate, threatening, close to one's contemporary questioning of
the meaning of love and sex.

At the very end I would read the beginning of the Gospel
according to St. John.

Many of the students and faculty members who came to this
place, The Golden Grape, were among the most imaginative,
stimulating, and promising people on campus. This former garage filled a need: creative writings could be read, original work
shared, offbeat and nonconformist ideas presented to others who
were sensitive and concerned.

Here, in this place, I could speak without pretense or accom-
modation about sex and love, the role of the rebel historically
and existentially in society, the meaning of individual and social freedom; because here I related the gospel to life. Even

those who might not accept the gospel would accept the fact that belief in it necessarily involves the believer in the social implications of that same gospel. My method was adapted to—indeed, grew out of—this rather unusual environment. Mine was in no sense a traditional mission situation, and strategy had to be altogether altered in order to permit the gospel to be heard here.

Fort Collins, the town that housed Colorado State University, had a Main Street out of any Hollywood movie. Mexican-Americans lived in a rural slum and their segregation was an accepted fact of life. Their women could work as maids in Anglo homes, but they were supposed to worship in separate churches.

It was both amusing and sad how many people in that small Western town fiercely resisted the existence and the work of that espresso coffee place where new ideas—in the form of poetry, drama, the novel, the dance, contemporary design, folk singing—could be presented. All this was somehow strange, foreign, and new to such people. Therefore, they felt threatened. Opposition became vocal. What had "the arts" to do with religion? The Golden Grape smacked of the avant-garde and allegedly had overtones of "beatnik"; it must be closed, they said.

My experiences in the place forced me to ask myself, What *is* a sermon? I concluded that the honest, searching, open dialogue was *more* of a sermon than what was preached from many a pulpit—for it involved "outsiders" to the church in a contemporary context.

The morning after a visit to The Golden Grape, I would find "outsiders" flocking into the Episcopal center across the street from the campus to ask frank, serious questions. They would come alone, in twos, or in small groups. "What, in your opinion, is immoral?" "Who is Jesus Christ?" "What is sin?" "What do you mean by salvation?" "What about other religions—are they false?" "Do you really believe in God or do you just do this for a living?" I became a close friend of several students whom I would not otherwise have known.

I was now putting to use in the college chaplaincy my experiences in Hollywood, as well as what I had learned in my first parish. A sense of the theatrical was clearly linked to the coffeehouse involvement, as was the theology of the English industrial missioners, the outreach of the house-church, and the concern for modern evangelism that I had learned at the Ecumenical Institute in Switzerland as a graduate seminarian.

For several months, after coming to Colorado, I had sat inside the expensively outfitted Episcopal center, seeing only the denominational students who came to see me. Their questions basically concerned sex or faith. Then, in an effort to relate my belief to my actions, I literally forced myself to move into the give-and-take of student life on the campus. Students welcomed me warmly, and we began communicating. My participation in The Golden Grape developed naturally.

When the next semester got under way, a student suggested using the name Expresso Night. The phrase had recently cropped up in an English film, *Expresso Bongo.* "It captures the feeling we have of wanting to express ourselves, of needing a way of expression which is uninhibited and free," the student said. (Later, when controversy was lashing at us, this name caused seemingly endless newspaper confusion. The names "espresso" and "expresso" were used interchangeably.)

No Expresso Night was in any way related to any church service. No sacrament of the church was ever administered at one of these events, nor did such an idea even remotely occur to any of us who were involved. Yet this absurd charge was soon to be leveled at us.

At one typical Expresso Night, the evening opened with dancing by a student from the Near East who was accompanied by bongos played by a student from New Jersey. There was folk singing, followed by a student's short original monologue. Espresso coffee and mulled cider were prepared and served by a committee of faculty wives. Everybody was seated on the floor of St. Paul's House. The room was dimly lit and all the furniture had been moved out.

Then a student and I combined various folk songs with readings. We called our offering "Songs and Words about Life and Love." Afterward we talked together—everybody in the room—for nearly an hour about conformity and nonconformity on the campus and in American society.

The Denver *Rocky Mountain News* headlined a story: MINISTER SANCTIONS RELIGION WITH A COOL BONGO BEAT, and went on to say:

> Flickering candlelight in a dim, smoke-filled room, the throbbing beat of bongo drums, the melancholy words of poets loved by the avant-garde set, the haunting rhythm of the blues. This is "expresso night" at the Colorado State University campus. . . . It is the 'out group' that Father Boyd is attempting to reach, as well as to serve the others through more ordinary church activities. . . . "Christ came not to save the church but the world" is one of Father Boyd's favorite expressions and he puts it into practice by putting himself into some unorthodox situations where he is available for those needing help.

Controversy erupted. In the April 1961 issue of *The Colorado Episcopalian*, the official publication of the Diocese of Colorado, the Rt. Rev. Joseph Minnis wrote:

> One of the signs that one is getting old is the degree of shock one feels when one is informed about some new, secular practice being injected into the worship of the Church, particularly in the administration of the Sacraments. "Beatniks" comprise a group of young people who seem to have a language comprehensible only to themselves and who are given over to the non-practice of bathing and the wearing of beards and black leotards! These beat the Bongo drums and mumble meaningless words, which, by the Beatnik, passes for poetry. . . .
>
> One thing I do know and that is that Bongo drums and the playing of them with doleful countenance or enraptured twisting of the body have no place in the worship of the Church. What I am trying to say is that I have no objec-

tion to a Bongo drum as a thing, but that is all
it is, a thing, and its association has been certainly in the past few years with the jungle, and
those who tried to transport the jungle into cafes
and drinking halls. Therefore, the drum suffers
by association, and therefore, it has no place in
the worship of the Church. . . .

> If the Beatniks get to heaven,
> They will find that harps are there,
> And they'll find their drums forbidden
> As they climb the heavenly stair.

You might like to sing this lovely poetry of
mine to the tune of the Marine hymn!

None of us should ever forget that we are
created in God's image and that dignity is a precious attainment. It comes as a result of a man's
having self-respect and appreciation of his position as the highest of God's creatures. You can't
think of yourself as a beloved son of God and at
the same time go around with matted hair, dirty
bodies and black underwear. I think that of these
three probably the black underwear is the least
objectionable. . . .

Heaven is your home. Don't allow the puny
minds of modern intellectuals to rob you of the
great truths revealed to us by the Holy Spirit
through the ages.

The fat was on the fire.

The bishop's newspaper comments were particularly surpris-
ing because I had not received a telephone call, a letter, or communication in any form asking questions or expressing concern
about my work. *You can't think of yourself as a beloved son of God and
at the same time go around with matted hair, dirty bodies, and black
underwear.* To me this was absolute heresy.

I offered my resignation in protest against the bishop's views.

"I find myself in fundamental disagreement with the bishop concerning the nature of Christian evangelism," I wrote in the letter that would sever my relations with St. Paul's House and the diocese.

"If a Christian church would ever express contempt of, or self-righteousness toward, any segment of the population racially, religiously, or socially, it would forfeit its claim to be the Body of Christ," I continued. "A Christian church would deny its dynamic and reason for being if it ever would bar anyone because of a label, be it 'Negro,' 'Jew,' 'wop,' 'dago,' 'queer,' 'Catholic,' 'Protestant,' or 'beatnik.' Underneath the confused and stereotyped images which comprise the popular image of beatnik, there is a valid element of protest as well as an honest searching for fundamental values rooted in truth. The church cannot turn away from this or any other manifestation of social change or unrest."

I received more than nine hundred letters, four hundred of them from Denver, all but a dozen endorsing my stand. On April 9, 1961, the *New York Times* gave me a new identification in a headline: BEATNIKS' PRIEST QUITS CHAPLAINCY.

The irony was that from the beginning I had simply been making a protest against stereotypes as a form of dehumanization. Now, maddeningly, I was the "beatnik priest"—stereotyped as a result of this very protest.

What does obedience mean? To whom is it given? If Christ is the head of the church, doesn't obedience have to be given to him? I agonized over these questions. I knew that the church is a basic social institution and not only a movement. Yet institutions can so easily fall into self-serving organization and stifling authoritarianism; their relationship to society can be open and receptive, or rigid and oppressive. How to be part of the church, and steer clear of these institutional pitfalls?

I kept reading, at the time of my resignation, about the worker-priest movement in the French church. I found it a beautiful example of people struggling in obedience to an authentic vision of the church as the Body of Christ. Not a comfortable, conforming bureaucracy. Not a dispenser of cheap grace and sacraments misunderstood as magic. Not a substitute for tranquilizers, outfitted with a plastic Jesus who is antirevolution and likes business-as-usual so that endless new buildings may be raised "to glorify God."

"The Apostles must most certainly have smelled of fish, Job was at his best when sitting on a dung hill, and it is to be presumed that Stylites had no bathing facilities on top of that pillar," one of my letter-writers said. "Our best Christians have been an odiferous and malcontented rabble, and you are to be congratulated for reminding us of that."

A priest in New York wrote, "Hunger and thirst are hunger and thirst wherever they occur, and those who seek to give food and water in what appears an unconventional manner will always be misunderstood and feared as enemies of the institutional church. My prayers are with you."

A woman in Ohio noted in her letter, "We, as a group, deride and use social pressures to exclude from parish life those who 'do not fit.' There is so great a need to give life to this great hulking corpse we call the church."

Why did I give a damn about this controversy?

When I came into the church, I meant it. I was not playing games, establishing a successful career. Active I had always been. I sought a commitment that would drive my life.

Again and again, I have been propelled outside my private life —that wall-to-wall carpeted ghetto—into involvement in battles outside. I have not been able to enjoy leisure while I knew somebody else was suffering poverty or ill-treatment. I could not pursue hedonism in an imperfect world that required my participation in the work of healing. I was not able to condense the meaning of life into a symmetrically perfect career of my own when, on the next corner, I met someone in awful need. Life as an exercise in *personal* success or *private* pleasure has always rather quickly bored me. I don't want to forget, but rather to find out and remember; I don't want mere activism, but rather involvement.

As I look back, I can see that the single great war of my life has been against fragmentation and for wholeness, against labels and for identity. As an American, I am not for my country right or wrong; the concept of one world commands my loyalty. As a Christian, I have struggled against the temptation to mold God in a Christian image and to believe in homogenized salvation for Christians only. As a white person, I want to think and feel black, yellow, or red, and I know this means placing my body and mind in actual situations outside the white reservation. In the heat of the Colorado controversy, all these feelings found expression in action.

Back in 1961, it could still be an occasion for raised eyebrows if a chaplain sat in a tavern with students late at night. Once a police officer entered a beer joint near the Colorado campus around midnight and was confused to find me sitting and talking with a group of students. "What's he doing here?" the officer asked one of the students somewhat angrily.

"Well, sir," the student replied, "I think he's saying good-night to his parish."

A few months before the Expresso Night controversy exploded in Colorado, there had been something of a furor when I spoke at Lehigh University, in Pennsylvania. I had joined students afterward at their local tavern. The Bethlehem *Globe-Times* reported that I heard a half-dozen confessions over the jazz. "For the modern priest, confession is not heard so much in confessional booths and in rigid form," the paper quoted me. "It is over the oatmeal or martini that people, without form, express themselves. They need to speak and be heard. They need to have layer upon layer of guilt taken away. . . . The church must go where people are. The theological point is that Christ is there—where they are—not confined to the church, but in the Lehigh Tavern, in Bethlehem Steel."

Incredibly, this story received national attention. It was headlined this way in Boston: PASTOR FINDS SINNERS AMID DRINKS, JAZZ.

The images set up by the story were quite false—I was not being a modern Carrie Nation, striding through smoke-filled bars to wreck them; nor calling people "sinners," exhorting them to church membership. In the Lehigh Tavern, I merely engaged in pastoral counseling (informal hearing of "confessions"). To my astonishment, this was "news." The Denver *Post* even commented in an editorial: "Father Boyd doesn't believe in what he calls 'dollhouse Christianity,' or lace-curtain religion. It must be real, lived every day, the motivating force in life. But to the Pharisees, when religion breaks out of the arbitrarily assigned confines of time and place, it becomes a threat. Father Boyd needs no defense. Religion could use more, not less, of his kind."

A number of people did not agree. I was accused of having heard formal confessions in the Lehigh Tavern. I wonder if my accusers pictured me sitting there wearing a stole while students, one after another, knelt beside me and shouted over the noise of the jukebox. I hastened to state that I had not heard formal confessions in the tavern or given formal absolution, and the wire services duly clarified this matter for the public.

The pain of such experiences grew out of the age-old dichotomy between "church" and "world." (It is akin to the dichotomy between "religion" and "life," or "priest" and "human.") This is a false dichotomy; I have warred against it.

•     •     •

There was a night in New York City many years ago.
An old man lay moaning in a doorway.
Was he drunk?
Had he suffered a heart attack?
The night was very cold. It was snowing. A fierce wind
     blew.
I held the collar of my heavy coat around my neck with
     gloved hands.
I saw the old man. I heard him cry.
I passed by.

The old man moves through the curious labyrinths of
     what conscience I may have, late at night, crying.
Did I see him at all, or merely look into a strangely
     misplaced mirror on the cold city street?

# Are You Running With Me, Jesus?

When *Are You Running With Me, Jesus?* was published in 1965, scarcely any attention was paid. Yet twelve months later it was selling 5,000 copies a week, and a British bishop wrote: "This is 'pop' prayer, prayer in the raw, with the last varnish gone— human life, in all its warmth and lovelessness, laid bare before God."

Five months after publication, the *New York Times* ran a major review ("a very moving book . . . these terse, slangy, always eloquent prayers"). Seventeen months after publication, the *New York Times Book Review* finally acknowledged the book's existence with a review ("blushing honesty and piercing ethical directness . . . crammed with understanding, compassion, indignation, love").

What had happened? I don't know, but there are clues. The book was original, breaking new ground. It fit the mood of the times. It was honest. The prayer about an inner-city window "where the old guy is sitting" was based on a street scene just five blocks from my lodgings near Wayne State University in Detroit. "The old house is nearly all torn down" was a view directly across the street. "They're in a golden world, Jesus" was a scene in a large downtown hotel.

The impulse to write the book sprang from my increasing inability to pray; I had assumed that prayer was necessarily verbal, and also tied to archaic language. I had grown disillusioned and bored, and now simply set out in a new direction.

As the book became celebrated, its title popped up in a poem by Ogden Nash published in the *New Yorker.* Senator Eugene J.

McCarthy, soon to run for President, wrote a poem titled "Are You Running With Me, Jesus?" that was published in the *New Republic:*

> I'm an existential runner
> Indifferent to space.
> I'm running here in place.

A poster carried in a San Francisco peace march asked: "Are You Bombing With Me, Jesus?"

In my introduction to *Are You Running With Me, Jesus?* I took note that "each of us is a person, with individual masks, scars, celebrations, moments of rejecting God, and experiences of conversion. Our prayers must spring from the indigenous soil of our own personal confrontation with the Spirit of God in our lives."

## For the Free Self

It's morning, Jesus. It's morning, and here's that light and sound all over again.

I've got to move fast . . . get into the bathroom, wash up, grab a bite to eat, and run some more.

I just don't feel like it. What I really want to do is get back into bed, pull up the covers, and sleep. All I seem to want today is the big sleep, and here I've got to run all over again.

Where am I running? You know these things I can't understand. It's not that I need to have you tell me. What counts most is just that somebody knows, and it's you. That helps a lot.

So I'll follow along, okay? But lead, please. Now I've got to run. Are you running with me, Jesus?

I'm crying and shouting inside tonight, Jesus, and I'm feeling completely alone.

All my roots I thought I had are gone. Everything in my life is in an upheaval. I am amazed that I can maintain my composure when I'm feeling like this.

The moment is all that matters; the present moment is of supreme importance. I know this. Yet in the present I feel dead. I want to anchor myself in the past and shed tears of self-pity. When I look ahead tonight I can see only futility, pain, and death. I am only a rotting body, a vessel of disease, potentially a handful of ashes after I am burned.

But you call me tonight to love and responsibility. You have a job for me to do. You make me look at other persons whose needs make my self-pity a mockery and a disgrace.

Jesus, I hear you. I know you. I feel your presence strongly in this awful moment, and I thank you. Help me onto my feet. Help me to get up.

You said there is perfect freedom in your service.

Well, I don't feel perfectly free. I don't feel free at all.
I'm a captive to myself.

I do what I want. I have it all my own way. There is
no freedom at all for me in this, Jesus. Today I feel
like a slave bound in chains and branded by a hot
iron because I'm a captive to my own will and
don't give an honest damn about you or your will.

You're over there where I'm keeping you, outside my
real life. How can I go on being such a lousy
hypocrite? Come over here, where I don't want
you to come. Let me quit playing this blasphe-
mous game of religion with you. Jesus, help me to
let you be yourself in my life—so that I can be
myself.

I know it sounds corny, Jesus, but I'm lonely.

I wasn't going to get lonely any more, and so I kept very busy, telling myself I was serving you. But it's getting dark again, and I'm alone; honestly, I'm lonely as hell.

Why do I feel so sorry for myself? There's no reason why I should be. You're with me, and I know it. I'll be with other people in a little while. I know some of them love me very much in their own way, and I love some of them very much in mine.

But I still feel so damned lonely right now, in this minute that I'm living. I feel confused about how to get through the immediate next few steps to the other ones afterward. It's silly, but I feel this way because I'm threatened by me, and I wish I could get through me to you, clearly and with a kind of purity and integrity.

And yet, while I say this to you, I've been unkind to certain people whom you also love, and I've added to misunderstanding and confusion, and I haven't been able to make it at all nicely or properly.

Take hold of me, and connect me with these other lives, Jesus. Give me patience and love so that I can listen when I plug into these other lives. Help me to listen and listen and listen . . . and love by being quiet and serving, and being there.

I'm scared, Jesus. You've asked me to do something I don't think I can do.

I'm sure I wouldn't want to do it except that you asked me.

But I don't feel strong enough, and you know that I lack the courage I'd need. Why did you ask me to do this? It seems to me that Jack could do this much, much more easily. Remember, I told you I'm afraid to stand up and be criticized, Jesus. I feel naked in front of everybody, and I can't hide any part of myself.

Why can't I be quiet and have peace and be left alone? I don't see what good it will do for me to be dragged out in front of everybody and do this for you. Don't misunderstand me. I'm not saying I won't do it. I'm just saying I don't *want* to do it. I mean, how in hell *can* I do it?

You know me better than anybody does, but then you go and ask me to do something crazy like this. I can't figure you out. I wish you'd just leave me alone today, but if this is what you think is best, I'll try. I'll try. But I don't want to. Pray for me, Jesus.

The drinks are tranquilizing me, Jesus, relaxing me and helping me to take it.

But even while I'm being tranquilized, I don't want to be.

I remember the cutting edge you lived on. You didn't get tranquilized. You went right on taking it, and then you gave back love. I seem to have run out of love, and I'm certainly taking it very badly right now.

Don't leave me alone, Christ, because I've left you. I just want the easy way out, any way out at all, but you know I really don't. I hurt inside and wish I could tear myself away.

This isn't me here, Jesus. This really isn't me. You know it, but nobody else does. I'm putting on a good act, but you know what a lousy act it really is.

Get me back on my own cutting edge. Help me to put away the tranquilizers and just be myself with you and the others you place with me.

I'm having a ball, and I just want to thank you, Jesus.

This is a good day for me. Yesterday I was down, but today I'm up again. These people I'm with are the greatest. The sun has really come out for me. I see everything in bright reds and yellows.

I hated the dark reds and the crying blues yesterday. I was mean, Christ, and vicious, and I can hardly understand how anybody put up with me. But they didn't beat me down. They let me know what it is to be human because *they* stayed human. Now I'm human again. I feel good, and I want to get out with the people and swing with them.

There's somebody I was mean to yesterday. I want to knock myself out to be nice to him today. Honestly, Jesus, thank you.

## For the Free Society

What was Hiroshima like, Jesus, when the bomb fell?

What went through the minds of mothers, what happened to the lives of children, what stabbed at the hearts of men when they were caught up in a sea of flame?

What was Auschwitz like, Jesus, when the crematoriums belched the stinking smoke from the burned bodies of people? When families were separated, the weak perished, the strong faced inhuman tortures of the spirit and the body. What was the concentration camp like, Jesus?

Tell us, Christ, that we, the living, are capable of the same cruelty, the same horror, if we turn our back on you, our brother, and our other sisters and brothers. Save us from ourselves; spare us the evil of our hearts' good intentions, unbridled and mad. Turn us from our perversions of love, especially when these are perpetrated in your name. Speak to us about war, and about peace, and about the possibilities for both in our very human hearts.

She doesn't feel like an animal, Jesus, even though she's being treated like one.

She looks sixty but she isn't yet forty years old. She is a migrant farm worker. She's working in this field all day—and day here means sunrise to sunset. Afterward, she'll go back with her family to spend the night in a one-room tin shack most people wouldn't let their dog live in.

Nothing seems to be gained by her suffering and deprivation, Jesus. She never gets ahead financially. The small amount of money taken in is already owed for back groceries. She needs a lot of medical care she'll never receive. Her husband is just as much a beast of burden as she. Their children seem already to be caught in the same vicious circle of exploitation.

There is still a vision of humanness inside her mind and soul, Jesus, although her body is broken and her face is wasted. Should she nourish any glimmer of hope, or would it be better for her to erase hope from her consciousness? What happens to a society that takes such a toll in human life and doesn't care?

Somebody forgot to push the right button, Jesus.

So all hell broke loose. Airline schedules are loused up, somebody is shouting at somebody else who can't help the situation, a lot of money has been lost, and about two dozen people are caught up in a cybernetic tangle. We've missed our plane, which isn't our fault, and I was due in Chicago to participate in a meeting forty-five minutes ago.

Please cool everybody off, including me, since I'm one of the people involved, and I'm hot right now and shouting angrily at someone else who can't help the cybernetic crisis any more than I can.

And, Jesus, please keep us human and capable of weathering such minor—and major—disasters. Don't let us turn ourselves into machines, no matter how hard we seem to be trying.

This is a gay bar, Jesus.

It looks like any other bar on the outside, only it isn't.
Men stand three and four deep at this bar—some
just feeling a sense of belonging here, others making contacts for new partners.

This isn't very much like a church, Christ, but many
members of the church are also here in this bar.
Quite a few of the men here belong to the church
as well as to this bar. If they knew how, a number
of them would ask you to be with them in both
places. Some of them wouldn't, but won't you be
with them, too, Jesus?

I see black and white, Jesus.

I see white teeth in a black face.

I see black eyes in a white face.

Help us to see *persons*, Jesus—not a black person or a white person, a red person or a yellow person, but human persons.

How may the heart be taught, Jesus?

When a mind is closed and communication has ceased,
   how may a person be reached? If a heart has never
   learned to love, or has stopped loving, how may
   the heart be taught, Jesus?

Three young children died in that room.

It's just a room in a slum, in a big American city, but when a fire started it became a very special room, a death chamber for three youngsters.

They tell me eleven people have died in this area of a few blocks, Jesus. All died in fires when they were trapped and couldn't get out. The people in the area can't move away because there's no place for them to go.

It doesn't seem fair for some people to have nice homes with safety, Christ, while other people can't get out of a slum like this except in a coffin.

It takes away my guilt when I blame your murder on the Jews, Jesus.

Why should I feel guilty about it? I wasn't there. If I had been, I can't imagine myself shouting anything about crucifying you.

The Roman soldiers were there, of course, along with Pontius Pilate. And the Jews were there, the Sanhedrin and those who cried for Barabbas instead of you.

I wasn't there, Jesus. I had nothing to do with it.

I *was* there, Jesus, as you know. I am a part of humanness, although I like to remember it only when I want something from my sister or brother or society at large, and like to forget it when it involves me in life outside myself.

I shouted for your crucifixion, Jesus. I taunted you as you bore your cross, and I stood in the crowd to watch you die.

I did this again just today, Jesus.

Forgive me. I ask for your mercy and forgiveness. But how can I ask forgiveness of Jews, after the pogroms, burnings, genocide, every form of discrimination, and most of it in your name? In your own humanity, you were a Jew. I am involved in your murder, Jesus, as in the lives and deaths of countless Jews. I ask forgiveness of you for the guilt I share in the deaths of Jews murdered by Christians in your name, for the guilt I share in the countless persecutions of Jews by Christians in your name.

I am shamed. I am mute.

We can't make it alone.

God knows, we've tried, and we've even reached the point where we could blow up everybody, including ourselves. Teach us how to listen carefully and patiently to other people. Teach us how to say what we have to say clearly, simply, and openly. Teach us what responsibility toward you and others really means.

Cut through all our egoism and self-interest, Jesus. Make us understand what patriotism must mean in one world of conflicting nationalisms. Educate us to support community wherever it brings people together in a shared sense of human concern. Work with us, Christ, to bridge gulfs and divisions between nations and persons.

I've searched for community in many places, Jesus.

I was often looking in the wrong places, but I don't
think my motive was altogether wrong. I was
looking futilely and hopelessly there for belonging and acceptance.

Now, in this moment, which many people would label
"loneliness," or "nothingness," I want to thank
you, Jesus. In this moment—in this place and
with these other persons—I have found community where and as it is. It seems to me it is your
gift.

I am here with these others for only a few hours. I will
be gone tomorrow. But I won't be searching so
desperately any more. I know I must accept community where you offer it to me. I accept it in this
moment. Thank you, Jesus.

## In the City

They're in a golden world, Jesus.

They're having a party in a hotel suite which is elegant and located in the best hotel in the heart of the city. There's music, jewelry, glamour, gin, V.I.P. status, and POWER.

But nobody's having any fun. They're too busy sparring with one another in the POWER game which, tonight, is also the sex-and-booze tournament.

Everybody looks slick and, underneath tans and wigs, somewhat lonely. I mean, they're not relating, Jesus. They're only observing the stiff protocol of small talk and ground rules. This informal gathering is as rigid as the court of Louis XIV, only the accents here are of Detroit, Houston, and Los Angeles.

The masks are on parade tonight, Jesus. The masks are smiling and laughing to cover up status anxieties and bleeding ulcers.

Tell us about freedom, Jesus.

It's a jazz spot, Jesus.

He's a musician who works here. Jazz for him is art and life. This is the way he expresses himself, tells it as it is, hangs on, and climbs.

But the night-club world is a tough one if you want to be free and be yourself. It's interested in top stars and pop performers. Steady work and the buck go together, and both are somewhat elusive. At least, that's his experience.

It's late in here tonight, Jesus. The customers are listening over their drinks; they're getting scared because soon they'll have to go into the dark night outside. There won't be any music or Scotch or lights out there on the early-morning streets. If there was someplace to go, they'd leave, but this is the last place open.

The musician is wondering if they're hearing him at all through their listening. He has something to say, and he's saying it. It's about death and life, sex and hunger, knowing yourself and being known, the dream, the vision. He's looking at the people, right into their dead and alive eyes, and he wants them to hear him.

Does he know you hear him, Jesus?

Look up at that window where the old guy is sitting.

See, he's half-hidden by the curtain that's moving a little in the breeze. That tenement—it's a poor place to have to live, isn't it, Jesus?

He is seated alone by a kitchen table and looking blankly out the window. He lives with his sister, who is away working all day. There is nothing for him to do. He doesn't have any money; all he has is time.

Who is he in my life, Jesus? What has he got to do with me? He's your brother, and you love him. What does this say to me, Christ? I don't know what sense I am supposed to make out of this. I mean, how can I possibly be responsible in any honest, meaningful way for that guy?

He just moved a short bit away from the window. Maybe he moved because he felt my eyes on him from the sidewalk down here. I didn't mean to embarrass him; I just wanted to let him know somebody understands he's alive and he's your brother, so he's not alone or lost. Does he know it, Jesus?

The kids are smiling, Jesus, on the tenement stoop.

The little girl is the oldest, and she's apparently in charge of the younger two, her brothers.

But suddenly she's crying and her two brothers are trying to comfort her. Now everything seems to be peaceful, and she's smiling again.

But what's ahead for them, Christ? Home is this broken-down dump on a heartless, tough street. What kind of school will they go to? Will it be hopelessly overcrowded? Will it be a place that breeds despair? Will it change these kids' happy smiles into angry, sullen masks they'll have to wear for the rest of their lives?

I look at their faces and realize how they are our victims, especially when we like to say they are beautiful children, but we don't change conditions which will make their faces hard and their hearts cynical.

Have these kids got a chance, Jesus? Will they know anything about dignity or love or health? Jesus, looking at these kids, I'm afraid for them and for all of us.

In this ugly red building, old people are waiting for death.

They're inside, Jesus, two or three in a room, and three times a day other people bring them food to eat. Otherwise, they generally don't have anything to do except watch television.

Is this death for them now, Jesus? Do they know they will have life afterward, when they die? Their families must hate to come and see them in this ugly old house—is that why they hardly ever do?

But these old people in this old house—are they happy at all? Do they know you're in here with them and also that you have overcome the power and loneliness of death? Do they? I hope the doctors who come here to see them have a lot of patience and kindness, and that the nurses do too. Help everybody in that house to have a lot of patience and kindness, Jesus.

I know pity is useless, Jesus, but I can't help feeling sorry for her.

She still has more writing talent than a dozen other people, but her life is going down the drain. She never learned how to live with her talent or use it. She starts drinking, and, when she gets tired of that, she takes heroin. She ran through most of the men in her life a long time ago.

But she always gives everybody that bright, energetic smile as if nothing was the matter, and she doesn't eat her heart out until she is alone. Her smile isn't jaded—she has a quality of innocence which is very real.

She gives with the assured patter she learned when she was enrolled in the best schools. She still wears clothes like the debutante she was fifteen years ago, although she has become very heavy and her coat is a rag. She lives in a run-down house in a slum. Her family is ashamed of her now and doesn't want anything to do with her.

Be good to her, please. She is so insecure and lost and needs your love badly. Of all your mixed-up loved ones, she is one of the saddest, even though she always wears this big smile. Jesus, underneath her tired, worn-out mask, let her know she is loved.

The old house is nearly all torn down, Jesus.

What became of the people who used to live here?
Where are they now, and what has happened to
the roots they had here?

The demolition men are doing a good job. A week ago
they started cold, and now the house is just about
down. I saw them taking it down floor by floor,
room by room. They tied a rope onto the wooden
frames of rooms and pulled them, bringing them
tumbling down onto the ground. Suddenly the
derelict old house is nearly gone. In a day or so
there will be only a patch of ground on a city
block where people made love, men and women
fought and relaxed and worked, babies were born,
and death visited from time to time. It will be
strange for people who used to live here when
they come back home and there isn't any home.

Help us to learn how to live with mobility and rapid
change and the absence of old securities, remembering that you didn't have any place to lay your
head when you lived among us.

*Meditations*

### A PRAYER OF DISCIPLESHIP

"Send me."

But where? To do what?

To bring pardon where there had been injury in a life
    I casually brushed against at my daily work? (But
    ᵀ had thought of mediating a teenage gang war in
    Chicago!)

To help turn doubt into faith in a person with whom
    I live intimately in my circle of family or friends?
    (But I had thought of helping a tired drunk from
    skid row!)

"Send me." Send me next door, into the next room, to
    speak somehow to a human heart beating along-
    side mine. Send me to bear a note of dignity into
    a sub-human, hopeless situation. Send me to show
    forth joy in a moment and a place where there is
    otherwise no joy but only the will to die.

Send me to reflect your light in the darkness of futil-
    ity, mere existence, and the horror of casual
    human cruelty. But give me your light, too, Jesus,
    in my own darkness and need.

Help us really to dig in, Jesus, and be with you.

After all the poor fiction and cheap biblical movies which have turned your life and death into almost bizarre superstition, Jesus, it's hard for me to see your cross as it really is.

They've even turned Jerusalem into such a tourist attraction that it's not at all easy, even while walking along the actual ground you walked, to visualize anything with honesty or accuracy.

I imagine it was sweaty and hot. When you said from the cross, "I thirst," I am sure you were very thirsty. It's easy for us today to say you were really thirsting for human souls (and I'm sure you were), but isn't this just a dodge that keeps us from accepting the fact of your real life? Why do we want to forget that you were a human, hanging on the cross for hours, who needed something to drink?

Can we somehow get through all the decoration which has been developed about the cross and just be quiet and be there with you?

Thanks for what you did about success and failure.

Jesus, you ruined all the phony success stories forever
when you didn't come down from the cross, turn
your crown of thorns into solid gold, transform
the crowd at Golgotha into a mighty army, march
on Rome, and become *the king*.

Now every success symbol looks so shoddy and short-
lived when it is placed over against your cross.
You accepted and overcame death. You showed us
the dimension of life in God's eternal dispensa-
tion which makes the careers we plan and the
standards we accept look absurd.

When you refused to play the role of a Great Celebrity, or the ultimate Big Shot, you really made us
level with you as yourself, Jesus.

What is love, Jesus?

It seems so important, Jesus, that you called on God to forgive your torturers because, as you put it, they didn't know what they were doing.

But you kept on loving, even then.

Help us to learn from you, Christ, how to keep on loving when we feel like hating. It's hard. Some of us have even turned your cross into a symbol of hate. When the Ku Klux Klan burns a cross, the blasphemy of it startles me. Doesn't this mean, in a very real sense, joining the ranks of your own executioners?

Nevertheless, you were actively, creatively, responsibly *loving,* even on the cross, Jesus. Help us to see that love for what it is—in all its fierce passion and sweep of forgiveness.

Teach us the path, show us the way.

They say that everyone has one's own cross to bear.
And once you said, "Take up your cross and follow me." What do these things mean? I think they
mean that every person ultimately has to face up
to reality—face one's own destiny, calling, nature, and responsibilities.

In your own life, Jesus, you faced reality directly and
unequivocally. You incarnated the truth as you
believed it. You didn't pander to any easy or obvious popularity. You attacked the hypocrisies of
the human power structure head on. You rejected
the status quo in favor of obedience to the ways
of God. And when it came to taking the conse-
quences, you didn't shy away from the most difficult forms of torture and execution.

The way of the cross was your understanding of your
mission and your faithfulness to it.

The way of the cross seems to be, for every individual,
the reality which dictates style of life, defines mission, and brings us into communion with you.

Help me bear my cross on the way of the cross, Jesus.

Here I am in church again, Jesus.

I love it here, but, as you know, for some of the wrong
    reasons. I sometimes lose myself completely in
    the church service and forget the people outside
    whom you love. I sometimes withdraw far, far
    inside myself when I am inside church, but peo-
    ple looking at me can see only my pious expres-
    sion and imagine I am loving you instead of my-
    self.

Help us, Jesus, who claim to be your special people.
    Don't let us feel privileged and selfish because
    you have called us to you. Teach us our respon-
    sibilities to you, and to all the people out there.
    Save us from the sin of loving religion instead of
    you.

## *PRAYER OF REPENTANCE*

God:

Take fire and burn away your guilt and our lying hypocrisies.

Take water and wash away our sisters' and brothers' blood which we have caused to be shed.

Take hot sunlight and dry the tears of those we have hurt, and heal their wounded souls, minds, and bodies.

Take love and root it in our hearts, so that community may grow, transforming the dry desert of our prejudices and hatreds.

Take our imperfect prayers and purify them, so that we mean what we pray and are prepared to give ourselves to you along with our words.

# Nigger

"Nigger Malcolm Boyd," said the scrawled postcard in my morning mail. It was September 1961. I was back in the North, having returned to Detroit from a freedom ride in the deep South.

At first I had been called a "nigger-lover," inasmuch as I was a white man involved in many civil rights demonstrations. Afterward I was often called a Negro. Some whites and blacks alike simply came to this conclusion on the basis of my ideas and my activity in the freedom movement. "You've got real thick lips and, because of the things you've done, we just kind of always took it for granted you were colored," a white woman once told me. When the Jackson, Mississippi, *Clarion-Ledger* (January 29, 1963) identified me in an editorial as "colored" and "Negro," I wrote the newspaper that personally I would be happy to be both. Yet I wondered why it was found necessary to bestow racial labels on people mentioned in the news. I asked if it were not sufficient, from a journalistic standpoint, to belong to the human race.

Finally I was being called "nigger." When one is called a nigger, one's identity as a person is being called into question. ("We got to make him a nigger first. He's got to admit he's a nigger," William Faulkner has a white Mississippian say. And one of Faulkner's black characters apologizes, "I just a nigger. It ain't none of my fault.") In this sense the term can be used for anyone whose human identity is being questioned, in the context of sexuality, work, education, artistic creativity, race, religion, or social protest. The name can accurately be applied only to someone who, in a given moment or situation, has been so utterly opened up to dehumanization by another or oneself that one characterizes or knows oneself as a subhuman, a digit, a thing, an object, a category, a label, *not* a *human being*.

•　　•　　•

Goddam nigger, I hate your guts.
Crawl, coon.
　　Don't stand up to me, boy.
Work, nigger. Move your black ass. Faster.
　　I can't even see you.
　　All of you look the same to me.
　　Your blackness is like dirt.
Hustle.
　　Your existence is disgusting.
　　Must you breed more of you?
　　I'd sterilize you.
*Boy*.

My world is insane.
How can I still be breathing in it?

•　　•　　•

Then came the freedom ride in the deep South; traveling together, blacks and whites, we could not get off the bus to eat, visit a lavatory, or drink from a water fountain if these functions required the use of public facilities. At the end of each rural stretch of road, we knew there might well be a gang waiting to attack us. In 1962, along with nine other men, black and white, I took part in a ten-hour sit-in at a segregated restaurant in Tennessee. After dark, a flaming cross exploded terrifyingly on the lawn outside. We watched the window as an angry crowd milled about restlessly, drinking more and more, getting noisier. In 1963, I marched in Medgar Evers' funeral procession through the streets of Jackson, Mississippi. I have marched for hours in a snow storm outside a segregated apartment house in Detroit that would not rent to a black student; carried a picket sign on a chilly, gray morning outside the Lovett School in Atlanta when it rejected the application of Martin Luther King III, among other young black students; stood on the steps of the Dearborn, Michigan, city hall—surrounded by egg-throwing, booing hecklers—protesting a de facto system of all-white real estate; marched around the General Motors Building in Detroit, a symbol of the pinnacle of the U.S. economic power structure, to demand increased black employment; integrated (along with another white man) a black motel in Natchez, Mississippi, as a half-dozen black women and men simultaneously integrated two white motels; marched with CORE in a Los Angeles suburb to protest the existence of a segregated, all-white housing tract; joined black students in Virginia to picket a movie theater in protest against a segregated seating policy; marched outside the Syracuse, New York, police department to protest alleged police brutality; worked in rural Mississippi and Alabama during the summer of 1965 with the Student Nonviolent Coordinating Committee; picketed the City and County Building of Detroit to protest discriminatory housing practices in the city; assisted in the work of black voter-registration in McComb, Mississippi, in 1964; worked with black people in Watts; was arrested in a civil rights demonstration in downtown Chicago; and explored racial justice with thousands of university students, white and black, in every section of the United States.

Why?

The main reason is people—and what I have seen of dehumanization. Personal experience breeds involvement.

A deeply affecting personal experience with segregation grew out of a visit to Louisiana in 1959. I was asked to be the convocation speaker for Religious Emphasis Week at Louisiana State University in Baton Rouge. At that time, while I would probably have described myself as "extremely concerned" about the "Negro problem," I understood little, if anything, about black culture, the realities of second-class citizenship, or the dynamics of the freedom movement.

Nevertheless, I knew enough about race relations to be frightened as I reached the L.S.U. campus: This was a bastion of white segregation and I knew I must use the platform given to me to say something about Christian doctrine and race relations. So, in my opening address before a large number of faculty and students, I made a clear, unequivocal statement opposing segregation. It was not meant to be inflammatory. Afterward I was accosted by only one person who disagreed.

My comments about race did not appear explicitly in the report of my speech in the *Daily Reveille*, the university student newspaper, on Tuesday, February 24, 1959. The lead headline on the front page read: CONFORMITY CRITICIZED AT REW CONVOCATION.

However, the story did contain a strong implicit reference to discrimination when it quoted me as urging students to become angry at the society that would have them be anything other than human beings. "Boyd attacked the conventional definition of sin. Most people, he said, think of sin as being only individual and do not realize that there is such a thing as cultural or social sin of which everyone is guilty."

An unusual feature of my visit was participation in a Religious Emphasis Week panel discussion on the topic "Prejudice and Exploitation in Our Society." The *Daily Reveille* report on the event included the following: "Presently the eyes of every country are turned toward America, Boyd said, and he explained that our solution of the problem [of race] will either 'make or break' us. Representing the theological viewpoint, Boyd said that racism is a continuation of exploitation and it is the Christian duty to ignore the viewpoint that certain races are inferior."

In my week there I crowded in a number of speaking engagements, running the gamut: reading a paper to an art class, talking informally with students at dinner, meeting with dozens of dormitory residents, addressing a large faculty group. The editor of the student paper told me he had received one or two negative letters about my visit, but that they were too vulgar and inflammatory to publish. On the whole, though, there seemed to be an unusually good response from the students. In fact, they asked me to return to Louisiana several months later for an Educational Spring Conference at Silliman College in Clinton, under the

sponsorship of the Student Christian Council of L.S.U. I accepted the invitation.

Several hundred brochures were printed announcing the conference for May 8–9. My picture was included in the brochure as
conference leader. The text mentioned me in the following way:
. . . [he] is no stranger to the students of L.S.U. for many will
remember his outstanding contribution in the 1959 Religious Emphasis Week program. He is well qualified to lead a study on the
problem of communicating a relevant Gospel in today's changing world."

In light of subsequent events, I find an unparalleled irony in
the announced "Purpose of the Conference" included in the brochure:

> This conference seeks to assist the professed
> Christians on the L.S.U. campus in making a
> realistic survey of the meaning of Christian disci-
> pleship in the non-Christian world that sur-
> rounds us. It will in no way attempt to avoid an
> honest, straightforward appreciation of the dif-
> ference in the various traditional concepts of the
> content of the Christian message, while it is
> hoped that many areas of agreement will be dis-
> covered. . . .
>
> This conference is for you . . . *if* you have felt
> the need for a relevant application of Christian
> insights as to the nature of man in a world which
> is confused; *if* you believe that though our soci-
> ety, as limited as this campus or as wide as this
> world, needs a realistic appreciation of the ulti-
> mate values as they pertain to daily life, yet the
> Church speaks with uncertain voice; *if* you your-
> self are an unwilling captive of a culture which
> is fragmented in its thought and you seek a unity
> of purpose and ideals for your life and of those
> about you.
>
> Now as never before the Church must speak

prophetically to our age. This conference will
seek to help you see what is involved in bringing
this great need into a fulfilled reality in your life
as well as the Church as a whole.

The brochures were destroyed.

The stencils of preliminary reports that I was assigning as
preparatory reading for the conference never reached the mime-
ograph—they were burned. It would have been meaningless to
duplicate them, for the conference was canceled. The lofty idealism of the brochure was buried deep in the mire of racism.

I was told of the cancellation in a telephone call on April 19,
from Baton Rouge. I was informed that if I returned to L.S.U.
for the conference, the university would not receive a million-
dollar grant in state funds. A formal letter would be sent about
the cancellation, but would not deal in specifics, its purpose being
simply to confirm the telephone call.

The letter, signed by the coordinator of religious activities at
the university, arrived on schedule, dated April 21. It noted that
the staff members of the University Religious Council "deeply
regret that the present situation makes it inadvisable to have such
a conference at this time. . . . This is to confirm our telephone
conversation of April 19 in which I related the circumstances that
have necessitated our cancelling all arrangements for the Educational Spring Conference on May 8 and 9 at Silliman College."

A typist's notation on the letter indicated that a copy had been
sent to Troy H. Middleton, president of the university. In a
telephone conversation with the *New York Times,* Mr. Middleton
declared that there was no truth in the charge that the university
would have lost financial support if I had come. He said that he
had not spoken to either the coordinator of religious activities or
me, and declined further comment.

Mr. Middleton said a bit more in a telephone conversation with
the Indianapolis *Times;* he termed my charges "ridiculous," but
went on to add that "some people down here can't agree" with
what he described as my anti-segregation stand.

I never heard again from the university. The *New York Times* reported the incident under the headline: NORTHERN CLERIC BARRED IN SOUTH.

The *Times* also reported a second cancellation of a scheduled speaking engagement I had accepted in the South. Mississippi Southern College (now the University of Southern Mississippi) had invited me to lead its Religious Emphasis Week. The chaplain of the school's Student Christian Federation wrote to me:

> . . . In the meantime, however, we received word of difficulties you met at Louisiana State University. We inquired into the nature of the difficulties and now feel that it would be an injustice to you and to the great cause of our program to have you appear as our principal speaker for 1960. Should the climate of our society change in the coming years, we will not only be proud but happy to present you as a main speaker of our Religious Emphasis Week.
>
> We pray that you understand fully the position in which we find ourselves doing the work of the church and of the Lord in an atmosphere that is filled with various tensions, which if unduly excited, will bring harm to the essence of our entire religious program.

I could only marvel at the perpetuation of Religious Emphasis Weeks devoid of religious emphasis. Hypocrisies such as those in the Mississippi letter on "doing the work of the church and of the Lord" seemed to be dreadful skeletons proclaiming the post-Christian era and the death of God in the lives of human beings.

In commenting on the two cancellations, I told the *New York Times:* ". . . when one becomes involved in such a situation, one must make a choice either to condone evil or stand up and fight for truth. . . . It is saddening as well as frightening for me to see such an example of fascistic tendencies, thought control, irresponsible slander and campus McCarthyism."

One extremely encouraging incident that emerged from these

events was a student action taken a few days later. Smiley Anders, then editor of the L.S.U. *Daily Reveille*, denounced the university's move in an outspoken interview with the New York
*Post*. He courageously criticized what he termed "the secret cancellation of a scheduled speech," pointing out that not even he,
although editor of the student paper, was aware of the cancellation until notified of it by me nearly three weeks later.

"This incident shows a great lack of courage on the part of
so-called religious leaders who have maintained silence about the
news event," he told the *Post*. "When the racial problem can no
longer be discussed, a great evil has been allowed to take hold in
the south." Anders continued by saying that, in my February
address, I had shown "a great deal of compassion and a desire to
create much-needed understanding between people. This is
something in the South we desperately need."

The incident was closed, but because of it the course of my life
had taken a different turn. I started to examine what it means to
be a human being and, conversely, what it means to be dehuman-
ized. This episode, more than any other, led to my serious involvement in the freedom struggle.

Violence was always present—whether overt or lurking just
beneath the surface—in the South during the summer of 1965. In
Selma, Alabama, I was in a car with seven black men and women.
The driver asked a white filling-station attendant to clean the
windshield. "I can't," the white man said. "Don't you have paper
towels? Don't you have water and soap?" the black driver angrily
asked. "I can't," the white man repeated, coldly resisting offering
anything but strictly minimal service. "We won't pay if we don't
get service," the black man said. "You'll pay or I'll call the sheriff
—there's a police car right over there," replied the white man, his
voice going out of control. We paid and left, having shared just
one more galling encounter in Selma, where, after the previous
spring's marching and publicity, the lot of the blacks was grimly
unchanged. In Natchez, Mississippi, stopping at a filling station
to get gas, we were confronted by signs reading FOR WHITES
ONLY over the drinking fountain and restrooms. Two days

later, driving to McComb, we visited another filling station. A young black worker in our group had stopped by the drinking fountain when a white attendant told him, "Boy, you can't drink water out of that fountain. If you want a drink, use a paper cup."

During the summer I was in Mississippi and Alabama, I lived and worked—shared my life—with four young men, all of them black and long-time veterans of the freedom movement. One had been sentenced once to a chain gang for a civil rights offense, and all had long experiences of jails, police brutality, and rejection by white society. They told me at the outset, "We can't make it with a white this close and for this long a time. You're not Negro. So you're going to have to be a nigger with us." In the eyes of White Power, we were niggers together. In practice, we lived as niggers: sleeping on shack floors, eating (if we were lucky) one meal a day given us by a poor black family, harassed by the police, our safety threatened many times.

One July morning, driving between Selma and Marion, we had a flat tire. We realized our jack was broken. Asking for help at a filling station across the highway, we were told there was no jack in the place. Within a half hour, several trucks filled with "crackers" (as poor whites who hated blacks were called by blacks) drove into the filling station. All had shotguns. Then two crop duster planes started flying over our car, swooping low over treetops, examining and frightening us. We suddenly realized we were in real danger, yet there was no way for us to help ourselves. No white car passing would stop to help us; two black cars drove by, but they were locals; the whites would not permit them to assist us. Then a car filled with black civil rights workers happened to come along. We borrowed a jack, put on a spare tire, and got out of there. But it had been a highly unpleasant situation, ominous in its potential danger.

The first Sunday morning of that summer I got up and planned to go to church. The white church was over *there* somewhere, a part of the power structure that oppressed blacks. Living with black youths who expressed their hatred of whites in dozens of ways each day, I constantly had to remind myself where they had learned their hate, and how. Being with them, I learned to see things more clearly through their eyes. What was I to do on Sunday morning? Leave my brothers, with whom I shared life and the fear of death, and go to meet "God" in a building that was angrily closed to them? Did Christ come only to the whites in their private club, in the rigidly prescribed form of bread and wine administered by an ordained priest? Was Christ not also with *us*, the four young men and I, in the broken-down wooden shack in which we had spent the night with an impoverished black family? Eating bread and drinking coffee together, did we not "receive" Christ? At such a moment, I could see the distance I had traveled inside myself, from the days when I worried about chewing the Communion wafer.

My involvement in the freedom movement has often meant fearing death—even as word has come that friends have been murdered in the struggle.

In the North, sometimes the fear has been as taut, cruel, and just as maddening. I have known the fear in a nice house on a nice street in a nice suburb. I rented the house one summer—it was located in the metropolitan area of a great Northern city—in order to complete work on a book. A black friend drove me to the house, stayed for supper, then departed. I was to be alone for an entire week, working in isolation. Then the telephone rang. When I picked up the receiver and said hello, I received no response—only heavy breathing. Was this a joke? I talked to the caller. Only the same heavy breathing came through the receiver. After quite a while I hung up. The telephone rang again. I said hello. The heavy breathing again. I hung up. It rang again. I said hello and listened, longer now, then hung up. Again. I let it ring for one, two, three, four, five minutes before picking up the receiver. I pleaded with the caller: What had I *done*, what was the *reason* for this persecution? (I knew the reason; the reason was a nigger driving into this neighborhood in the liberal North and stopping for supper at this house.) I was terrified by the unknown person who could permit himself to be so driven by hate and possible madness. The calls continued. One, two, three, four, five, six times. Then I realized that he *must have seen my friend—*

so the caller must live nearby, might be looking right now at this house.

Not long before coming to this house, I had attended the funeral of Medgar Evers in Jackson, Mississippi. Arriving early on the morning of the funeral, I had stood outside the Everses' home. It looked like a house on a Norman Rockwell cover for the *Saturday Evening Post*, clean, friendly, pleasant. Only it had a bullet hole in a windowpane. Across from the Evers' house was a field of tall grass; the murderer had crouched there with a gun, stalking his victim. *This* house, so neat-looking on the nice street in the nice suburb, looked like a Norman Rockwell home, too; *this* house (the telephone was ringing again) had next to it a field of tall grass, extending all the way to the next street. Answering in despair now, I shouted into the phone: Leave me alone, what do you want with me, what's the matter with you, why don't you tell me who you are, are you sick, why do you hate me? . . .

I tried to sleep at night. I felt a cold breeze coming in through the window from the field of tall grass. My room was in inky blackness; if I did not put on a light, I would wait here in terror until sleep came from exhaustion. (The telephone rang.) Morning brought no relief, for light without cheer can be a mocking thing; the morning light was flat and stony. (The telephone rang.) I stayed on inside that house. I did my work. And from time to time the telephone rang. One, two, three, four, five, six times. I let it ring. After several weeks, when I had finished my work, I left.

# *Black Face, White Heart*

I was afraid
    standing guard in the shadows
    a freedom house in McComb, Mississippi
    3 A.M. October 1, 1964
    night watch
    17 hate calls, 8 death threats
    16 bombings rocked McComb this summer
    no arrests made
    tense when I heard a sound
    footsteps, a car, a dog

I was afraid
    bunking with a black freedom rider
    in a black home in an Alabama town
    wrong side of the tracks
    listen to the stillness of the night outside
    wind blows through leaves like paper
    moonlight shines through heavy foliage
    shadows move across the window
    my heart pounds
    will they torture us when they drag our bodies
    out underneath the trees?

I was afraid
    driving at midnight through rural Mississippi
    only white in a car filled with blacks

suddenly, a car looms up behind us
lights blinding
see only white faces
we are civil rights workers
who are they?
car stays behind us, abruptly speeds past,
vanishes into the night
but at a fork in the road,
there it is again
lights turned off
waiting
now it follows
along deserted, eerie road
pass through ghostlike towns
lights of TV sets flash behind half-closed windows
fear local police
as much as danger on the dark road

"Don't burn. Soul brother"
sign in store window
in ravaged Detroit black slum
July 1967
whites are here, looking at gutted buildings
whites didn't ever come here before
politicians argue on front pages
about who is responsible
this place never on any front page before

A gifted white woman talks loudly at a smart cocktail
party
dressed fashionably
wears a bit too much jewelry
drinks too much
keeps saying
"I want to work with the poor
in Africa"

A black woman cautions her daughter
    employed in a white office
    "You're starting to laugh white"
An artist creates a stained-glass window
    depicts a black angel
    plays a saxophone
A white man on a race relations panel
    reaches out to a black man beside him
    put his arm over his shoulder
    smiles, says
    "Despite the fact your face is black
    I want you to know that
    *I* know your heart is *white*"


During Watts
    a black woman remembers
    "A white cop stopped my car
    gave me a ticket.
    just stood there and said
    'Get out, nigger bitch.'
    I'm not going to take that
    any more from the blue eyed devil."
    A Watts exhibit of black art
    Aunt Jemima
    black Jesuses
    a lacerated black man lies dead
    on a bloodstained bed
    20 pairs of eyes gaze
    "I've Got Rhythm" made up of
    a metronome, photo of a lynch mob
    tiny hanging black figure,
    miniature American flag, crucifix
    "Summer Vacation" shows a teen-age black youth
    hemmed in by tree branches,
    steel spikes, fire, a wall

In an L.A. suburb, a sanitation truck
    moves slowly up the street
    everybody has placed garbage cans
    and bags of trash
    in front of their houses
    it's Thursday morning
    trash collected on schedule
    four sanitation men move
    quickly, efficiently
    the only black people
    in the neighborhood

A black man wears a red shirt
    blue coat, checkered vest
    striped pants
    walks across a yellow bridge
    water underneath silver
    trees bright green
    sky trumpet blue
    the black man in the colored world
    and I pass on the bridge.

# Study in Color

Following the experience of a freedom ride in 1961, I wanted to make a dramatic statement about humanness. At the same time, bail money was needed for arrests in connection with the freedom ride. As a result, I wrote a short one-act play called *Boy*. In its premiere performance I played the part of a black shoeshine man, wearing a black mask, while a black actor, Woodie King, Jr., played a white man and wore a white mask. The drama was performed on a small stage area in the center of a coffeehouse, surrounded by a dense crowd.

> Just don't you go gettin' into no trouble, black boy. Damn it, boy, spit on that shoe. . . . Make it shine like your face, black boy. . . . Spit on it, damn it. Where's your spit? . . . You ain't gonna get nowhere in this white man's world if you're so damned lazy—if you won't spit. (From *Boy*)

*Boy* has been performed in every section of the United States by university, civil rights, and religious groups. It was presented in 1964, on a tour of Eastern university campuses, and in April 1965, in the National Cathedral in Washington, D.C., NBC–TV televised excerpts from it.

The play was given its most exciting production at the Concept-East coffeehouse theater in Detroit. The Concept-East was originated and run by black artists, actors, directors, and playwrights. A number of young men—including Ronald Milner,

Woodie King, and Cliff Frazier—were driving forces in its life.
The theater was housed in a converted store in the black poverty
ring that circled the inner city. The first time I saw the building
it was filthy, with great piles of refuse and layers of dirt. Soon
it was transformed into one of the most intriguing theaters-in-
the-round that I have seen. Its importance as a vital testing
ground for young black talent—which would otherwise have no
outlet—cannot be estimated.

I next wrote three plays, contained in a trilogy: *Study in Color,
They Aren't Real to Me,* and *The Job.* When the plays were first
presented in Detroit coffeehouse theaters, in 1962, I told the *New
York Times:* "I've written these plays because I believe that the
most powerful sermons of our time and culture are to be found
in the theatre, the novel and occasionally in the medium of film.
I have something to say about race—or, as I prefer to call it,
human—relations. Many people do not attend a church or synagogue; some persons who attend seldom listen in depth to sermons, or are seriously moved by them." I pointed out that the
plays represented a frank attempt to disturb audiences and punc-
ture smugness about human injustice.

All my plays have the same theme: affirmation of humanness
in the face of powerful, sophisticated forces that try to break a
person, compelling one to settle for less than personhood, and
become a stereotype, a "nigger," "boy," "queer," a thing.

In representing the confrontation of a black shoeshine man
and a white man who brutalizes him, *Boy* has proven to be a
painful experience for both blacks and whites. In a number of
situations, it was banned or angrily attacked. When a tape-
recorded performance of it was played in a high school social
science class, the teacher was reprimanded by the principal. The
manager of a radio station, who played a tape recording of *Boy*
on the air, told me this was a contributory factor in his subsequent dismissal.

Difficulties, hell. I get sick and tired hearing
about the difficulties of the whites. Why do they
want to integrate with us? If they'd keep in their

place I wouldn't care about their existence. But,
as my father has always said, give a white man an
inch and he'll want to take a mile. . . . Stepping
on my toes? Let him try, let a white man try
stepping on my toes and you'll see one less white
man in this man's world. They aren't . . . real
. . . to me, I can't really see them on an individual
basis, but I hate them, Frank. I just don't like
whites. I can't stand their lack of color. (From
*They Aren't Real to Me*)

The trilogy was given its premiere in the spring of 1962 in an
experimental theater located in an upper-middle-class, all-white
suburb of Detroit, with an integrated cast and racially mixed
audiences. Again, I appeared in two of the three plays during the
initial run of several weeks.

My last play in the antibias trilogy, *Study in Color*, has always
aroused strange and paradoxical audience reactions. It opens
with two players seated on high stools on the stage. One player,
a white man, is dressed in a black T-shirt, black trousers, and
black socks and shoes, and wears a black mask with Caucasian
features. The other player, a dark-skinned black man, is dressed
all in white, and wears a white mask that has Negroid features.
The white player in the black mask is reading *Ebony;* the black
player in the white mask is reading *Town and Country*.

The player in the white mask speaks first: "I become so bored
with color. As a matter of fact, I wish I had some. (He self-
consciously stretches and yawns.) All this race jazz. I mean, what
*is* color: Well, you know, on a human being? Is it like being a
painting, you know, walking around like a painting among a lot
of non-paintings? What is a non-painting? It's so complex, it's
hard to talk about intelligibly."

He tosses the magazine on the floor. "My God is a nigger. Jesus
Christ. Nigger Christ. Christ nigger."

After each character delivers several monologues, during
which they show no recognition of each other's presence (they
are lighted by separate spots on a dark stage), one puts on a small

mask of colored stripes while the other puts on a small mask of colored polka dots. The overhead light comes on and the two men talk together. But they do not truly communicate or reach each other.

> FIRST MAN: I've wondered what it's like, what it must be like, to be colored. You know, in a white society. I hate all this race prejudice. . . . It embarrasses me a bit, even makes me angry, when I realize that I have all the advantages of being white, and I just wear this mask when I *want* to, but you, you're colored all the time, you can't take a mask off or put it on when you want to. It makes me really angry.
>
> SECOND MAN: Why?
>
> FIRST MAN: It's . . . so unjust.
>
> SECOND MAN: (Abruptly removing his striped mask) I'm not colored. I'm black.

The conversation continues, involving each man more deeply in the encounter than he had wanted to be. The play ends in a theatrically violent treatment of the question of color.

When involved in a performance of one of these plays, I sometimes thought I would orbit away in an explosion of memory or fantasy. Both as author and actor, I profoundly felt the plays' statement about life. In addition, my relationship with an audience was sensitive and intimate. It seemed that we were openly exposed to each other—unable to hide any feelings or responses. For I *knew* these people seated before me—in laughter or silence, in a nervous cough or the sound of a chair scraping the floor—and they *knew* me, vulnerably standing on the stage wearing a white mask, a black mask—or my own.

Reactions to my plays differed sharply from one audience to another. My favorite audiences combined blacks with whites—but not when they were seated in color blocs (a black theater party on one side of the aisle, a white theater party on the other, with no communication or interaction between the two). The best audiences have had blacks and whites seated close together in a polka dot: whites, tensely waiting for a black response in order to feel free to react, have been able to sense and pick up this response, somehow uniting it with their own feelings to form a "white reaction"; blacks, being sufficiently dispersed among the whites to alleviate social fear of a monolithic white block, have felt free to respond spontaneously and naturally—thereby breaking through the racial tensions that had initially been present.

> Are you self-conscious about being too light or too dark? Would you like to try new skin tints or shades, to vary your whole personality make-up, make new friends and bring out hitherto unknown facets about you? Now you can feel *free*, now you can change the *old* you into the *new* you you have dreamed about. Did you dream about it in black and white? Now you can make your dreams come true in Technicolor. Now you can be as stark white or jet black, as rosy-cream or golden-brown, as you have secretly always wished to be. Liberate your secret dreams. If you feel washed-out and pale, *think* color, *feel* color, *be* colorful. If you feel more colorful than you want to be, *think* white, *feel* white, *be* white. Use Black *or* Tan—get *both* in the giant economy size. (From *The Job*)

One such night, when the audience was mixed and responding warmly and naturally—with considerable gusto—to the plays, a prominent white reviewer and his wife left their seats in the second row and stood for the remainder of the show in the back of the theater. "Those blacks were sick," the reviewer later informed me. "They were laughing at things that aren't funny."

When Lorraine Hansberry's play *A Raisin in the Sun* was playing to black-white audiences in a major American city, another prominent white critic admonished blacks, in his review, for laughing at lines that were "not funny."

Whites have a smell. I can't describe it, but in a crowd sometimes I sense it. Weren't they better off as slaves? They were treated well, especially under the late paternalistic movement. . . . Did you notice that report over the weekend on the increase in white teenage crime? Whites breed like rabbits. They are destroying the moral foundation of our whole society. I even wonder if the white race isn't biologically inferior. (From *They Aren't Real to Me*)

One night I noticed a clerical collar in the audience when we were playing to an all-white audience that was responding with icy reserve. Afterward I stood at the door to shake hands with members of the audience on their way out—after all, these plays were my sermons, and it is customary after giving a sermon to stand at the church door to shake hands with people. I noted that the white collar did not pass by. Later I was informed that the priest had simply jumped out of a ground-floor window, rather than shake hands with the author.

*Each* audience—even on successive nights in the same theater—was different. A laugh would not emerge at all where, the night before, the rafters had shaken with laughter. But, without warning, a laugh would suddenly crop up at a place where a laugh was *impossible* before. So I would ask myself, What did the laugh mean, what precisely was the audience expressing?

And then I discovered how useful laughter can be as a means of focusing soberly on a serious question. Laughter is a common acknowledgment of the absurd. An experience of the absurd, shared openly by a vulnerable audience, permits a storyteller to work in a dimension of truth that would otherwise have remained hidden. Now the chips are down. Now people are compelled to focus together—even if only for a moment—on a single shared experience.

Out on tour, the cast would be housed in the homes of people generous and kind enough to take us in. An encounter with our host or hostess might reveal either deep-seated racial prejudice, well-masked but clearly focused in a brief moment of clarity, or a sincere desire to become engaged in the struggle for human freedom.

During a brief Eastern tour of *Study in Color*, a black woman in the audience extended a blanket invitation to the cast, and those local whites who had been involved in the production, to come to her home after the performance. This marked the first time the whites had ever been inside the home of a black family. The conversation that emerged seemed almost an extension of the play itself.

> FIRST BLACK: Exactly what do you propose doing with the national constitution? The white man now possesses equal rights under the law.
>
> SECOND BLACK: Equal rights to touch my daughter? Equal rights to marry my daughter?
>
> FIRST BLACK: It's impossible to discuss any of this rationally with you, Art. It's just not possible.
>
> SECOND BLACK: Then let's not talk about it, Frank. Let's not talk about it at all. . . . Damn whites. Dirty whiggers. Dirty whiggers.
>
> FIRST BLACK: I've asked you not to use that term in speaking about whites, Art. I find it offensive. After all, we've got to try our best to get along with them. (From *They Aren't Real to Me*)

In 1962, I wrote a play called *The Community*. Its second act takes place in a darkened apartment; a segment of the church has vacated its public buildings and gone underground in society. Throughout this act the telephone rings intermittently. Someone in the underground says:

> They have somebody just calling the number nearly all the time. I have to let it ring. It's a very steady testing of my nerve that it will never go away. I have to live with it, day and night, as a

condition that does not change or go away. It tests my faithfulness and my hope.

The theme is revealed in this speech:

> The church will never be a building again. For a while it was apartments but that was something like being a building too. Now it won't be even that. But it gets stronger all the time. It moves to essentials. It becomes itself, a body, a community of persons in love with God and in a tight, close communion . . . but the very closeness springs it loose, out of the tight body, back in dispersion into the city. So the church is whatever each of us is. The church goes out into the city with each one of us. The church is like the salt of the world there. It is alive, it is active, it is in danger, it is in ferment.

In *The Community*, a white person tells someone black:

> I know all the Christian answers on race. They've been fed me like pablum and they've been force-fed me by an ugly tube run down my throat when I didn't want it there. But I still don't want you to live next door to me, or go to the altar rail with me to drink from the same chalice, or kiss my daughter on the mouth. . . . And so, in living, I am dead in the ways of false death and false life. Why can't I learn to live by dying to the things I ought to die to?

The black responds:

> Where was the white Christ when I was crucified by white Christians? *Where?* The white Christians respectably praying to the gentle white, blond-haired, blue-eyed Jesus with caucasian fea-

tures, while I felt the black lash on my black back
. . . and I was forced into a black, black cloud
without light or hope? And then I found the black
cloud was a vision of light. And then I found the
black was beautiful and the white was ugly, and
the light was black! . . . We are alive and dead, dead
and alive. The church is not dead. Only the
church I see is dead. It is a part of my sin that I see
it in this way. I have faith that there is a newborn,
a reborn, church. I cannot see it but only know it
is here. I feel its life. But when I look to see it, I see
only the church which is dead.

Under the sponsorship of the Student Nonviolent Coordinating Committee, I toured Mississippi, Alabama, and eastern Ar-
kansas in the summer of 1965, giving readings from black writers
and presenting my own plays before rural black audiences in
freedom houses, churches, and community centers. Four young
Afro-American veterans of the movement, the Freedom Singers,
accompanied me. The audiences seemed as integral to the program as we actors. We were all part of the Mississippi drama, the
deep South cycle, the Alabama passion play.

Everybody in the deep South seemed to be playing a role,
speaking given lines, responding to cues; every so often when the
dramatic action seemed to lag, one instinctively knew this was
pure deception; suddenly there would be a new shock, a thrust
in the movement, drawing very tight again what had momentarily seemed to be a slack in the plot. (The blood was real.) In our
drama, stage lights could change, in a flash, to hard headlights of
a car cutting through a lonely stretch of highway late at night.
We never forgot that we were performing within the context of
this greater drama of the South—this life-and-*death* reality.

•     •     •

We had a performance to give at 8:30 that night, but as we
speeded along the highway toward our destination, the odds

seemed to be moving against us. It was 7:30, we weren't even within miles of the town, and four cops were tailing us.

Those headlights shining back there on the dark, menacingly swamp-lined highway seemed to be out of a romantic, very old Bogey movie. But, we realized with clammy discomfiture, they were indeed as real as any other part of our incongruous situation.

If we were stopped, on a real or an imaginary minor violation, it would probably mean at least one night in jail. In this part of Mississippi, white and black workers in the freedom movement had learned to anticipate incarceration instead of a traffic ticket, along with a likely beating and a very high bail—for people invariably short on money.

Miraculously, there *was* a performance that night as scheduled, for we were not picked up by the gendarmes. After tailing us for an interminable length of time, they had either had their sport for the moment or were called to better pickings, and without warning, they zoomed ahead of us and swiftly out of sight.

In the town, an audience awaited us in a haggard, flea-bitten cavern that was the "Negro theater." The owner, of course, was white—and was on hand. He had, in fact, been told by local civil rights workers that our performance would be a "cultural event" without racial connotations. So, instead of the usual innocuous B film, we were present that night inside the seedy hall, which, with its ancient red plush seats, seemed to be a huge mouth from which all the shiny clean teeth had been extracted, leaving only empty space and blood-red cushy holes.

Youngsters under ten years of age completely filled the first row of seats. Men and women were scattered throughout the house, and wishing to create as intimate a setting as possible, we asked them all to move down and fill up the seats near the front.

Now I was on stage before the all-black (with the exception of the white owner) audience. The Freedom Singers had sung four freedom songs, and the wary, weary crowd had begun to respond to them. "Oh, freedom." *"This* . . . little light of mine." "Whadaya want?" "Freedom." "When?" "NOW." The white theater owner was becoming visibly agitated. He stood up, walked to the back of the theater, where he used the phone, and then remained standing there, smoking in an unrelaxed way, observing the rest of the performance with the air of a Madrid censor. Time was golden: we breathed and worked in it.

I explained to the audience that I am a white man. "Or a white devil, if you see it that way." There was a warm hum of appreciation from the people; the white theater owner took a long drag on his cigarette. "Yet white blood has been shed along with black. Viola Liuzzo . . . Jimmy Lee Jackson . . . Jim Reeb. No white is free, despite what one may think, so long as anyone else in the society is not free. We're here for freedom." I explained something of what it has meant to be white in the movement: one has the seesaw experience of being called, in one moment, "a white nigger," and in the next "a white devil." There were laughs in such a situation, and tears, I said. I attempted to share some of both with the audience. Suddenly, all of us in the theater seemed to have acknowledged relationship. The theater owner was fighting it, but I felt he had nonetheless experienced it, too.

"How many of you know the name Richard Wright?" Just a few hands went up. "He lived here," I said. "Do you know what a freedom school does? One thing is teach black culture and history. It's important for us to know black writers . . . Richard Wright, for example . . . and to understand what is their experience and what they are saying." I read Wright's short story "The Man Who Went to Chicago."

After another freedom song, I asked: "How many of you know who Ralph Ellison is?" Hardly any hands were raised. I told them about Ellison. Then I said I felt it was important for Mississippi to know about Harlem, and for Harlem to know about Mississippi; and I read the Harlem funeral scene from *Invisible Man*. A pin, had it been dropped, would instantly have been heard inside that old theater; the youngsters in the front row seemed not to breathe or move. This reading is a long one, and not uncomplicated, but the people heard it and shared its meaning. (Later, over a urinal in the men's room upstairs, I would see scrawled these words: "The Peoples Wants Freedom.")

Now, we would perform my one-act play *Boy*. This required

me to don a black mask, for I would play the role of a black shoeshine man; a black actor would play the white man. Here the audience had to work hard and try to make difficult adjustments. What *right* had the white man (white nigger or white devil) to become a black? How could he *know* what an Afro-American feels? Was there any *justice* in such a performance?

No audience before had ever laughed at any part of *Boy,* but, when the white man, wearing the black mask, knelt on the floor to shine the shoes of the Afro-American wearing a white mask, appreciative and joyous laughter swept through the theater. "Shine my shoes, nigger. . . . No, dammit, *spit* on the shoe, boy. Spit. What's your spit worth, boy? Make it shine like your black face, nigger." The audience roared. The white owner tried to stop the performance, but the people decided that *Boy* would be completed.

The Afro-American wearing the white mask left the stage. The white man wearing the black mask placed a white mask over it, and started playing an imaginary scene; the white man playing the black had become a black playing a white man, addressing an imaginary black. "Who do you think you are, nigger? Do you think you're a big shot, nigger?" The laughter snapped off like a light switch. Then the white mask *and* the black mask came off, and the face was immediately not a masked but a human one. "Who am I? *Who am I?*" Into a moment of desperate questioning the audience poured the epithets and inhumanly murderous names used by racists: "Boy! Boy! Where are you, boy? Boy! Come here, boy! Boy! Boy! Boy!" The cries rose and filled the theater, then ceased as abruptly as they had started. The man on the stage slowly stood up. He was human and white, white and human, and he had been playing a black man. "I am not boy. I . . . am . . . not . . . boy." The applause, in that old Mississippi theater that was segregated for "niggers," rose, in a giant roar, and sounded like London or Broadway. The theater owner was clapping his hands in a staccato movement against the people's applause and he was shouting in counterpoint to the roar: the performance is over, you must leave immediately, quickly, *get out.*

But still it could not be stopped. The crowd and the performers clasped hands. "We Shall Overcome." The words were shouted, the music was starkly simple.

So went one night of our tour. Filing out, the people shook hands with us. Shortly afterward, we joined them at the restaurant that was the black gathering place in that town, and talked for several hours about the readings, the plays, the movement, the young black nationalists, riots, LBJ, Adam Clayton Powell, and whether freedom would ever really come.

Every night of the tour was different. But always it was hot . . . sometimes 110 degrees . . . and in the crowded, airless centers where we played, we would sweat, and be wringing wet by the end of a performance.

One night, when the white man in *Boy* hurled a coin at the Afro-American shoeshine man and ordered him to "pick it up," a small black youngster—seated quite close to the small wooden stage in the packed community hall—ran in front of the actors, picked up the coin, and handed it to the black man wearing a white mask, telling him, "You dropped this." The audience laughed and applauded, but immersed itself almost immediately back in the flow of the drama.

In Palmer's Crossing, Mississippi, I read the "Jerry and the Dog" sequence from Edward Albee's play *The Zoo Story*. ("We neither love nor hurt because we do not try to reach each other. And, *was* trying to feed the dog an act of love? And, perhaps, was the dog's attempt to bite me *not* an act of love?") The individuals in the audience identified either Jerry or the Dog with black or white, and also related themselves, in various ways, to each one. (When I had read this speech, a year before, at the Ecumenical Institute of the World Council of Churches, in Switzerland, a white man from South Africa had come up to me during tea the next afternoon and said, "The dog was the colored man.")

After I read the Harlem funeral scene from *Invisible Man*, at several of our stops, people would often ask me questions about Malcolm X, although he is not mentioned in any line of the reading, and again I found how deeply imbedded was his legend in the consciousness of Southern blacks.

One of the Freedom Singers often read the fantasy TV commercial from my play *The Job*. ("Now you can be as stark white or jet black, as rosy-cream or golden-brown, as you have secretly always wished to be.") In the North, on college campuses and at civil rights meetings, I was warmly received when I read this; but not in Mississippi or Alabama, where only a black actor could be accepted reading these lines. A Freedom Singer and I portrayed, several times during the tour, the two roles in my play *Study in Color*.

Within each audience that saw a performance, we were really playing to four different audiences: local black adult residents, black and white volunteers from different parts of the country, local Afro-American youth, and staff members of the Student Nonviolent Coordinating Committee and the Freedom Democratic Party. Most people seeing our performance were looking at a play for the first time in their lives and had never before been inside a theater. A man in southern Mississippi, after the reading from *Invisible Man*, told me that he had once read it but now understood its meaning for the first time. And I remember the elderly lady who, after *Study in Color*, said simply, "That's it. That's the way it is."

Our tour was entertaining; but the audiences did not appreciate it so much as entertainment as an "identifying-with"—an expression of what had been individually known but not shared, corporately. In getting across a human message—directly and disturbingly—at best our art seemed to have all the impact of a freedom ride.

# *I Lay Doing My Exercises*

I lay doing my exercises as the air raid sirens blew.

Touch the right knee to the forehead, once, twice, three times: Is it real this time? Is it the Chinese, the French, the Russians, the Germans? Will civilians be killed this morning, or just oil tanks pulverized? Touch the left knee to the forehead, once, twice, three times. Easy?

Draw the right knee up to the chest, one, two, three, four, five, *six* times: Isn't the siren blowing longer than usual, doesn't it seem to have lost control? Are bombers only ten minutes away? Are submarines surfacing on both coasts; has radar been knocked out? Draw the left knee up to the chest, one, two, three, four, five, *six* times. Tired?

Push-ups: one, two, three, four—*one* more—five times this morning. I should have put the life insurance policies in the lawyer's safe. What if the house burns? I should have placed a supply of fresh water in the fridge—God, what if the TV doesn't work? The mail delivery won't come, and I wanted to see the Pauline Kael review of the new Spielberg film. The phone lines will be jammed. Do you suppose we're really going to *die?* Push-ups: one, two, three, four—*one* more—five times this morning. Rest.

• • •

A long white snake—(see it there?)—*there* . . . is tensed and waiting for me to walk by. I am almost even with it now, where it lies by the roadside.

What does it want of me? What possible satisfaction can it give to wound me? Does it hate me? And, if it does, why?

Could the white snake and I relate? Does it know the meaning of loyalty? (Do I?)

If I manage to slip by it this time, won't it still be waiting for me—outside a garage, in a stack of old newspapers by a cellar stairway, in a fruit tree, at the bottom of a pool?

I must greet it (how? by a word—or a stone?), demand our moment of encounter. But one of us might die or be wounded, and I would rather both of us might live and go our own ways. Of what use will its death be, or mine, out here on this lonely road?

*Does* someone care if a sparrow falls, or a white snake or a person dies? I want answers and help. Please. The white snake is moving.

·    ·    ·

"Peace," she says, "why don't people talk about peace?"

She's nervously lighting another cigarette. Her manner, professionally controlled, cannot conceal her basic unrest. She's successful in her career, but, at least at this present moment, not in her private life.

That's the problem she faces, the split in her life between two worlds: the public one is wide open, electrically charged, something she's conquered as her own preserve; but her private life is fenced in by barbed wire, a bewildering jungle of hurts and dangerous hidden places, a kingdom at war against its queen.

"Goddammit, it's peace we need to hear about," she says, starting her first drink of the day. "No. I don't mean just tranquillity. I understand the paradoxes. But still, I want to hear about peace. *I'm* at peace now. Finally. For the first time in years, slowing down, doing some things for *me*. At last I'm finding answers."

She moves her famous head. "I'm no one special. I'm not *terribly* rich. I can earn a good solid income for a good number of years. I don't have to buy love. I have love."

She takes a long-distance call when her maid announces who

is calling from California. When she hangs up, she smiles. It is a celebrated smile. She tosses her hair. "But there's too much emphasis on problems. War. Race. Poverty. Hunger. Damn it; I want to hear about peace."

•     •     •

Our leader is lonely.
   So are we.
Our leader wants to be understood.
   So do we.
Our leader wants to be loved.
   So do we.
Our leader wants a rest.
   So do we.
Our leader feels imposed upon, overworked, and at the
      end of his resources.
   So do we.
Our leader feels like blowing his cool.
   So do we.
Our leader feels like making a major speech.
   So do we.

## TO A PROPHET DYING YOUNG

It wasn't easy knowing you, or even hearing you. I felt, in fact, that you were often strong-willed, uncharitable, and impolite.

I saw you pouring out your life. I resented that, too, as I safely clutched my own. But I *did* see you, though I sometimes didn't want you to know it.

Yes, I heard the criticism—and joined in. At times I thought I hated you, because what you said and did cut so painfully against my mask, my security, my being.

I miss you very much. Thank you—for who you were and whose you were. You wouldn't want me to wish you "peace," and I could never think of you in any misalliance with a false truce or easy compromise.

But I do, with all my heart, wish you peace with deep restlessness, a cock crowing at dawn to announce battle, and love to heal the necessary wounds.

## TO A PROPHET DYING OLD

You had mellowed, they all said, before you died. I questioned what I know they meant by "mellowed." Softened to the point of atrophy. Sold out for final honors. Quit keeping up with new thoughts, and, indeed, thinking them.

I saw and heard you the week before you died. You were as exasperating as ever to everything in me that wanted to be complacent. You rubbed me the wrong way when you bore down, ungraciously, I felt, and with unneeded force, on some highly sensitive areas in my life. You tenaciously caught hold of some issues we just don't talk about, and you talked about them until I honestly thought my nerves might give way.

In other words, you were as independent, strong-willed, arbitrary, fierce, unrelenting, uncouth, and saintly as always. You made my blood flow faster, nettled my slumbering conscience, opened up my caved-in thoughts, and dragged me outside my wall-to-wall-carpeted ghetto into involvement again. Involvement with raw sunlight, raw ideas, and raw commitments. Damn it, I wanted you to leave me alone, and deeply resented you and your coming. When you forced me to look honestly at myself and my world, you hurt me, embarrassed me, scalded me.

Yes, you had mellowed. Your old anger was more suffused by loving. But the embers of old fires still burned me when, seeking comfort and release, I came too close.

## GUERNICA

The small Spanish town bustling around the market. Men and women talking, buying, moving in the streets. Children playing, no sense of danger. Suddenly, from open skies, planes swoop low, bombs dropped, guns blaze. Blood soaks the sun-baked earth.

The cry went out from Guernica to all the corners of the earth, heard by men and women who wept and swore an oath, then were mute. Cry went out, did not prevent Dachau and Hiroshima, World War II and Vietnam, Pearl Harbor, Hungary, Tibet, Algeria, Cambodia, Czechoslovakia, Biafra, Afghanistan, Beirut, El Salvador. . . .

Is there no resolution in the cry? Perhaps it is only against war, not for peace. Possibly the cry has been too frenzied, even hysterical, not enough a claim for change and a new world. Not only must the voice, screaming terror and death, be in the cry for peace. The whole body, whole mind, the full power of the soul, these must be heard in the cry for peace.

●　　●　　●

The young man is going to war.

He doesn't want to lose either precious time *or* his life, yet is anxious now to get into the uniform and fight. He's been told it is his duty.

He asks himself, "What does war mean?" It seems to him it's madness, murder, pain, the denial of love.

A priest is saying a prayer over him and other young men and women who are going overseas with him.

"O holy God, bless these our young men and women who are about to go forth into battle. Strengthen them for victory over the enemy as they prepare to render service to Thee and Thy Kingdom. O God, preserve our nation and our way of life, execute this war according to Thy holy purpose, and give us victory, through Jesus Christ our Savior. Amen."

He listens to the words, unable to pray them.

●　　●　　●

A smokestack means burned bodies.

A freight train moving along the tracks means people being transported like cattle to a concentration camp.

A large shower room means a gas chamber where men and women were killed when poison gas was released into the chamber, and they clawed at each other's bodies as their lungs seemed to be burning up inside them.

A charred log means a roasted human stump after a screaming, hours-long lynching party when gasoline was poured sparingly and with delicate deliberation upon a human being who begged in vain for a quick death.

A whip means being lashed to a post, hands tied together in an upward position, while the hot leather (one, two, three times— twenty-one, twenty-two, twenty-three times) draws circles of blood on one's back—screams from deep within one's self—a satisfied response from hard-working torturers.

Wire means death by slow strangulation. A hook means a bobbing, jerking body, impaled.

A bucket of water means a bucket filled with one's own urine, vomit, and spit—forced to drink.

At least, that is what these things mean to some people.

●      ●      ●

Looking out the old window
Past midnight

         I hear jazz
         So bright, the neon hotel sign

It is red
Lively

         Even so gay

Presumptuously alive
   Lights shine on the streets
They are wet

         oh, the traffic lights

Red, red,
It is a jagged bleeding wound in the street
   Turn green

         cool, cool

Christmas tree green

         in the gutter
         blaze

Dirty, dirty
    cars roll past
    tires hiss on the wet
           order in white-marked lines
           stability and order
           in white-marked lines
      I am so hot
           flash cool
           rain, fall
(do you extinguish the fires burning underneath the
    pavement?
I am so hot
           gently, quietly
I can't hear the rain for the hiss of tires
           in cracked cement
           under a bright white light
I am in a concentration camp, it is 2 A.M.
I am in a supermarket at 4
I am washed in the incandescent brightness of a clean
    dawn
           God
I am restless in a beating light
           Christ
I see the tired, tired, light of a street
long, long
hot red, cool green
water falls in a cement crack
I can't hear it for the hiss in an alley
           Lightness
           Lightness
The brightness
           out of the window
The brightness
           has killed the night
           *Pace, pace*

# Street Priest

On a cold winter's night I arrived at my first parish. After six years of seminary studies I found myself as a priest suddenly surrounded by *people*. They worked at hard unrewarding jobs, laughed, sweated, liked a beer, snored, had sex, and came to church on Sunday mornings.

They asked my advice about how to live. One night a member of my slum parish, a laboring man, asked to see me in the church. We sat together in a pew.

"My wife and I are having sex problems, Father," he said.

"Oh. What kind?"

"I need it more than she does. Sometimes she says she has a headache."

"Well—"

"But then, there are times when *I'm* tired and she seems over-eager. Like, you'll forgive me for using the word, Father, a whore. Like she *wants* it too much. I want her to be a lady, you know, restrained. *She's my wife.* I want to get everything back to normal between us, Father."

I had stirred uneasily during the man's litany. But now all my seminary training suddenly became relevant. I began to preach to him, albeit in a low-key way. I used illustrations to indicate God's gift of freedom by grace, and expressed myself humanly in a one-to-one encounter.

Just as I built into the climax of my panegyric for the Christian sexual person, my listener stood up. He was sweating profusely. His face darkened by wrath, he told me to go to hell. Then he walked outside the church.

Soon word reached my ears that I had been too earthy and direct in what I had to say about sex. The couple transferred their membership to another church. Yet, as fate would have it, I inadvertently saved the marriage. The man and his wife were so furious at me, they simply forgot their own differences and apparently came together like peas in a pod.

*But,* the man was really saying, I had not acted *as a priest should.* This same criticism would follow me later during civil rights and antiwar arrests; as I read my prayers from *Are You Running With Me, Jesus?* at San Francisco's hungry i; and when I came out of the closet as a gay man and priest.

The crux of the matter was that, increasingly, I did not see Jesus Christ as conventional. I saw Jesus as someone whose views and lifestyle cut sharply against strictures of merely hypocritical respectability, and judged the too-often lukewarm, safe, status quo reserve of organized religion.

Human beneath my armor image-trappings as "the rebel priest," I found myself in Newport, R.I., one weekend in the later sixties to read prayers at the Jazz Festival, accompanied by guitarist Charlie Byrd.

One of my favorite recollections of that turbulent decade has its origin in an invitation I received during my Newport stint to be the guest of Hugh D. Auchincloss at elegant Bailey's Beach. Presumably I would not meet my host; the invitation was a courtesy arranged by friends.

On the designated day I occupied a cabana belonging to Auchincloss, Jacqueline Kennedy Onassis' step-father, at the exclusive beach club. I had sunned and swam, and was relaxing inside the cabana while reading a book, when Auchincloss suddenly walked in.

He struck me as being an extremely formidable man, a near contemporary clone of the legendary J. P. Morgan. He evidently tolerated little nonsense and knew his own mind.

Without making a prefatory remark of small talk to soften the bluntness, he blurted out, "Why don't you write some prayers for stockbrokers?"

I looked sharply at him. My initial reaction was to say something like "I thought most prayers in the Episcopal Church *had* been written for stockbrokers." An eye for an eye. A deep bow to the Establishment-on-its-knees.

But he looked tame, and I thought a bit sad, under his lion's mane as drag.

I smiled instead and said, "It's one of the things I intend to do." After which he guffawed and wheezed, busied himself with the *Wall Street Journal* or a towel, and in a few moments was gone.

Auchincloss had probably encountered my image that same year in the pages of the *New York Times Magazine.* An article entitled "And Now Even Prayers Are Pop" had said: "[Boyd] is an angry man and his prayers are written in a jarringly modern language because he says he feels 'there is something phony about praying to God in Old English.' "

Oh, well. How intense all of us seemed to be in the sixties. Idealism percolated like coffee. We had civil rights, the Peace Corps, demonstrations against war at the Pentagon, assassinations-on-TV followed by mass outpourings of passionate feelings, black consciousness pointing the way toward feminist and gay aspirations, and, it seemed, the last suicidal hurrah of primitive American nationalism.

*Everything* seemed bigger than life. In Dallas to speak at a conference, I awoke to find myself on the front page of the *Morning News* (February 16, 1967): "The Rev. Malcolm Boyd, the controversial priest-laureate for today's 'hip' generation, turned Wednesday morning's session of the National Council of Churches education conference into a shouting match."

However, this was nothing compared to what happened the next day when I casually referred to the existence of an "Underground Church," describing it as a movement characterized by zeal for unity and social concerns.

You would have thought the Red Sea parted. Dutch television was on the phone (there were language difficulties) requesting an immediate interview; newsmagazines vied with newspapers for full details. The enthusiastic panic that greeted the announcement might have momentarily eclipsed the Second Coming if its time had come.

All in all, it was hard to sort out events in the sixties. They kept hitting our collective consciousness like unexpected explosions. There was little or no perspective, and virtually no shading.

The Cuban missile crisis had already scared most of us nearly to death. I remember walking around New York City on its eventful climactic day, wondering if this was to be my last. Heady stuff for Americans, who had long lived as the world's gods. Experiencing stabbing pains of anxiety, now we had a glimpse of our mortality.

There was a youthful, fantasy, golden, god-like aura about John F. Kennedy. As members of a nation, we wept bitter tears when he was entombed. Yet not for a moment did we doubt that his mission would continue and find its vessel in us.

*Life* published a special issue in 1962 that heralded "The Take-Over Generation—Its Breakthrough in Government, Science, Space, Business, Education, Religion, and the Arts." The magazine selected "One Hundred of the Most Important Young Men and Women in the United States." What cheek, what chutzpah. It was an era of a legion of new Caesars.

This made the twenties with its Charlestons and bootleggers a faded glittering footnote. The "take-over" elite included—let's see—Theodore Sorensen, Leontyne Price, John Updike, Thomas Eagleton, Lukas Foss, John Lindsay, Daniel Inouye, Harold Prince, Andre Previn—and me. Oh, wow.

"Any young American who aspires to join these movers and shakers can find an inspiring model somewhere here," said *Life*. "The 100 had to meet a rigid set of criteria: 1) tough, self-imposed standards of individual excellence; 2) a zest for hard work; 3) a dedication to something larger than private success; 4) the courage to act against old problems; 5) the boldness to try out new ideas; 6) a hard-bitten, undaunted hopefulness about man."

"Man." *Life* would say "humanity" today, or else "people." But the idea of the *Life* special issue was an uplifting one, meant to inspire people and move them to social action. I sincerely felt that our generation would turn America around, taking monumental, giant strides to eradicate racism. The "dream" of peace seemed a viable goal.

I tried to follow and serve Christ. In the "foot washing," the service of others, which has always been recognized as a traditional form of discipleship, one perceives, and serves, Christ in others. This is simply an extension of the meaning of the incarnation. And Christ identified himself with the poor, the outcast. Surely, this addresses those "theologians" of our day who call loudly for *less* "social action" and *more* spirituality.

The struggle of the sixties took its toll in my life. I had understood human sin theologically, but it was awfully hard to take it out of comfortable academe and deal with it in chilling life-or-death terms. I had so many close calls with violence, it became a wonder to me that my life was spared. However, my mind, soul, and body were not. They were scarred.

The close encounters with racism seriously isolated me from other people I knew who were scarcely able to imagine this precise kind of experience, let alone deal with its implications and revelations, its fury and dread. How could I easily move back from a world of abject poverty, police brutality, a double standard in "law and order," and gun shots fired through glass windows from speeding cars—into a seeming never-never land of choreographed polite manners, rote materialism, trivialized cultural religion, unswerving allegiance to convention, and locked closets containing unmentionable subjects like racism?

Trying to make the move, I stumbled repeatedly. I wondered: Whom could one trust? How could one respect an outer facade of values that seemed to be a visible contradiction of inner truth?

I came out of the situation with far more hope, and much less optimism, than before. God who did not stop the human-packed trains moving toward Auschwitz is God whom I came to know intimately in moments of dire crisis. I knew God to be alive and well, and present, *and yet* respecting human free will by not performing movie-miracles on demand.

In the fall of 1966, I performed at the hungry i, a nightclub in San Francisco. I read selections from my writings and then replied informally to people's questions. Nothing in some years intrigued me more than the uproar that greeted my performance.

What was a priest *doing* in the hungry i? Wasn't it heretical for him to be in a nightclub? This priest was taking a knife and slashing through the utterly false, dreary, pretentious, theologically unsound, personally burdensome dichotomy between "church" and "world." Being at the hungry i meant the same to me as reading my prayers to jazz accompaniment at the Newport Jazz Festival, or appearing in one of my plays in a coffeehouse theater.

There is another reason I played the hungry i. It is akin to why I went on the freedom ride in 1961. In each case I was invited to put my body where my words were. When I was asked to take part in the freedom ride, I sat up one night, trying to weigh all the factors that seemed to be involved and make a decision. I decided that if I didn't go I should shut up on the subject of racial justice. When I was asked to appear for a month at the hungry i, I felt that if I didn't accept I should have the decency to shut up forever concerning the church's involvement in the world. I decided to complement rhetoric with action.

Critical reaction to my performance was extremely varied: The San Francisco *Chronicle* deplored it; the *New York Times* strongly recommended it; the *Christian Century* attacked it; the *National Catholic Reporter* praised it; *Life* said it "bombed"; the NBC-TV Evening News said it succeeded.

Dick Gregory headlined the show at the hungry i. We had become friends after once being jailed together in Chicago during a civil rights demonstration. We appeared twice on Monday through Thursday nights, three times on Fridays and Saturdays. The club was closed Sundays. Never have I worked harder. I tended always to stay on stage too long, trying to answer too many questions. On weekends, when we had three performances, I had to cut my reading due to the pressure of time. Sometimes during intermission I would take friends who were catching the show out into an alley behind the hungry i and read for them the prayers and meditations that had been deleted, as a young student accompanied me on guitar. Generally, between shows, I was in the club's bar talking with people who had either seen one performance or were waiting to catch another. People

were intensely anxious to ask questions; often a virtual mob scene
built up inside the bar, with men and women shouting comments
and questions.

What did I feel? I was scared. There were flashing, agonizing,
confusing images between people in the audience and myself—
could they see me at all or only my clerical collar and "Father"
sitting up on the high stool in the hard light? Would it be possible
for us to annihilate isolated roles and rigid separation, and to
construct bridges of feeling and encounter between ourselves? I
knew that silence could speak louder than articulated responses
or applause. Yet, in my weakness, I welcomed the audience
reactions I could *hear*. They were comforting and reassuring.
Though I kept an inner silence and cool, I drove myself to the
edge of physical and emotional exhaustion during that month.

The hungry i experience deeply affected the way I look at a
number of things. For example, I used to enjoy the challenge of
speaking to large groups of people (I once gave an address before
ten thousand). Now I dislike the element of show business that
seems inevitably to be a part of keeping a large number of people
responsive to a speaker. Technique has a way of taking over when
it is needed; this includes the injection of humor, dramatic emphasis on key points, shifting of mood, projection of "sincerity,"
and the necessity to have an irresistibly strong opening (which
may determine the course of the whole presentation) and ending.
Now I prefer speaking to a very small group of people; the
give-and-take is simpler, less mannered, and genuine conversation seems to result. A university student, a good friend of mine,
walked out of a meeting of around sixty people that I was addressing. "I never intend to listen to you speak again to a group
or more than five or six people," he told me afterward; I knew
exactly how he felt.

What I disliked most about the hungry i was that technique
had to take over when I was too fatigued or concerned about
audience reactions to be human. One night NBC-TV's crew
photographed my presentation in front of an audience at the
hungry i; on the next two nights CBS-TV and ABC-TV sent
crews to do the same thing. It was almost impossible to relate to

persons in the audience amid the physical distraction of cameras and technicians operating, as well as the psychological distraction of knowing they were there merely as observers and not participants. This virtually precluded the possibility of everybody in the room becoming a community.

It's hard for me to remember hard specifics concerning what happened at the hungry i. The *New York Times* reported one question that I was asked and my response to it. " 'Are you bringing Jesus to the hungry i?' a patron in the basement establishment of Enrico Banducci asked the cleric. 'How can I?' he replied. 'He's already in the hungry i.' "

The *Times* continued:

> One much appreciated prayer beginning, "They say he's rocking the boat, Lord," was about a professor. "I think he's at Berkeley, unless he's been canned," Father Boyd said. "But your Mr. Reagan hasn't gotten there yet and I hope to God he doesn't," he added amid a burst of applause. This was a reference to the announced intention of Ronald Reagan, the Republican nominee for Governor, to appoint, if elected, a blue-ribbon commission to investigate the University of California at Berkeley.

On the stationery of a San Francisco hotel, someone wrote the following letter, having put pen to paper following one of the hungry i performances.

> The lights come on. Bright. A man stood there. A priest! After the manner of Melchisedek?
> He spoke. Of man's inhumanity to man. The church. Life. Injustice. The march. His compulsion to march. Black. White.
> "I am told I am white. What is white?"
> Who was he asking? You know no color.
> Only the heart. You know pure. You know

impure. You do not know white. You do not know black.

Jesus.

The church was a building he said. He said the church is really people. Selah.

His language. Coarse. Offensive. Shocking.

At times. A woman rose—protesting—to leave.

Music, lighting effects, photographer, dark.

Light, strange prayers, music, dark.

Light, strange prayers, music, dark. Photographer.

Sensationalism? Sham? Irreverence? Blasphemy?

Only you know

Jesus.

He's not an ex-father. In. Stay in.

Not out. In.

In. In. In, Father Boyd. Stay in.

He heard you. Is he in?

Jesus.

Living at Yale as an associate fellow in the early seventies, I lunched one day with a group of students.

"What do you do?" one of them, a newly arrived freshman, asked me. Quickly, without missing a beat, another student replied: "He's a celebrity."

The celebrity part of my life started when a book I wrote that no one took very seriously became a runaway bestseller. The media expressed interest in the author of *Are You Running With Me, Jesus?* "Will the *real* Malcolm Boyd please stand up?" "What is Malcolm Boyd really like?" I cooperated happily with the developing media blitz, enjoying the excitement of recognition, and even believing this was a truly marvelous way to communicate. I was sincere. I believed. I played it straight.

However, the irony of the celebrity description, which had significantly been offered without irony, did not escape me.

In just a few short months I was arrested inside the Pentagon for demonstrating against the Vietnam War. The ambiguities of celebrity seemed to crush me beneath their weight. For, at the time of the Pentagon arrest, I was described in news headlines and photo captions as "the nightclub priest." That handle was considered okay. But it was asked: Why didn't the nightclub priest stay inside his nightclub instead of getting mixed up in heavy politics?

Yet, several years earlier when I appeared in San Francisco's hungry i and earned the monicker "the nightclub priest," I heard the same kind of thing, only in a different way. Then, I was labeled "the coffeehouse priest." Because I frequented coffeehouses and read my prayers and poems inside them for audiences. Okay. But it was asked: Why didn't the priest, coffeehouse or whatever, stay inside his bloody church instead of moving into the secular playpen?

Even earlier, when I participated in civil rights demonstrations, I heard the same thing according to still another variation. Then I had a pulpit. Okay. But it was asked: Why didn't I stay in *it* instead of answering Martin Luther King's Macedonian call to become an agitator in a clerical collar for human rights?

There seemed no end to the dilemma. Apparently, if I stayed where I was supposed to be in a concrete mold, instead of getting mixed up in activities that did not fit the accepted image, there would be no problem.

On those occasions when I consciously relinquished celebrity, it had the damndest way of bounding back like a rubber ball. When I publicly announced that I am gay, I believed that I risked my future security altogether. I was bowing out of the ballgame. But *The Book of Lists* appeared. Incongruously, I found myself listed as one of "67 Renowned Homosexuals and Bisexuals" throughout history, along with Alexander the Great, Julius Caesar, and Richard the Lion-Hearted. What could I make of celebrity, its ebb and flow, gifts and price tags, and ironies?

# *A Small Streak of Color*

When I was a child
    God looked something like Lionel Barrymore
    old
    craggy
    no-nonsense
    voice resembled
    FDR's in a Fireside Chat

Priests were perfect
    appeared to move about inside bodies
    but one knew they had only souls
    minds too? we-l-l, for theology
    God was their turf

God had nothing to do with
    controversy
    racism
    sensuality
    sweat
    poverty
    funky things
    crucifixions of people

When I was a grown-up
    cast wistful glances at the church
    did a heart beat
    under stiff trappings?
    a soul stir
    amid counting of monies?

anybody give a tinker's damn
about people, about sinners?

My heart burned
    with same fire
    Moses saw
    in a burning bush
    an angel
    put a burning hot coal
    on my tongue
    death of old self
    born again

One Sunday morning just as
    the procession was about to start
    up the center aisle
    a woman approached me
    apologized
    asked "What was Jesus' religion?"
    "He was a Jew," I replied
    "Oh then, my husband was right,"
    she said thoughtfully
    "We were arguing about it last night
    My husband told me Jesus was a Jew
    but I thought he was a Lutheran"

"When my wife and I
    are engaged in
    the sexual act"
    (a man told me)
    "God turns his back"
    ashes to ashes, dust to dust,
    but let the spirit burn

Burnt-out people
    play with fire again
    light candles in darkness

            moral minority emerges
            integrates diversity
            feminine, masculine
            heterosexual, gay, lesbian
            black, white
            Latino, Anglo
            European, Asian, African
            new breed
            sophisticated beyond belief
            innocent as lambs
            tough survivors, tender lovers

        God isn't Lionel Barrymore anymore
            glimmer of deity
            along lines of
            Dorothy Day, Barbara Jordan
            Eleanor Roosevelt, Georgia O'Keeffe

        Endless procession
            chanting, robed
            women and men
            (a place for me)
            here, tiny seashell
            on floor of mighty sea
            there, small streak of color
            in blazing sunset

                    •    •    •

A television crew visited the monastery.

The TV producer, worried about his program's sagging ratings, felt it was a fresh new angle for a ten-minute time slot. The prior of the monastery believed that the national publicity could help evangelize the nation, assist fund-raising efforts, and possibly bring in a few badly needed new recruits as novices.

On the day when the TV crew visited the monastery there was a sharing of chaos for everybody. The monks could not pray on schedule because they were kept busy rehearsing various scenes before shooting them. The TV crew had to haul equipment inside the tiny Romanesque chapel, wire it for sound, and set up lights.

The Mass needed to be simulated for filming. So did the ceremony of a monk's taking his life vows. The sacred words were halted again and again by shouted instructions from the TV director to the monks, instructing them to change positions, to kneel facing a camera for a close-up, or sometimes to pray more loudly.

Tempers became frayed as the monks felt divine ground was being trod upon by hard secularists, and the TV staff abhorred the monks' sheltered life that seemed not to complement the rhythms of the complex life they knew in the world.

Finally the work was completed, five hours late. Everybody was exhausted. Driving away, the TV producer sped along a country road toward the city in his Porsche. He contemplated a hot shower and a cold martini. Back in the monastery, the prior pondered the theology of modern culture and asked himself if this momentary absorption in secular involvement was really worth the alleged benefits.

Why couldn't the monks and the TV crew relate to each other as human beings?

## MOCK PRAYER

O Thou who art omnipotent, omniscient and
    omnipresent,
  Forgive us our human life.
Hurl down hot coals to cause us pain.
Send Thy pure white light into our loathsome
    blackness.
Preserve us from the wicked, naughty world.
Thou art divine,
  We are of dirty and despicable flesh.
Thou art holy,
  We are diseased, corrupted and dead.

Thou art the First,
   We are the least, the last and the lost.
O flail and burn us,
   punish us with Thy staff and rod.
Sprinkle Thy holiness down upon us from above
   as we cringe at Thy feet,
   slaves who are unworthy to love Thee.
                           Amen.

•    •    •

Memo from a press agent to the producer of a multi-million-dollar biblical spectacular movie:

> Last night, when I saw the rushes, I wondered about the orgy scene. Could you possibly underplay it more? Remember, the N.Y. critics lambasted you for the same thing before. Couldn't you make a concession to them without losing dough in Indianapolis?
>
> I suggest, in line with your new image we talked about over lunch Tuesday, that you join a panel of biblical scholars for, say, an eight-minute segment of a TV documentary. This will NOT, repeat NOT, be an ad lib. I will brief you carefully. The association with biblical scholars will lend you dignity.
>
> Be sure to save the seventy wigs of Esther you had made in Kansas City, the eighty robes of Potiphar's wife done in Paris, the thousand spears you ordered from Cairo for the desert army. I can use these in exploitation.
>
> There may be a national mag cover story on the 120 elephants you got for the battle scene. Especially if you can provide some of the female extras to pose with them. Maybe, for one shot, a female extra could be chained and we could get

a photo of an elephant about to crush her. A hot
item. It's got sex, animals, danger, and a built-in
plug.

Hold your breath for this one: Invite the snot-
tiest reviewers of them all—yes, sir—invite them
NOT to a week in Vegas. NOT to Hawaii. NOT
to an expensive junket in Hollywood or N.Y.
But get an out-of-the-way monastery (in Wyo-
ming? Utah?) to cooperate. Promise to build the
monastery a chapel or something, explain how
you're doing God's work. This is a *solid* idea. The
reviewers would have to get up early to attend
religious services. Eat monastery food. Do you
realize that after all that, they couldn't *ever* attack your sincerity again? You and the prior (I
believe that's the term; all this can be researched
and checked out) of the monastery could hold a
joint press conference. I can just see all the space
you'd get. And IN DEPTH.

P.S. The Interfaith Council is giving you a
plaque tomorrow at lunch. It'll be in the Sistine
Room at the studio (that's the new name we just
gave the Lobster Room in the commissary).
Don't smoke. Watch your language. Don't take a
drink before lunch. And I'll get you a copy before 10 A.M. of the ancient Hittite grace you're
to say aloud just before the group sits down to
eat.

All for now. God bless.

•  •  •

I cannot kiss your ring or salute you.
You ask for my obedience. Earn it, then.
Who are you? Who am I? Master and servant? *No.* If you wish
me to recognize your authority, show it to me in your*self,* your
actions and style of being. Don't read any more words to me from

statements you have composed in cool isolation and now seek to pronounce from a throne or platform.

Come down from your high place. Mingle with us, listen to us, speak to us without notes or a loudspeaker or a press agent as interpreter.

I will honor not your rank but only your person. I will pay respect not to your role, but only—*if* you earn it—to your*self.*

•     •     •

During my senior year in theological seminary, I was, on Sunday mornings, "seminarian-in-charge" of an old mission church in San Francisco that had never achieved parish status or had a full-time priest.

The people there were remarkably kind to me. I presented my first confirmation class to a bishop. After the service, all of us sat around a table in the church basement drinking coffee, eating cake.

It had been a pleasant occasion. But after everybody had departed and I was locking up, I cried. Many thoughts overtook me. I felt my inadequacy to teach the confirmation class properly. And I perceived the frail, mundane, unrelated life of that little church to the terribly real life in the great world outside its decaying walls.

I recalled a recent Sunday morning in the church. At most, a dozen persons had comprised the congregation. Three young boys and I formed the procession that marched up the center aisle. One youngster, his robe almost tripping him, led the way and carried the cross.

The processional hymn was "Onward, Christian Soldiers." It staggered me. It caused me to glimpse the great, good humor and very real sadness, the glorious poverty and mad pomp of the whole thing. As I followed up the aisle toward the altar, I was shaking, half laughing, half crying.

# Sermon at St. Augustine by-the-Sea

I shall probably never forget the sermon I preached on Sunday, August 16, 1981, at St. Augustine by-the-Sea Episcopal Church in Santa Monica, California.

> Father Fred has asked me to do something that I find rather difficult. But I sense that he is being an instrument of the Holy Spirit. And I sense that God is also asking me to do it. You see, the subject requires humor, patience, lots of understanding, and love.
>
> As you are no doubt aware, the parish has been holding workshops on human sexuality. And, this week, will host the national convention of Integrity International, the organization within the Episcopal Church of gays and lesbians and their friends.
>
> *Our* friends, I should say. For I am a Christian and a homosexual. A Christian and a gay.
>
> Of all the subjects, this seems nearly the most bizarre—outrageous—misunderstood—controversial. There has been so much discussion about it and so little information."

I had actually come "out of the closet" earlier, in 1976 to be exact; and had written two books on the subject: *Take Off the Masks*, published in 1978, and *Look Back in Joy: Celebration of Gay Lovers*, published by Gay Sunshine Press in the spring of 1981.

After a lifetime in a closet that became increasingly claustro-phobic, I decided that I would henceforth cease to "tell a lie for Christ."

Yet most of the people in the parish of St. Augustine's were unaware of my gayness. They pursued their own busy lives, worked hard, raised families, paid mortgages or rent, and, if they knew of me at all, probably vaguely recollected me as the author of *Are You Running With Me, Jesus?*

So, it was a bit of a shock, that sermon on August 16, 1981. A few people had very serious problems with it. One even said: "A homosexual *priest?* But is that *possible?* I've never *heard* of such a thing."

Shock or not, Fred Fenton, the rector of St. Augustine's, was right in asking me to preach it. For the subject of my being gay *had* to be dealt with—in, and by, the parish. I was "out"; gossip and rumor would have had their way if the issue was not con-fronted honestly and openly, without equivocation.

That morning I told the parish that I consider myself "whole, healthy, blessed, happy, created in God's own image, free of the past horrors of human slavery, and able to combine my sexuality and my spirituality."

I said that, for gay men and lesbians, strong feelings of same-sex erotic attraction and love are the norm, the normal. I ex-plained how, with understanding and compassion, this can be expressed, placed in its proper focus and context, and life goes on at its accustomed clip.

> But when there are awful shadows cast on such love—bitter faggot jokes at work and whis-pers of perversion around the corner in the neighborhood—something dirty, ugly, gro-tesque—queer—is pictured. So, the self-esteem of the gay or lesbian person is called into ques-tion; sometimes he or she feels too hurt or anx-ious and vulnerable to tell a mother or father, and certainly an employer or co-worker. Because so many gay men and lesbians therefore are clos-

eted, their very existence can come to seem entombed: an existence in only partial light; a life
pattern that is rigidly choreographed to avoid
inadvertent disclosure; verbal communication in
code; an underground of surreptitious meeting
places that are 'hidden.' In time, such a lifestyle
can become a self-fulfilling prophecy of half-
truth, distortion, masks, charades, sophisticated
games, innuendo, and double-entendre.

Looking out at the faces in the congregation, I said that gay is
not exotic or glamorous; it describes something real, basic, vital,
indigenous to some 10 percent of the nation, the culture, the city
—and the church.

I made an appeal from the pulpit:

For gay and non-gay alike, let communication be
an event that involves people, not a charade of
puppets. For gay and non-gay alike, let's be ourselves. Relate to other selves without inhibition
or pretense. Help others to be themselves, too. It
isn't just gay people who occupy closets. *Think* of
all the various closets of *all* our lives! Opening
doors . . . walking outside, sharing "closet experiences" as past history, can be liberating, a gospel
experience in Jesus Christ.

Having no idea what would be the parish's response to this
sermon, I went further in my appeal:

Don't let's label each other, place each other on
convenient shelves, and therefore keep each
other in our places! Let's let each other breathe,
grow, develop as daughters and sons of God. To
do this, we must truly *see* each other and *share*
ourselves. Then, in that mutual vulnerability
which is surely a gift of grace, we can *all* grow

to the fullness of the glory that is God's call, and
gift, to each one of us. Thanks be to God!

The roof did not fall in. There were growing pains, problems,
and human interaction involving mutual suffering and growth,
but we *made* it. This, with the never-failing compassionate help,
and leadership, of the two priests in the parish, Fred Fenton and
Carlyle Gill, and a wonderfully supportive and loving group of
women and men in the church.

Looking back—not only to August 16, 1981, but to August 1976,
when I came out to the Integrity convention meeting in San
Francisco, and September 12 of the same year to the media—it's
very clear that it was absolutely essential to me to "come out" if
I were to continue to function as a priest.

The long-established lie masking the fundamental part of my
being had become acid of sorts, eroding my sacramental, pastoral,
and prophetic work in the church, as well as *all* the various
relationships of my life. It also seriously damaged my writing,
where openness is essential. A lie is deadly, for it touches *every*
part of one's life. Also, it's contagious. It contrives against wholeness.

Acting affirmatively on the request of the rector, Bishop Ru-
sack of Los Angeles licensed me (I am canonically resident in the
Diocese of New York) to function as a priest in the diocese. The
vestry of St. Augustine's called me to function as a priest on staff
in the parish. It is significant beyond words that I always felt
secure in the abiding love and deep trust of Paul Moore, the
bishop of New York, whose spiritual and emotional support
were steadily and unstintingly given to me.

It *can* be done. One *can* be honest and open about being gay
*and* function as a priest in the church—in the best sense of community and spiritual health. I feel accepted and loved, even as I
appreciate and love.

At St. Augustine's parish, I am the active third member of a
team ministry. We share equally liturgical and preaching responsibilities. I edit the parish newsletter, *Ebb and Flow*, and the
Sunday bulletin; arrange themes and invite guest speakers for a

vital, exciting Sunday-morning discussion series, "Sunday Focus"; do my share of calling and bringing private communion to people who are elderly or ill and therefore unable to get to church; and have conducted a series of evening workshops dealing with such subjects as commitment, the meaning of being male in this society, prayer, taking off the masks, and finding a new start in one's life.

I honestly feel that I'm generally accepted in the parish now as Malcolm—myself.

It was in 1955, thirty years ago, that I was ordained as a priest. Now, I find myself engaged in the most challenging and demanding period of my priesthood. I have acted as celebrant of the AIDS Mass and preacher at AIDS Mass II, held in the church, and blessed the relationship of two gay men in a Covenant of Commitment. Let the church *be* the church, a vessel of loving and healing, a sacrament of blessing.

# To Be Alive and Well, and Gay

## WHERE ARE THE GOOD PEOPLE?

Why does antigay feeling run so high in our society? I'm beginning to sense the shape of the answer. Could it be that many people, however reasonable they think they are, in fact are intellectually trapped by the stereotypes of gay men and lesbians?

The stereotype does not fit.

We gays work in business, government, academia, the media, religion, sports. We do volunteer work, teach school, practice law and medicine, cut lawns, and cook meals; we report the news, say Mass, and serve in the armed forces; we play tennis and cards, watch TV, and grouse about the freeway traffic. We live up the street from you, or next door. If you look closely, maybe you'll find one of us living in your home.

Since much of gay identity remains closeted, co-workers frequently do not identify us as gays. Neither do many mothers and fathers, even wives and husbands. This vastly complicates open communication, multiplies problems.

There are analogies. Jewish stereotypes, buried deep in the hatred of anti-Semitism, lose potency in one-on-one contact that contradicts them. Black stereotypes diminish in intensity when people are given an opportunity to interact as themselves, not as figures of myth or imagination.

The gay population is all-American in its utter diversity. We are thin and fat, old and young, dark and blond, attractive and ugly, sexy and asexual, rubes and sophisticates, puritans and libertines, rural and urban, Latino and white and black and

Asian, Christians and Jews and Muslims and atheists. And we lack easily identifiable outward marks, the cliché limp wrist notwithstanding.

To change public consciousness about gay reality will not be easy. There are several obstacles. The most obvious one is the current messianic movement of biblical fundamentalism-cum-politics, Khomeini-like in severity and disproportionately well-financed, which attempts to link church and state through punitive legislation aimed at gays and others.

Then there is the problem with the very word *homosexual.* It conjures up imagery rooted in present discriminatory acts and past savage persecution, as well as the repressed fantasy and fear concerning one's own androgyny and full range of sexuality.

A related problem is how the truth of AIDS is distorted, often cruelly manipulated against gays. AIDS is *not* a "gay disease." It is, instead, the number one health problem facing the nation. To twist its meaning, to try to "use it" against gay people as a political tool of homophobia, is reminiscent of demonic Nazi methodology at its worst.

It required "black power," the concentrated effort by black Americans to assert self-acceptance and pride in the face of rejection and contempt, to change both blacks' and whites' attitudes towards blackness. I remember Rosa Parks, who prepared the way for Dr. Martin Luther King, Jr.'s, leadership, reflecting on her refusal to sit in the back of a bus in Alabama, recalling "the appalling silence of the good people."

Where are the silent "good people"—including the "good," still-hidden gay people—who will come forward to advance the cause of gay people's rights?

## THE TWELVE

Twelve people, an astonishingly diverse group of celebrities, are seated at a table before reporters and TV crews. Picture a *Dinner at Eight* cast for a 10 A.M. all-star press conference.

Jeff Nile's familiar face has looked at the public from front pages and the network evening news for years. Presently he works in the White House as an assistant to the president.

Erica Fitch, a beloved sports star, comes close to being America's sweetheart.

John Mason is an internationally famous bishop who fights for causes and makes news.

George Peck, resplendent in his uniform, is a general.

Daphne Cristie, patrician and elderly, is the author of three classic American novels.

Guy Stevens is the host of a TV news show that is secure for the second consecutive year in the top twenty ratings.

Arturo Vitale, the symphony conductor *assoluto*, is as well known for his temperament as for his musical ability.

Adam Washington, who resembles a founding father, is a bank president and philanthropist.

Bookish-looking Douglas Epstein is editor of a top-circulation magazine.

Johnny Cracker, his media smile flashing, is a mass evangelist of TV fame.

Smokey Faith, the Hollywood superstar, is the world's reigning sex goddess.

Timothy Lewis, tall and austere, is one of the best-known university presidents in the United States.

Nile opens the press conference by reading a short statement on behalf of the twelve.

"We are here today because we are gay men and lesbians. We seek openness and honestly about our lives. We sincerely hope that the true diversity of all of us may be celebrated with tolerance, mutual respect, and goodwill."

Although the roof does not fall in, no one seems to breathe for a long moment. The eyes of the women and men of the media search the naked, renowned faces for clues to restore shattered images and myths.

Immediately questions explode.

"Mr. Nile, do you believe that the announcement of your sexual orientation will change your White House duties or your responsibilities for the president?" asks a woman from the *Times*.

"I have no reason to believe there will be any change," Nile replies.

A hand is raised by a reporter for the Washington *Post*.

"Miss Faith, will the public accept your decision and continue to attend and support your films?"

"I honestly don't know the answer to that question," she replies. "I hope they'll understand. I hope they'll let me be a person and not just an image."

The *Wall Street Journal* has a question for Adam Washington.

"Sir, do you think that your announcement this morning will affect the Dow tomorrow?"

"Well, if it should do so," Washington replies, "the market has needed such a lift for some time, in my studied opinion."

Hours later, the twelve gay men and lesbians are observed by the public on TV news programs. A few days later a newsmagazine, with a bow in the direction of Oscar Wilde, christens them "The Wilde Twelve." The name sticks.

•     •     •

This gay fantasy about "coming out of the closet" won't happen—at least, not now. Yet America needs to be told who gays are and the contributions that gays make to society. Conscious awareness of an experienced relationship between gays and non-gays is needed if there is to be an equivalent development of communications and respect. And rights.

The continued hiddenness of the overwhelming majority of gay people plays into the hands of those who denounce visible gay role models, even as they call for more closets. "You're not O.K., so hide who you are," critics of gays declaim. "Stay in the closet and tell a lie for Christ" is a message of negativism from many churches.

Yet after our tragic Watergates and Vietnams, surely all of us have had enough of both social and private lies. Honesty and openness and mutual human respect point toward hope. But if hypocrisy and lies hold the day, that hope cannot be realized.

Liberation from past repression surely needs to include the freedom to become one's self, not a figment of someone else's imagination. That is why acceptance of differences under the gay label is so important. One of the contributions that gays can offer to the rest of American society at present is a sharp image of diversity over against sameness and conformity for its own sake.

## *HIS SUICIDE*

His suicide shocked a large number of people.

He was a gentle, scholarly man. When he spoke, it was with a faintly discernible hesitation, which caused him to express himself laboriously and with long pauses. He was an incredibly kind man. In his rooms at the university he would invite for lunch small groups of students who felt alienated from life there.

I was one of the students. I knew that he was gay; surely he sensed that I was. But in that closeted environment, we never spoke of it.

After I graduated, we wrote occasionally. His last letter to me was written only four days before his suicide.

I believe he took his life because the academic community in which he existed was a cold, airless ghetto within which, at a certain moment, he had needed a strong, unsentimental support it could not give. There was a stifling absence of love.

Why?

•     •     •

My lover
stirs in my arms
    his head nestled
    between my neck and shoulders
    strands of his hair
    fall on my forehead

I love him
    hold one arm around his shoulder
    the other rests
    on the ivory
    rise
    of his
    ass

surely
one of the seven wonders
of the modern world

Warmth and desire stir in my groin
that sensitive seismograph
energy lifts me
desire seizes my willing body
curious mind
groping spirit.

He moans ever so quietly
in his sleep
happy to have me
for his lover
trusts me in the
labyrinth of his dream

I kiss his forehead
neck
slowly, turn his face
tenderly toward mine
kiss him on the mouth
he awakens

## *LOUISE AND HENRY ARE NICE PEOPLE*

They've lived in their suburb for years, raised a family, paid taxes, gone to church, taught Sunday school, supported culture and good works in the community, and generally shown a smiling face to the world.

But now the unbelievable has happened. As Henry put it to Louise, they've got "a goddam queer in the family." Henry always suspected it, yet managed to repress his anxiety to such an extent that he previously never mentioned the subject to Louise.

It was Louise who happened upon the terrible news. During a visit to her Aunt Martha's house, the fact that a male homosexual bears the proud family name was ferreted out, amid tears and cups of camomile tea.

The first question for Louise and Henry: What should one *do* about the children in the family? Obviously, they cannot be told. They must never know anything at all about the leprosy.

The second question is: What should one *do* about everybody else—friends, business associates, neighbors, church members? They must never know, either. The rain falls on the just and the unjust alike—but *why?* Why is this unmentionable sinner of their own blood—call him a queer, faggot, homosexual, gay, or whatever one damned well likes—visited upon a God-fearing, decent, hard-working family that never blasphemed or committed evil in the sight of heaven?

It boggles Henry's mind. It takes Louise's spirit. As Henry just said to Louise, they had invited him to dinner next Sunday *before* they found out he is a queer. What shall they do?

God, what shall they do?

•       •       •

Suddenly, I was alone.

I hadn't wanted to be ever again. What had gone wrong? I felt awkward and out of place in the space we'd shared. Survival worth the name would take doing. Instinctively, I knew that I must gather together loose, out-of-sync fragments of my life and try to make a new whole.

I cleaned out closets, wrote to friends who hadn't heard from me in years, listened to old recordings of favorite operas. The latter caught me in emotional quicksand. I lost control, and cried for the first time, when I played the love music of *Tristan and Isolde*. I had better not do that again, or play either Act III of *La Bohème* or the trio from *Der Rosenkavalier*. Not for a while.

Later, I feared an overwhelming experience of loneliness as I lay alone in the large bed that we had shared, but, to my surprise, yawned and stretched out contentedly. I had always slept on the left side. Now I seized possession of the right side, too. It was like a friendly but autonomous province. Could I use my American Express card over there? I astonished myself by enjoying the conquest.

Shopping alone at the supermarket Saturday morning proved

to be sad. We had always shared this task, compiling lists of needed items, placing our goods in one shopping cart, bumping into one another in aisle four and remembering to get matzos, holding a conference about a roast at the meat counter. This time I plodded up and down the dismal, neon-lit aisles all by myself, casting secret envious glances at happy couples and feeling camaraderie with singles. I momentarily forgot that I live alone now when I placed two cans of sardines in the cart. I never eat them. Sheepishly, I returned them to the shelf before making my way lugubriously to the checkout line.

Abruptly one evening the phone rang sharply in the apartment. I lunged out of my chair, sprinted across the room, and picked up the receiver on the third ring. An old friend of *ours* was on the other end of the line. How are you both? she asked. I caught my breath and strove to put a good face on the situation; she didn't know. Nothing was really different or had changed, a seductive inner voice coolly informed me. I transmitted that information intact.

Yes, I said, it would be great fun for all of us to get together in the near future. When I hung up, I felt like an alcoholic who had downed a bottle of booze. It shocked me to realize how deeply I apparently felt embarrassed, guilty, or worthless about the end of the relationship. *Did* I feel that a major challenge of my life had been irretrievably lost? I was distressed by my awareness that I was playing an absurd game with the facts.

When I telephoned the friend to correct the information, she was sensitive, understood what had happened, and was supportive. I would tell no more lies, accept the reality of the present.

I was gaining ground.

•    •    •

My lover is adding a new room to the house
plays god each day in the back yard
digs a trench, pours cement, selects wood
pounds nails, erects walls, places windows

I watch him, a deity who creates out of a vacuum,
    and quietly marvel
this god with tape measure and tools
infinite energy and ineffable skills
    is mortal when he sleeps
    snoring gently beside me
    bare shoulder alongside mine


Out of bed, out of the house
he is Prometheus building his room
    a cigarette protrudes from his mouth
    glowing
he's here, there, everywhere
    a master builder
gives orders to a small blue bird
    excites the cat


Garbed in overalls
    clutches a hammer and nails
    entrechats through the framework
    in his liturgy of the new room
    his daily Mass
wonder if he may have a stroke
    godhead be unmasked


His male beauty is a marvel
    prancing unaware beneath a vaulted sky
innocent moments of being
    a most likable god
    disguise his mortality
incredible, how little can make him happy
I stand by as unseen servitor
    carry a nail
    a coke
    a god's helmet

I envy more than marvel as the new room
    actually takes shape
    grows bigger before my eyes
I cannot add a room to my life
    a foyer
    sweep of laughter without tears
    one extra year of my own

•     •     •

From the outset of my consciousness as a gay man, survival dictated I learn how to read between the lines and understand social shorthand. Acting lessons were de rigueur in order to participate in the life drama that lay ahead.

To provide an automatic, apparently sincere, and easy laugh for fag jokes.

To talk to other men with absolute confidence, employing explicit details, about making it with women.

To learn universally accepted manly ways to cross one's legs —the ankle should be balanced firmly on the opposite knee; to laugh, to swear; to pick up a knife and fork; to eat an ice cream cone; to hold a martini; to open an envelope.

To be sexy to women by means of wearing cowboy or military drag, developing bedroom eyes, stuffing a handkerchief in one's crotch, speaking with a French accent, or getting a Robert Redford haircut.

To master the ritual of lavatory behavior with heterosexual men. To practice how to walk up to a urinal, unzip one's fly, take out the pecker, aim it, hit the water with good force—make it sound like Niagara Falls—get the pecker back inside, and withdraw heartily in the mood of *The Charge of the Light Brigade*.

Although I saw Marilyn Monroe as a beautiful woman, she never aroused me erotically. I was turned on instead by Marlon Brandon as Stanley Kowalski in *A Streetcar Named Desire*, Paul Newman as the stud in *Sweet Bird of Youth*, Montgomery Clift as a soldier in *The Young Lions*, and over the years by a long line of men on the screen.

Being gay inescapably conditions the way one looks at the world, knows it in the gut, and experiences it.

The family doesn't mean "nuclear" to me. I know the family as an extended one.

Religion does not mean to me "what the Bible says." In my view it is an everlasting trust in the breadth and depth of God's mercy and love. I feel especially close to Jesus because he was single.

My prayers are frequently addressed to God the Mother, not God the Father. St. Paul's mysterious "thorn in the flesh" has never been a mystery to me.

### *NATURAL SOUL*

Emptiness is a better gift than fullness
Let me come to you as I am
An unvarnished wooden floor
Is more beautiful than one painted

When I come to you empty
I am not filled with sound and fury,
Braggadocio and the lies of the world,
Artifice and makeup, bright blond and bold black

I trust you to see my natural soul
    early-morning eyes, tousled hair
    know my bad breath as you do my snoring
    smell my feet out of dirty socks

Perceive me as one who can betray
    Tell a lie about minutiae
    Conceal surface feelings
    Plot world wars silently

If I come to you in the effulgence
    of a Thanksgiving basket
    packaged, ribbons tied

The lie of perfection conceals my fear
    An illusion is your gift,
    but this is not the way it is

When I do not fear you, I come as
    an unframed picture
    a face that sports a pimple
    a character with a flaw
    a personal history with ambiguity

It is better to hold emptiness than fullness
    love it in its announced need
    fill it with good things
Better to clothe nakedness with loved garments, one by one,
    than strip excess without finding bare skin
Better to make love to what is
    than what is not

## GREGARIOUS LONER

You are as leathery as a saddle
lean as a penciled shadow sparsely drawn
your eyes questioning, abrupt, hurt
gaping, burning holes in a tentative face

Gregarious loner, your shyness is sophisticated
its mask of mockery and irony awry
the child looks out from layers of skin
asks for mercy, rejects pity, half laughs
    half cries
    says shit, fool
    this is the way it is

It's take you or leave you, right?
you can't change, won't change,
you tell the world adamantly
    with the wiry edge of a cigarette cough
    the full roundness of a zero
    the finality of an exclamation point

But you can change your course like a river
when you decide you must
    or want to
silt shifts, villages disappear overnight
trees uprooted, waters roll by
    in a new direction

You are as ugly as a weathered wooden shack
paint peeled away, gaping roof open to the rain
you are as gorgeous as a dying manzanita bush
red veins recklessly splashing blood on grayed limbs

You hide your beauty with studied deftness
let the world observe plainness and ordinariness
keep it always at a distance, you in quiet control
not wishing to stun it with an epiphany

You are secrets wrapped in secrets
inside gauze of a mummy's binding
half of your life is in a quiet interior
yet you are always friendly to strangers
    always hold children so tenderly

The mystery of you as a separate universe
    meets the orbit of mine
    when our bodies touch in ecstasy
our minds meet for a panel discussion
    over morning coffee
when we look at the same object
    in the same moment
    see the same thing

Then the mystery of you
    falls away
in my consciousness of
    your flesh
    breathing
    your eyes, closed or open

I accept this moment of truth
tread on its shore
   gaze in wonder
   at its source
   of light

        •      •      •

Memories.

So many of mine will always include you. Our years together—turbulent, funny, touching, never dull. Your crackling rage at the time of a full moon; and your otherwise unending, never-failing grace and sense of humor.

If someone asked me to describe you in a single frame, what would I say? Would it be one of lovemaking as I held you? A frame of you laughing or crying, angry or peacefully content? None of these.

It is a picture of us at a seashore—I wading out into the water, but turning to watch you, making a sandcastle.

        •      •      •

## CANUTE

Was it his shyness that attracted me to him? Or, maybe it was the curious mix of the devilish and the angelic in his easy smile.

I met him in a gay bar in Denver in the late '50s. It wasn't very gay because there were implicit threats of police harassment or arrest, and blackmail, in making the public disclosure that one was homosexual by appearing in the bar.

Merman and Garland played on the jukebox. I nervously sipped a watered-down scotch. We made contact. We went to my motel room. Shortly, we found that we were deliriously happy in each other's company.

Every Friday night I met him in the bar. He stayed with me until the next Saturday afternoon, when I must drive back alone to the small Colorado town in which I lived a closeted existence as a priest.

He earned his living as a short-order cook and a waiter. We were uninhibited in our free play, innocents who defied all the odds and claimed a small stake of pure happiness. But, it was doomed. There was no support system for our transitory relationship that was limited to an existence twenty-four hours a week inside a curtained motel room. There, we hid, loved, and earnestly tried to shut out the rest of the world.

Like King Canute trying to hold back the waves, we failed.

## GOLDEN HAIR

His fey expression and golden hair made him resemble a wondrous figure in a panel of medieval stained-glass.

His smile was elfin. A young Irish priest, his manner was marked by a strange sort of enchantment and mischievousness. Whenever I found him in an occasional uncharacteristic dour mood, all I had to do was speak gently, and gaze tenderly into his momentarily intractable eyes. In a flash, the fog of his nature would clear, the clouds disappear, and he smiled back at me from an illuminated expression.

I could not imagine living an earthly existence with such a creature from another world. However, I was delighted to be with him for a short time.

During a walk one afternoon we stopped to examine a stream alongside our path. A leaf which had been captured there inside winter ice was now free, a part of the springtime's running stream.

I never told him that I loved him except with my eyes and by my actions.

## THE OPERA

Always we made love before we went to the opera.

Our night on the subscription series was Wednesdays. So, on the late afternoons we got inside the covers and relished each other. After that, a light supper with a glass of wine. Then, off to the opera.

*Norma. La Bohème. Tosca. Fidelio. Der Rosenkavalier. Turandot. Lohengrin. Don Carlo. La Gioconda.* At intermissions the men attending the opera, dressed in everything from tuxedos to jeans, took close measure of one another climbing the marble stairs or conversing under the great chandelier. Always we waited for the coming of the last intermission to drink a glass of champagne.

To spill over with emotion is something that I have always done in the presence of beauty that touches me in an opera, at the theater or a museum. I savor the sense that it is my likeness to Zorba.

Yet I could not dance to express my grief when we parted.


## THE RAINS CAME

He had shining, explosive, dark eyes. His body was lithe, his smile warm and open. We met in a Greenwich Village bar.

Explaining that his father and mother were away, and the house he shared with them was empty, he invited me to his home in a distant suburb. We boarded a train and reached our destination after what seemed an interminable length of time. We were maddeningly ready to tear off our clothes and make love.

He unlocked the front door and opened it. As we walked inside the house, excited voices rang out. His parents' plans had obviously changed, and they were at home. He and his family were clearly involved in a crisis of dire proportions. He begged me to leave immediately, for my presence was proof that he was gay.

Out on the street, I realized it had begun to rain hard. I did not have any idea where I was. For hours I walked block after block, each containing similar locked, dark houses. No phone booth was in sight. I was drenched.

I walked all night. Half-drowned, chilled, and shaken by laughter at the lunacy of my predicament, I managed to hitchhike a ride into Manhattan in a truck.

What had I learned? Never trust a stranger? Yet I knew that would mean I could not trust anyone.

## THE LABORING MEN

A cousin of mine, a U.S. businessman who was as straight as American Gothic, took me with him on a short auto trip into Italy.

I tried to disguise my sharp looks in the direction of lusty Italian men, finally endeavoring not to look at all after my cousin expressed implicit disapproval. But this made me tense and edgy. My cousin and I, sharing a hotel room at nights and spending hours alone in his car during the days, began to fall into long, awkward periods of silence.

He was keenly aware of something different in me that he did not like. I was frustrated and miserable. We found little to talk or laugh about.

Near the end of our journey, as we drove in his open convertible along a highway near Milan, we were behind an open truck occupied by five laboring men. They were stripped to the waist, revealing bare, bronzed shoulders and lean bodies. My intent gaze caught the eye of one man. His sensuousness responded with alacrity to mine. He winked at me, smiled broadly, and happily caressed one of his bare nipples. I smiled back and started to make gestures of friendship.

My cousin became furious. He gunned the car's motor, took a dangerous swerve around the truck on the narrow road, and raced toward our destination. Not another word was said between us on the journey.

## THE MAN ON THE ROAD

Driving along the Mediterranean from Cannes to Monaco, I noticed the flowers in bloom along the road. The sun shone on the blue sea below.

He walked on the side of the road ahead. When he turned to cross the road, I slowed the car.

It was then I saw him, my quintessential ideal of male beauty. He seemed perfectly formed without self-conscious excess or arrogance. His movements were graceful and natural.

Our eyes met for an instant.

I seemed to gaze into the depths of an ocean, a rose, softly falling snow, an idyllic forest. I loved him.

He returned my look with simplicity, openness, and acceptance. He focussed intently on me, shutting out the world, expressing love and desire.

I have already driven past him on the road, helplessly as if I were drowning. Should I have braked the car, run back, and taken him in my arms under the noon sun?

I drove back to the same place on the road the next day, and the next, and the next, but did not find him again.

## THE KEY

We drove up the Oregon coast into Washington, then headed for Seattle.

We stayed at the "Y."

I had known him for years, yet he was a stranger to me. He was a tortured enigma of a man, a combination of loner with a short fuse of anger and sophisticated extrovert who generated the laughs in a crowd.

He was rugged, physically handsome, and in control: he did the driving, made most of the decisions about our trip, and I settled back and enjoyed not having to think.

We stayed in Seattle for several days. During the days we saw the sights, and he introduced me to a couple of friends of his who were women. I sensed the sadness they felt about him, the inability of such a sexually arousing man to become aroused by them. It was clear that they saw him as a Gary Cooper or a Steve McQueen, and that he had no idea what they felt about him.

At night, we drank. Heavily. We moved from bar to bar. Then we returned to the "Y" and fell on our narrow cots. I couldn't find the key to unlock the truth buried in him.

Why couldn't we make love instead of drink? Because he was afraid, sorely afraid, and I knew that if I touched the live wire an explosion could blow us up.

## AN OLD FRIEND

The intensity of seeing him again made me drive the car with dangerous abandon.

Our time together would be no more than an hour. I drove across France from Paris, accompanied by two people who did not know of my feeling for him, or what emotions were aroused in me by making the trip.

His life was settled now. He was well known. Our brief reunion would have to appear utterly casual and low-key, almost as if it were something trivial and entirely by chance.

So, as I drove the car, I talked of every possible subject except the one that mattered to me. My two companions must have wondered about the frenzy of my driving, yet my seemingly relaxed laughter no doubt kept them from worrying about it.

When we reached our destination, the three of us had lunch, shopped, went through the ritual of sightseeing. Then, I mentioned that I wanted to look up an old friend just to say hello, if he happened to be in. Could we meet in an hour? They went off to see a church or a castle, I to see him.

We held each other. I hoped that my eyes would be clear after shedding tears when I rejoined my companions.

I searched his life, he mine. Everything to do, say, feel, experience in an hour. Sixty minutes.

Then, somehow I said good-by and walked away.

## THIS STRANGER WHOM I LOVE

I struck you. Both of us fought with our fists. Later, shouting, we lay on the floor of the room and wrestled. Finally we were exhausted.

Somehow, we stopped shouting and fighting and got into bed. We had agreed long ago never to sleep in separate beds away from one another. Now, too, we slept in the same bed, as if by some reflex action.

Exhausted, we fell asleep right away. I awoke sometime in the middle of the night. I gazed at your naked body lying beside me. Who is this stranger whom I love, I wondered. How can I live without him? But I can't live with him. It's hopeless, the whole thing. Apparently I don't know him at all.

But you no longer resembled a monster with tongues of fire streaking out of your mouth. You looked very tender and likable. I wanted to kiss you. I desired more than anything to take your sleeping body into my arms and love you.

However, how could I do this if I were leaving you in the morning? I sighed. Shortly I fell asleep again.

When I awakened in the morning, I heard you brushing your teeth in the bathroom. A moment later I was beside you, and we embraced. We made a decision to stay together. We would find a way through our problems.


## TACITURN

The weather was freezing cold. It was after dark when I arrived at his place, having driven in my car most of the day to get there.

His was a rural church out on the plains. He lived next door to it in a small frame house.

A taciturn young priest, he was seemingly tied in knots emotionally. He was cold as ice. His laconic manner spurred my feeling of necessity to start a conversation. However, I found myself giving a monologue.

We ate dinner which he had prepared. The food was sparse and the silence bleak. I yearned to get to bed as a way of simply being alone, putting an end to unpleasantness. The next morning I would preach the guest sermon in his church and be on my way.

I was startled when he said there was only one bed and we would share it. When we undressed, I noticed the pure whiteness of his naked muscular body.

One side of the bed was placed against the wall. He asked me to climb into bed first, and occupy the side against the wall, so that he could get up first in the morning to start a fire.

After I climbed into bed, he turned off the light and followed me. The sheets were bitter cold. However, his body was warmer than a fire when he took me in his arms.

• • •

Why am I gay, God?

No one can really explain it to me.

Yes, I like to have sex with members of my own sex.

Yes, I've yearned forever for what was mysteriously and stubbornly called forbidden fruit.

Yes, I've fought and struggled, tooth and nail, against the tyranny that would kill my nature, mercifully changing me to a vegetable—albeit a socially acceptable one.

I'm tired of Bible-spouting hypocrites who talk about love in your name, God, while they hate my sisters and brothers—and me.

I'm sick of self-righteous inquisitors who quote scripture even while they light the faggots to burn, turn the screw of the rack to draw more blood and screams, and hammer nails into countless bodies on numberless crosses in order to murder the human spirit.

At long last, I have come to know myself as free. I have taken off my mask, and the sun and rain upon my naked face feel marvelous. The mystery of my gayness I celebrate with joy and thanksgiving.

Thank you, God, for making me gay.

# In Jerusalem

I caught a New England limousine for New York's Kennedy Airport. The car was filled, except for an empty seat next to the driver. I occupied it. The driver asked us which flights we were taking that day. The names were called out. United. American. TWA.

"El Al," I said. El Al is the airline of Israel.

We motored along in silence for a while.

"Last week I drove two Jewish girls who had just got back from Israel," the driver said. "They had fresh fruit they had brought home with them. They were telling me that the fruit was confiscated. They couldn't bring it through customs."

Nobody in the limousine was talkative, but I allowed as how customs could be difficult. The driver lapsed into silence.

"I was reading a book," the driver said after another half hour had passed. "It was about Germany. Most of the Germans, according to the book, didn't know what was happening. It was just a few Nazis who were guilty, and they didn't tell the rest of the people."

Neither I nor anyone else felt like making a response to the driver's remark, so the trip continued quietly and uneventfully. El Al was the car's first stop at the airport. But moments before the limousine reached the entrance to the terminal, the driver turned his head toward me and asked, "Why do you Jews want to go to Israel?"

The El Al dinner aboard the plane was kosher, but the meal included meat. When fruit was offered to the passengers after the meal, I asked, "Is there some cheese?"

The stewardess opened her mouth to say no. I knew the answer, and why, and was suddenly embarrassed. A kosher meal cannot combine meat with milk or any food that contains milk. This is according to strict rules of Orthodox Judaism. I must watch myself and not be an intolerable tourist.

My seat companion on the flight was a taciturn young man who never spoke a word, not even to a stewardess in acknowledgment of being given dinner or in response to questions. He appeared to be an athlete or a soldier. I assumed he spoke another language and dismissed the matter from my mind.

I had homework aboard the plane. Once inside Israel, I intended to explore the matter of Jewish-Arab relations there. One publication I had with me was a transcript of conversations between Arab and Jewish students at the Hebrew University.

Now the time was 2 A.M. Most of the other passengers, including my seat companion, had apparently gone to sleep as I began to read the document.

"Why are you doing that?" the young man abruptly asked. He spoke English with only the slightest accent. He explained that he was a Sabra, a native-born Israeli, who had been visiting relatives in the United States as their guest during a holiday. I put aside my reading in favor of a long conversation.

It was his arrogance—there is no other word to describe his facade—that initially struck me. As we talked, this outer roughness or seeming harsh unfriendliness gave way to warmth, marked by an abrupt directness in getting to the heart of issues or ideas.

I thought of him several days later when I visited Yad Vashem, the Holocaust memorial in Jerusalem. Buchenwald, Auschwitz, Dachau: The names of the death camps where six million Jews perished are written inside Yad Vashem. Ashes of victims' bodies were brought here from the camps. A flame burns by the graves.

I found written upon a wall the words from a letter by Opher Feniger, a parachutist and member of Kibbutz Givat Haim, who fell in the Six-Day War:

> I cannot say that I feel what they felt, they the
> doomed who lived without hope in the shadow

of death, but I sense it in all the hell and the terror that shows in their Jewish eyes, the wise eyes that know so much suffering behind the electrified fence—I have the feeling that out of all the horror and the hopelessness there rises and grows up in me an enormous force to be strong, strong even to tears, strong and sharp as a knife, silent and threatening—that is how I want to be. Only when I am strong will that look disappear! If we will all be strong! Strong and proud Jews! No longer will we be led to the slaughter.

The young Sabra on the plane had made "that look disappear" in his face, his manner and style. He was "strong and sharp as a knife, silent and threatening," yet he carried this with an innate relaxation and overpowering sense of confidence.

There was the aspect of—what can I call it?—a personal odyssey that contributed to my wanting to visit Israel. It was an almost lost fragment in my history. Three of my grandparents were Anglo-Saxon Protestants. The fourth, removed early from my consciousness by a divorce followed by death, was a Jew. I knew that in Nazi Germany this fact of my having a Jewish grandparent could have led to my imprisonment, possibly to my death. What significance could it hold for me now? Was it simply a meaningless statistic that brushed against my life?

I grew up a Christian and remain one by the commitment of faith and personal belief. During high school and college days I thought of Judaism as an alien faith utterly distant from my own experience. (Sunday school raised the insistent question, Hadn't the Jews killed Christ?)

Jewishness as a life-style often seemed forbidding and even odd. What was kosher food? What in the world was a bar mitzvah? What tradition did Jews observe at Christmas? My separation from Jews, already a fact of life, increased in college when

I joined a fraternity. It was Christian; there were separate Jewish fraternities, and the twain never met.

I remember a voting session in my fraternity when new pledges came under consideration. A particular name was called.

"He has a car," one member said. Applause.

"The guy's an athlete."

"He's sexy, man." Whistles. Laughter.

"He's got grades."

"You guys, listen. I'm serious about this. He looks Jewish. You know? He's got all that kike hair on his face that doesn't shave clean. I say no."

The prospective fraternity brother was blackballed.

During my days as a college student, I was invited home over a Christmas holiday by a girl whom I dated. To my consternation, I encountered another example of prejudice toward Jews, an overt expression of anti-Semitism that was couched behind an easygoing smile. On Christmas Day the entire family was seated around a table laden with foods. A fire crackled in a grate. The atmosphere was *gemütlich,* one of cheer and friendliness. The girl picked up a morsel of leftover food on her plate and started to place it inside the mouth of the family dog that was begging.

"Don't give that damned Jew any more to eat," her mother said, smiling warmly. "He's had too much already."

The specter of anti-Semitism had recently become locked inside my mind. For my worldview now included Hitler and his mobs, goose-stepping Nazi soldiers marching in shiny black boots, Herr Goebbels who acted like a devil and resembled an ascetic monk, and a rich civilization that was bent on persecution and its own ruin.

The staccato quality of Hitler's voice stuck in my awareness. It was accompanied by the rhythmic, measured cries out of thousands of Nazis' throats, growing in intensity until a blood sacrifice insinuated itself into one's own blood. The imagery of flailing whips and broken bones caused me to cower in evocative fear as if before an incensed serpent-god that demanded one's essence, identity, blood, body, mind, soul—one's very being.

I remember with some horror a moment inside a church, prior

to my departure for the seminary, when my heart constricted and I did not know where to go spiritually, or what to do. Recently I had concluded a long period of agnosticism and struggle with the meaning of faith. I had started to attend a church in Los Angeles occasionally. It scheduled a fund-raising drive. Because I worked in Hollywood, and therefore possessed numerous connections in the entertainment industry, I was asked to obtain celebrities as volunteers to appear at a benefit program in the church. My efforts were aided by those of a close friend, a songwriter who was Jewish.

When I walked into the church on the evening of the benefit, I saw its young rector. Surrounded by a half-dozen high school students, he was gesturing angrily with his hands. His voice boomed out. I heard him say, "I knew that damned Jew would be late."

Apparently the songwriter who had volunteered to help me was a few moments late—as I must have been, too. My idealism was stained and shattered. The joy of the evening benefit—what there had been of it—was drained. I turned and fled. I wondered, What could I do? Religion seemed a terrible thing to me in that moment, something infinitely more complex than I could cope with as an individual who sought communion with God and love of humanity.

Years of preparation lay ahead before I would become a priest. Inside the seminary I studied Judaism for the first time. Classes were devoted especially to the Old Testament and church history. I visited, over a period of six months or a year, a different Conservative or Reform synagogue every Friday night, because I wanted to participate in worship with Jews. I had a vision of universal love outside the strictures of my own religious doctrines and practices.

I asked myself: Why does religion separate people instead of unite them? Why must universal love give way, in the priorities of organized religion, to erecting high walls between people in whom God's spirit dwells?

Across the street from the first church that I served as a priest was a small, very poor Orthodox synagogue. I was asked to turn on the lights inside the synagogue every Saturday (sabbath) morning, thereby becoming a *shabbos goy*—a Gentile who performs this sort of task for strict religious Jews, who are not allowed to do such things.

When I moved away from the parish to become a college chaplain, I found myself involved in pragmatic interaction and a new dimension of life with an altogether different group of Jews—students and professors. A few of them became intimate friends. One graduate student and I held long discussions during which he explained the dynamics of his personal faith.

"Auschwitz and the simple truth that the Jewish people still exist are the central religious facts in my life," he said. "I can't adjust to myself a truth that encompasses both of them. Hope seems to betray a black truth that is truer than hope. Yet I simply can't live without hope."

He spoke of Yom Kippur: "There is a long blast on the shofar. It represents the slamming shut of the gates of heaven in the pure, straight legend terms in which it is given. Even on Yom Kippur, however, I always permit myself an escape clause. It seems inevitable that I'll get it together on that last moment when my lack of perfect faith will be taken back and forgiven."

I remember how the same student spoke of the Passover. "There is the allegory of the four sons—the smart, the bad, the simple, and the one who didn't know how to ask questions. I always knew, even at the age of eight, that I was in one of the first two."

Soon I entered actively into the tests and turmoil of the civil rights era. I went to jail with Jews. We faced death together on stretches of Southern country roads in the cause of equal rights for blacks, which we defined as obedience to the will of God for human justice.

A rabbi who was with me said that his participation in the movement was directly related to Jewish teaching that any suffering, anywhere in mankind, was therefore his suffering, his concern. This reminded me of Jesus' words in the New Testament.

It seemed to me that the rabbi and I shared consciences that had been informed by a common Judeo-Christian heritage. "Let justice roll down like waters," the prophet Amos cried.

Upon my arrival in Jerusalem, I stood past midnight before the Western (Wailing) Wall. The lines of a letter—written to a kibbutznik at the conclusion of the Six-Day War and later published in the popular Israeli book *The Seventh Day*—expressed poignant feelings that I found myself able to identify.

> As I stood weeping by the Wall, there wept with me my father, my grandfather and my great-grandfather. . . . I caressed its stones, I felt the warmth of those Jewish hearts which had warmed them with a warmth that will forever endure.

My Jewish grandfather never managed to reach Jerusalem or the Wall, except in the presence of his *goyische* grandson. The irony did not escape me.

On the eve of my departure for Israel, I had talked one evening at Yale with one of the foremost Jewish novelists in America, whose celebrated writing themes have not included either the Holocaust or the Israeli experience.

"I'm going to Israel on Monday," I told him. "Tell me about it—what to do, whom to see."

"I have never been to Israel," he said.

"Don't you want to go?"

"No. There's a boy-scout aspect to it. I'd keep looking into faces that said over and over again, 'What have you done for Israel?' I wouldn't like that."

Our conversation came to my mind two weeks later when I sat in the Tel Aviv suburban home of Moshe Shamir, the Israeli novelist and journalist. His wife had poured Scotch on the rocks for us.

"I think many American Jews are afraid of Israel," Shamir said. "Israel is too strong a dilemma. As a Jew, you cannot be an onlooker. You have to participate fully and say good-by to America and everything in which you have participated. A serious Jew has to answer the question: Why am I not staying in Israel? There is something of desertion, of being a traitor, in not being here."

The definition of "a Jew" came under discussion during my stay in Israel. I reflected upon words written by Arthur Koestler in his novel *Thieves in the Night:* "For Jews were not an accident of the race, but simply man's condition carried to its extreme—a branch of the species touched on the raw."

I chatted in Jerusalem with Rabbi Jack Cohen, director of the B'nai B'rith Hillel Foundation in Israel, who spoke of "the myth of Jewish peoplehood" inside Israel.

"There is the self-identity problem," he said. "Jews are battling among themselves as to who they are. Traditionalist and democratic pluralistic views are worlds apart. Then, too, Jews do not come to Israel as Jews, but as men and women characteristic of various cultures. It isn't easy to get a Russian Jew to understand what an American Jew is talking about—for example, when he discusses feelings of loyalty to America. To create a people out of this cannot happen overnight."

Moshe Shamir spoke of a "crisis in Judaism" during our conversation in Tel Aviv.

"If Judaism is a religion first and foremost, then it is in a very dead condition," he said. "What saved it from total collapse is Zionism—the opportunity to try again in a different dimension as a nation on its own land. As pure religion, small societies spread all over the world, there is a total bankruptcy. Intermarriage. A lack of believers. Religion becomes a monopoly of small exotic sections. The beautiful thing about Israel is that it started really as a rebellion against Orthodox Judaism. Zionism is a branch of assimilation—let's not use such a strong word. Of secularism. Let's stop praying for the messiah to come and save us. Let's do it with our own hands.

"In a miserably small way, Zionism is a success. The most fascinating aspect of it is the revival of the Hebrew language and the experience of Jewish history. Out of legend or myth has come a unified power, and, with it, something like a religious renaissance. This is not taking place so much in Israel as in Jewish communities outside of Israel. There is a great change of heart in Western Jewry. Personal edification instead of personal philanthropy."

The question of self-criticism arose in my conversation in Tel Aviv with David Ben-Gurion, then prime minister of Israel, when I asked him if he had read Amos Elon's book *The Israelis: Founders and Sons.*

"I wish you would not speak of that book," he said. "I wish it had not been written."

What did Elon say in his book that disturbed some people inside Israel and aroused controversy? For one thing, he alluded to the existence of a "spiritual vacuum created by the receding future of the classic Zionist dream, a vacuum that cannot satisfactorily be filled by feats of arms."

In other words, a number of Israelis—and Jews throughout the world—realized that the dream of settling and establishing Israel has been completed. What then, would be the substance of the people's new visions and dreams? What would be the sources of Israel's spiritual and moral power? Could there be peace?

When I spoke with Elon during a visit to his home in Jerusalem, I asked him to comment on the spiritual, or deeply moral, questions that confronted Israel.

"This is a functioning society. A youthful society," said Elon. "What am I afraid to lose? We must never forget that the idea of creating another state was, at the start of Zionism, subservient to creating a better society. Yet Israel is the closest thing to a Greek city-state that exists today.

"Only in raucous, nearly anarchic freedom can you get this kind of strength. There is an electricity in the Israeli society. It comes from a deep spiritual source. It is understood that freedom is more effective than tyranny. There is an element of not wanting to force anybody to do anything. It also comes from an essential gentleness that remains in this society."

Meron Benvenisti, a member of the city council of Jerusalem who had previously resigned, amid controversy, as administrator of East Jerusalem, expressed self-criticism, as well as consider-able optimism, during a conversation.

"We know from history that a national movement, once it has begun, cannot be forgotten. A moral danger in Israel is that the occupation of the West Bank will become permanent. However, I don't like to think this will happen. People would like Israel to be both democratic and Jewish."

Inside her East Jerusalem apartment, I chatted with an Arab woman, a social worker. "I have a Jordanian passport," she said. "I am just a question mark. Nothing. Imagine this feeling: You are in your own country, and at any moment a military order can kick you out, put you in a car, and drive you across a bridge. Jews don't know what they want to do with Arabs like myself on the West Bank. They want the land but not the people."

There is logic in both Jewish and Palestinian claims. Intellec-tual comprehension of such logic, however, does not solve the dilemma of having to adopt a psychological point of view, an emotional reaction, and even a moral posture.

"Arabs and Jews are doomed to live together until the end of time," a Jewish teacher told me. "We can make it a better pros-pect instead of an impossible one. Coexistence means keeping a certain distance between Arabs and Jews. I speak of a distance of honor, not a hatred distance.

"This can allow two peoples to live together without being exposed to old abrasiveness. It is tragic that, in effect, Arabs and Jews are in the Alamo today. We don't want to absorb each other. An adequate distance will allow people to smile. It won't go deep in the heart, but it can keep people from killing each other."

Late one night I drank coffee and talked with an Arab news-paper editor inside his office in East Jerusalem.

"Peace must be based on justice for the Palestinian," he said. "The other side must respect my rights if he intends to live with me in peace. I would like to see peace, but I cannot live under occupation forever."

I drove from Jerusalem to a town on the West Bank to meet an Arab lawyer. We chatted over cups of Turkish coffee.

"The world has solved the Jewish problem while creating an even more difficult one—the Palestinian problem," he said. "What I want is the right of statehood."

Walking in the Old City of East Jerusalem, one is thrust into the midst of people who are baking bread, carrying sacks of corn seed, selling produce, animatedly talking in small groups, or dozing in the noon sun. Smells of orange juice, meat cooking on an open stove, moisture of a wet wall, spices from a shop, and even a latrine close to the street assault one's senses. The daylight is blinding, for in Jerusalem the air is clear and there is extraordinary brightness.

"There is peace in Jerusalem," an immigrant to Israel remarked during a stroll through the streets of the Old City.

"No," replied a long-time occupant of the city. "We can't have peace in Jerusalem unless the wish for it exists also in Saudi Arabia, the United States, the Soviet Union, the Vatican, Egypt, and Syria."

Jerusalemites have so many conflicting views about this subject. A thirty-year-old Arab social worker in East Jerusalem explained why he does not envision peace for many years.

"I think the Palestinians like myself will suffer more," he said. "I have no hope whatsoever of living a normal life. I never remember a day in my life when we had peace. All I remember is war and war, promises and insecurity. Not even one Arab in East Jerusalem is happy. How can you live under occupation and annexation? If I weren't married, I would have left for the States."

He sipped an orange juice and puffed on a cigarette.

An Israeli teacher, an intense, chain-smoking woman with tired eyes, looked at the situation differently.

"We Jews lost so many lives in the Yom Kippur War and sustained tragic injuries," she said. "Out of this vast Middle East we occupy a tiny piece of land. It is the homeland for us following the murder of six million Jews in the Holocaust. We have no other place in the world.

"Many of us sympathize with the Palestinian cause and seek a just solution to it. But we can't say that we are willing to be pushed into the sea. We must survive for the sake of millions of Jews who have perished as well as those who are still unborn."

A lovely incident during my visit to Israel served memorably to underscore a significant aspect of my life. In lifestyle I am a highly mobile person. Interiorly, I am not a stranger to restlessness, either. I have been forcibly struck by Karl Barth's stinging words, "There is suffering and sinking, a being lost and a being rent asunder, in the peace of God."

One afternoon I visited a distinguished Jewish theologian in his Jerusalem home. He received me graciously as a guest—an American Christian who had written a book of prayers entitled *Are You Running With Me, Jesus?* We enjoyed an hour of conversation. Suddenly, I glanced at the clock and realized that I was late for another appointment.

"I must run," I exclaimed.

"God has placed a curse on you for writing that book," he said levelly, with only the slightest suggestion of a smile at the corners of his eyes. "God will make you run forever." He put his arm around my shoulders, and we both laughed.

## CHILD IN THE CITY

I ride a glassed-in elevator
    all the way to the 34th floor
    see reflections of the city in windows
    cars swirl into freeways
    "Jesus Saves" sign blends into a swimming pool
    keep riding up and down until
    people stare, whisper, point in my direction

For a while I sit and look at fountains splash
    in a plaza
    Ten small fountains, a sophisticated shimmy
A man with long matted hair
    wears loose, tattered brown pants
    sandals on his bare feet
    asks me for money
    says he's hungry

In a Japanese garden in the sky
    small leaves, red, green, brown
    bob up and down at the base of a waterfall
    ships of an armada caught in a storm
Two white stone dragons, eyes blazing, teeth bared
    guard a corner
    pine winds blow
    see empires rise and fall

A tall building reflected in a quiet pool of water
    seems to shake, totter
    speed as if animated
    want to jump into the pool
    climb the building that moves so fast

Pause on a freeway overpass
    drivers of speeding cars don't see me
    seem lost in their thoughts
    pace of cars hypnotic
A man seated on the lawn across from City Hall
    barks sharply like a dog
    every 30 seconds

I see myself cloned ten times
    in the glass windows of an office building
Ride escalators down into the bowels of skyscrapers
    look up, see glass-sheathed structures
    mirrored in each other
Play with three giant waterfalls
    inside a garden below street level
    alone here in the midst of ten million people
    waterfalls cascade, thunder
    shoot in a perfect arc
    like quicksilver before my eyes

On the street a man wears red shorts
    carries a baby on his back in a harness
    holds the Hound of the Baskervilles
    on a short leash
I watch a sensuous woman
    in tight white slacks
    long black hair falls down her back
    she is a movie queen
    restless, in search of anonymity
    wears sunglasses on a cool day
    on her way to meet Howard Hughes

Two elderly women drag heavy suitcases
    One stops, says
    "God bless! I'm tired now"

Inside a high-ceilinged hotel lobby
    expect to see Douglas Fairbanks
    moustached and costumed
    swing from one chandelier to another
But a Science Fiction convention is in progress
    an unsmiling man, an unsmiling woman
    wear long black robes that sweep the floor
    their faces painted chalk white
    sit self-consciously in the entrance of a public room
    hold each other, kiss perfunctorily
    seem bored with everything,
    even their performance
I sit and watch a man who bites his fingernails
    talks into a pay phone

## TO MY DOG AND CAT

If the truth were known, I like you equally well.
This is not to say you are in the least the same.
One of you is quite patient with me, hardly ever selfish—
except at mealtimes—very easy to live with although surpris-
ingly easily hurt, and always around to meet my every need.

The other is easily put-out and impatient with me, extremely
self-centered and selfish (therefore, mysterious and puzzling),
awfully complicated to live with—but never boring, absent on a
whim, secretive, and making me aware of meeting *your* every
need.

One of you invariably makes a good, firm, steady impression
on guests, obeys orders, retreats when commanded, and sleeps as
late as I do in the morning.

The other can, with malice aforethought, make a most sinister
impression on guests, even frighten them. You can callously dis-
obey orders, cling onto guests who find in you the very incarna-

tion of a medieval devil, and wake me up at dawn by getting upon on my pillow and purring.

One of you wags a tail in devotion, the other rotates a tail in anger. One of you licks my hand as a sign of affection, the other sits on my lap and scratches my knee, even to the point of drawing my blood, equally affectionate.

Both of you have four legs, are the same color, take an afternoon nap, and possess healthy appetites. I must bathe one of you, whereas the other attends personally to such an intimate matter.

Each of you is something of an intellectual, and also has a hard core of integrity. You know very well when you have done the right or the wrong thing. You are both capable of the worst mischief and the greatest kindness.

I like you equally well—one at a time. One of you is like salt, the other pepper. There is a moment and a place for you both. I'd rather not mix my moments and places, and, for once, you *both* agree with me.

## THE FILM AND I

It is being projected onto a screen at the other end of the long room. Images are moving. I hear words and music. All of us seated here in this room are very silent, absorbed.

Is *that* reality or fantasy? It seems to me somehow more real than my own life. Yet it is a film. The actors are actors; they do not live in the poor hovels I see on the screen, but in grand houses and great hotels. They are not hungry and emaciated as they now appear. The terrible dilemmas of the persons are scripted; the actors can check out at 5 P.M., have the make-up and costumes removed, and drive home for a drink before dinner.

But I am absorbed in what seems real. Of course, it is real for the characters who are portrayed. However, have they a life? If so, what is the relation between their lives, under greasepaint, to mine without it?

A few minutes ago I was laughing out loud at something very funny up there. Now I am sitting in stony silence, unaware whether my own heart is beating, closer to tears than I am aware.

These may be brought over the brink by the right use of music, or a clever use of the camera if it moves—right now—from the exterior snow scene through that window into the room where a father and his son confront each other.

Images. Sounds. Light. Greasepaint.

Soon I will be outside the theater, walking on the street. Will the only reality then be inside myself, or will I have returned to fantasy from the reality on the screen?

• • •

This is *serious* drinking.

Drown out the seashell music, blot out all the pain, make a new pain that can be *felt* to take the place of the other.

Death, are you quiet or loud?

You frighten me, yet I feel I could embrace you in this moment of pain and fury. You couldn't hurt me more than I am hurt. You couldn't depress me more than I am depressed.

But don't come. Stay wherever you are.

I know you're close. I feel your not breathing. I hear your heart not beating. In pain, I still want the aching restlessness of a heartbeat. In fury, the unbridled movement of breath. Don't come.

## DUET ON DEATHS

*How many deaths must we die?*

We must die deaths until we die.

*What is the difference between death and deaths?*

Our deaths are in the spirit, affecting our pride, our isolation, our spiritual murdering and exploitation of others, our greed. Our death is in the body as well as the spirit, and marks our physical annihilation on earth.

*How are deaths related to death?*

Deaths diminish our egoism and multiply our open relationships with other people, and increase our awareness of the universe of life surrounding our own personal islands. When we have become accustomed to dying—or, living in a broader and deeper sense—we are naturally adjusted to the final act of death itself, which is an act of life.

*Why is the act of death an act of life?*

Death is inseparable from life. A seed dies, buried deep in the earth, and after a time new life is born. Death is dynamic, never static or isolated from momentum. Its pause or evident lack of rhythm is deceptive; forces of life are gathered. While a body is still and decaying, a personality is a great force of incredible diversity. At death, it is like a symphony that awaits the start of a new movement. If there seems to be silence, listen: that dead life makes a sound that is like the reverberation inside a dead shell torn from the sea. Death is very real, and exists, but not apart from life. Life is very real, and exists, but not apart from death. The finality of each is required of the other.

*How are the acts of death related to the act of life?*

Unless we die many deaths in the spirit, we cut ourselves off from living itself. We come to misunderstand life, fear other people, break the very rhythm of living. Life, in its openness and continued vulnerability, absence of hardness or cynicism, is marked by the scars of such deaths. They are the very signs of life.

## SURPRISE FROZEN WALTZ

Gone to the movies
    double feature, old downtown theater
    mediocre cinema at best
    win some, lose some

Lights came up at eleven
    saw audience, handful of us
    felt sense of tribalism

better stick together
we'll be safe from
old movie stars' ghosts
celluloid gangsters
crawling out of woodwork

Outside, everybody scattered
all alone
car parked across street
use cross-walk
step out
car a block away
moves closer, speeds
strange unease

Frozen in path
feet cemented
car bearing down
headlights make macabre glow
hypnotized
jump backward
car fills space

Face staring
muscles slack
mouth opened wide
horror in eyes
drunk driver confused
car lurches forward
vanishes around corner
in urban crossword puzzle

Feel bruised
death brushed against me
our gazes locked
in surprise frozen waltz
felt neither resentment
nor dismay
only recognition

Odd, to walk away
    with jaunty step
    we'll meet again
    death and I
    in a hospital or airplane
    at home or urban wasteland
    wasn't a dress rehearsal
    death will come
    on its own terms
    its own choreography

Disinterested in death
    don't want it to come
    to break lean
    singular continuity of my life
    not now.

•    •    •

*I don't want them to give you my body, you goddam black hearse.*
I don't want you to have me, you flashy junkpile owned by a vulgar cat who mauls dead bodies. I don't want to be stifled inside you, beneath a mound of sweet-smelling flowers.

I don't want traffic to stop at an intersection while you bear my body on exhibition down a street. I don't want somebody to make the sign of the cross, and somebody else to curse because of the traffic jam as you bear me by.

I don't want some paid minister who doesn't love me to read prayers out of a book while you wait ominously outside a church, and people cry to the accompaniment of unctuous organ music.

Let my body be used for medical research, then burned, and the ashes scattered where they can't hurt anybody or pollute water or poison the atmosphere.

I don't want them to give you my body, you goddam black hearse.

•    •    •

## URBAN SAILOR

In 1955
    vacation from studies at Oxford
    traveled to Greece
    to Mount Athos
Early-morning mists closed tight around island
    approached in small open boat
    filled with sheep, feet tied together,
    a donkey
    coming from Ierissos

    wandered on beach near Vatopedi
    stone ruins nearby
    chimes pealed inside walled monastery
    rare moment following sunset
    darkness about to fall

Now in 1981
    yearned to get away from it all again
    unwind, relax,
Find crucial new focus
    become quietly at peace with myself

Boarded flight 866 in Los Angeles
    flew to Jamaica
hours after arrival in small sailboat
    on dark blue sea
    Cuba next stop
Quickly follow Ulysses
    become seagoing philosopher
Universe breathes in motion of waves
    splash on my shoulders
Sky, close, filled by huge faces, shapes
    reach out
    try to touch

Tiny boat soars to peak of watery hill
    plunges into valley of foam
Exhilarated, sense overpowering decadence
in overripe, lush, dying colors

Morning beach walk ends abruptly
    pile of rocks
    "No trespassing" says sign
Remark to young black man
    have apparently lost
    knack with nature
    He says, follow me
    climb along narrow ledge
    let body drop from scary height
Stay intact, decide upon return to Los Angeles
    perhaps should enter Mr. Universe contest

At midnight
    lay on dark beach
    waves wash over body
    stars remain constant
    century after century
look up at sky, laugh out loud
    unchanging galaxy preserves objective view
    of all the characters
    including me
    in a chorus line
    on the world's stage

Strong wind moves in from gulf
    take final sailboat ride
As a youngster was afraid of water
    now Caribbean waits inches away
    plunge me into coral reefs forever
    drenched with salt water
    floods boat with makeshift sail
    three-foot waves beckon me to lively oblivion

am Zorba about to dance
on the waters
Urban sailor
rides fury of waves
Vacation was splendid
questions not answered
new focus on life eludes me
to be quietly at peace
remains distant goal

Yet, who knows?
might even pay return visit to Mount Athos
stand there once more
in rare moment following sunset
when darkness about to fall
Look up, ask why
roar with laughter

# PHOTO ALBUM

Malcolm Boyd, as an infant, with his parents, in New York City.

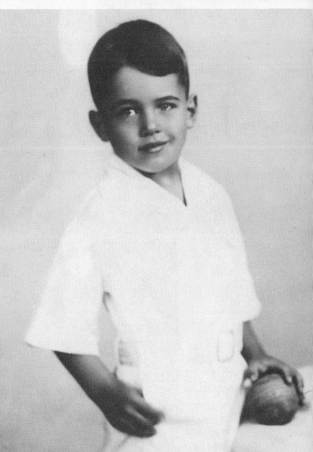

Malcolm Boyd, as a boy.

Malcolm Boyd
hands bouquet to
Gloria Swanson as
Buddy Rogers
looks on.
Hollywood, 1949.

The young TV
producer in
Hollywood.

With Mary
Pickford at the
Hollywood
Advertising Club
in 1949.

In seminary, Berkeley, California, 1954.

ABOVE, RIGHT: With actor Woodie King, Jr., in a performance of Boyd's one-act play on race relations "Study in Color," in a coffeehouse in Daytona Beach, Florida.

At Colorado State
University's Golden
Grape coffeehouse, 1960.

With Woodie King, Jr., in a performance
of Boyd's one-act play "Boy," in Detroit,
Michigan, 1962.

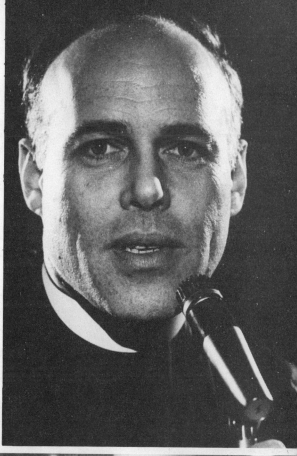

At the hungry i.

Arrested at the
Pentagon "Peace
Mass," June 15, 1970.

In Jerusalem, at the
Shrine of the Book.

Malcolm Boyd now. (*Joe
Doherty; used by permission*)

ABOVE,RIGHT:
At Big Sur, 1985.
*(Mark Thompson;*
*used by permission)*

Shelley Winters with Malcolm Boyd (President of Los Angeles
Center of P.E.N.) and Norman Mailer (President of P.E.N.
American Center in New York) at a Los Angeles literary party, 1985.
*(Kathy Weiss; used by permission)*

# PART II:
# IMAGINATION

# Images and Incense

I sat eighth row center as a guest critic for the *New York Times* at the Broadway opening of a new rock drama in October 1971. Can Jesus survive *Jesus Christ Superstar?* was the question that I asked myself.

Jesus had recently become the newest pop phenomenon. He was on the stage in both *Jesus Christ Superstar* and *Godspell*. A sporadic religious movement used his name in association with self-styled "freaks." A bumper sticker on a handful of cars even announced: "Honk if you love Jesus." I could not help but wonder if Jesus as a woman (a capital idea) might be offered to us next. If so, would the model be Princess Diana or Bette Midler, Nancy Reagan or Bella Abzug?

It could only be presumed that cultural interchange with China would reveal a strapping yellow Jesus. Perhaps a Henry Kissinger would bring a young Chinese actor from Peking to Hollywood in order to help set up a new biblical spectacular with the surprise element of a wholly new image for the treadworn ones of the past.

Can Jesus ever simply be himself? It is apparent that many people want to create Jesus in their own image. Activists want an activist Jesus. Several years ago, Pier Paolo Pasolini added pepper to the scriptural stew by giving us an angry cinematic Christ, played with a mystic electric quality and restless vigor by Enrique Irazoqui in the movie *The Gospel According to Saint Matthew*. He overturned the money changers' tables in the temple with a zeal close to fury, becoming a great overnight favorite cult figure with social activists. This was the best religious picture in years. John the Baptist was not a bearded Charlton Heston in furs, but a man of the people, sweaty and crude. The disciples had wonderfully unhandsome faces, lined by anxiety and suffering but young in new commitment. One saw Jesus with his disciples as a band of poor men, despised by power structures and marked off from respectable dry rot and hypocritical niceties in the face of human need and pain. Pasolini caught on film the offense and scandal of Jesus.

Contemplatives want a pious figure of Christ locked inside the confines of the Twenty-third Psalm. Whites have always demanded a snow-white Lord, preferably with blond hair and blue eyes. Asserting that "black is beautiful," blacks began to pay public attention to a jet Jesus.

Of course, we have grown accustomed to Jesus' face in a spate of Hollywood biblical films. Yet Jesus as a superstar seemed a devastating irony. Most superstars are not executed as common criminals after being flogged half to death. However, Cecil B. DeMille indulged in a Garboesque sign of Christly superstardom when he made *King of Kings* in 1927 and ordered H. B. Warner, who portrayed Jesus, to wear a veil on his way to and from the dressing room and to eat his meals alone.

R. Henderson Bland played Jesus in *From the Manger to the Cross*, a 1912 movie. He later noted in a memoir how crowds gave him superstar treatment precisely because of the part he played. "The crowds around my carriage were so dense that police were told to keep the people back," Bland wrote. "When I left the carriage to take my position in the scene a way was made for me with no word said. Women stepped forward and kissed my robe."

Stage and screen portrayals of Jesus raise a storm of protest and questions from church officials. Is the mystery of Jesus compromised by literal depiction that adheres to such a detail as accurate historical costuming while it falsifies truth in the very presumption of revealing it before one's eyes?

Yet it is absolutely proper for Jesus to be portrayed on the stage and screen. Christian theology teaches that Jesus does not dwell in holy ghettos separated from the joy and misery, the sordidness and beauty, of human life. Jesus, we are told, lived as a human being for thirty-three years on solid earth and continues to dwell at the central and intimate places of people's lives, where he shares profound involvement in human politics, work, leisure, sexuality, life, and death.

Instead of merely criticizing the portrayals of Jesus on the stage and screen, it behooves churches to ask what images of Jesus they have been communicating to the public—and to what extent they have happily succeeded or deeply failed in that task. I am inclined to see considerable failure. Partially it was erroneous images of Jesus conveyed to me as a child in a plethora of Sunday school classes that led to my being a cynical and sometimes angry atheist in college.

Still another in a long procession of Jesus images awaited me as I sat inside that darkened Broadway theater in the fall of 1971 to watch the premiere of *Jesus Christ Superstar.*

The young actor who portrayed Jesus reminded me of Lauren Bacall, especially in the repeated gesture he used to push back his hair. His was a sensual, soft Jesus: often petulant, self-centered, a figure of flaming youth who enjoys flattery and publicity.

Superstar? I am more inclined to share the view expressed to me one day by a student at Yale who said: "I don't think much about Jesus. But to say he's a superstar is all wrong. He's the lost face in a crowd. He's the woman in *La Strada.* He's the leper. But he's not a big celebrity standing up over other people."

Many church folk are thankful for any religious or secular crumbs that fall from a fattened table in these lean days. A great big commercial hit that pays attention to Jesus might even make the church seem to be "relevant." (Power to the Apostles.) Youth might be attracted by means of exploitation to unchanged dogma, ritual, and social attitudes. Best of all, Jesus might become news. He might become (say a prayer) a real superstar to fill all the church buildings again. These church folk say, in effect, "Don't criticize this show. Thank God for it."

The god of technical tricks and slick majesty? For this is the god whom director Tom O'Horgan—shades of Cecil B. De-Mille's biblical spectaculars—gave us, with enough brashness thrown in to induce praise from the late Mr. DeMille. And also enough theological travesty to boggle the mind. In a myriad of details gone wrong, the Broadway show bore little resemblance to the New Testament. Yet, what is most important, Jesus' mission got misplaced somewhere from drawing board to Star Chamber.

Sometimes *Jesus Christ Superstar* was *Love Story in Jerusalem*. Other times it sadly seemed to be only *The Greening of the Box Office*. But was it a serious work of art? And how did it deal with the Passion of Christ? Since this show was built on the Rock, I decided that one had best look under it.

I asked myself: Is this the Jesus of a significant counterculture? Not at all. For we see him reject the sick and distressed victims of society who come to him for help. We see a restless and tired "star" Jesus arrogantly send Judas away to the work of betrayal. Fatigue and introspection could have legitimately been portrayed. But despair looms too centrally in Christ, conveying a sense of mission lost and purpose forgotten.

In the absence here of depth of feeling, I recollected the profundity and integrity of the multiple crucifixion that is implicitly portrayed in Eugene O'Neill's *Long Day's Journey into Night:* a calculated reach into the recesses of the soul, a confrontation with quintessential actors who trod the stage of life and wore flesh and bones, as well as lines upon their faces caused by pain.

As in Dali's concept of the Crucifixion, there was clearly the absence of a cross rooted in earth in *Jesus Christ Superstar.* Such lack of specificity leads to those quasi-religious fantasies that obliterate detailed truth. I am not one of those purists who decry the show's bypassing of the Resurrection. After watching Jesus hang on a Daliesque golden triangle (an avant-garde symbol of the cross?) for a glamorous simulation of the Crucifixion, I offered thanks to the pantheon of gods that we were indeed spared a Resurrection. But in its failure to come to terms with the sacrifice of a Christ-figure, or the Passion of Christ, the celebrated Broadway production of *Jesus Christ Superstar* also failed to become a seriously motivated and constructed rock opera.

It was several things: a Rockette operetta, a Barnumian put-on, a religioso–cum–show biz pastiche, and a musicalized "Sweet

Sweetback's Baadasssss Judas Song." The Jews seemed to be guilty, once again, of causing Jesus' death. Jewish priests were seen in ominous, gargoylelike costumes straight out of medieval caricatures. We were thrust against energy without exuberance, torture without tragedy, in this collage-in-motion based upon a celebrated group of musical numbers, several of them splendid and memorable.

Tim Rice and Andrew Lloyd Webber, who wrote *Jesus Christ Superstar*, had something interesting going for them with their best-selling album of songs. The Broadway production changed all that inexplicably. A clean, unambiguous concept became a muddled, religiously controversial show.

The sexuality of Jesus undoubtedly comprised the exhibit A controversy about the show. He and Mary Magdalene fondled and kissed each other; I felt an implicit acceptance of the fact that they had enjoyed intercourse. The exposure of this side of Jesus' humanity understandably drew cheers from the audience, no doubt in reaction against the celibate Jesus of the organized church who has been used traditionally as a major argument against sex outside of (and before) wedlock as well as against homosexuality.

Looking at Jesus as a human being (as well as the Son of God) with sexual feelings is far overdue in our puritanical, sexually hypocritical society. I applaud it. Yet I feel that his sexuality was not handled sensitively or with taste in the inhuman Broadway parody.

I remain critical of other things in the show: a glittering gold shaft descended from "heaven" onto center stage to indicate, I suppose, the presence of God; Jesus looks up when he asks the Father to spare him; the—excuse me—queentessential Herod ruins "King Herod's Song" by making it a campy nightclub number instead of a piece of the mosaic in "the last seven days in the life of Jesus of Nazareth," to quote the program.

The show gave us a confused, tired but plucky Jesus who is going to the cross even if it kills him. Mary Magdalene is a cool, mod, and sincere chick who digs Jesus but senses that he is very different from other men whom she has known. She sings a gentle ditty about the love for him that she feels. However, it is clearly not sufficiently deep a love to bind her to him through his torture and death. My bet is that Mary Magdalene, after a few bad days, a lot of cigarettes, and a gallon or so of black coffee, would be able to submerge memories of Jesus long enough to shack up with next week's superstar in Jerusalem.

Judas' feelings about Jesus provides the real basis for what utterly fictional story line exists between the musical numbers. Judas feels that he is trapped in a terrible role, one scripted by God and directed by Jesus. In this show, four demons assist divinity with the pragmatic dirty work of haunting and wrestling with him. Judas' acceptance of predestination to damnation smacks unappetizingly of Calvinism with bitters. So Judas ended up playing a role instead of himself.

It is an absurd irony that a simplistic success—with a $1 million advance sale—emerged from the ambiguity and violent paradox of Jesus' Passion, presented on Broadway with all dimensions flattened. Even the controversy of Jesus, intellectually ignored in this show, was made marketable in a plastic-ware production that didn't have a soul.

When it was announced that *Jesus Christ Superstar* would be filmed, I only hoped that the movie would not become a star vehicle and that distant locations would not serve as a substitute for the intimacy of human beings engaged in interaction on dusty Palestinian roads, inside simple dwellings and occasional palaces, and at Golgotha. Well, the movie that resulted simply brought to mind my favorite spiritual, as I noted when *Newsday* invited me to review the film.

> Were you there when they crucified my Lord?
> Were you there when they crucified my Lord?
> Oh! Sometimes it causes me to tremble, tremble,
>     tremble,
> Were you there when they crucified my Lord?

The nails were pounded into the old rugged cross with familiar precision. I asked myself: Why do festering illusions leap like full-grown demons from a filmmaker's mind when the time comes to place this hardy perennial story on celluloid?

The film *Jesus Christ Superstar* offers us the same self-indulgent Jesus who screams, "Leave me alone!" when the sick and needy crowd about him for help; sadistically and mercilessly—he's not even a decent guy, but a temperamental superstar—sends Judas off to finish his work of betrayal; and stoically offers his Wotan-like Father—before whom he seems to be more Job than Jesus—his life.

Jesus' sacrifice is portrayed here without perception of its mystery, awareness of its context of victory and joy, or even personal resources that would open up his death to others instead of let death simply close in upon himself.

For example, the only words spoken by Jesus from the death-cross in the movie version of *Jesus Christ Superstar* are "Father, forgive them; for they know not what they do" and "My God, my God, why hast thou forsaken me?" We do not hear those words, or perceive those related actions of Christ's, that concerned the thieves with whom he was crucified and his compassionate response to them; the very human interaction concerning Jesus' mother and his beloved disciple, which reflects Jesus' deep concern for others even at the moment of his own torture; or Jesus' own intense humanness as it reached out to the circle of people standing about the cross and was expressed in the words addressed to them: "I thirst."

Jesus is portrayed in the movie as an athlete-for-Christ, blue-eyed, blond, Anglo-Saxon, muscular; and one can almost see him in a men's after-shave lotion commercial made for television. Why—for Christ's sake—didn't they let Jesus be a Jew in *Jesus Christ Superstar*? After all, they took the cast to Israel to shoot the picture there. Doesn't historical location call also for historical accuracy?

Now we come to the heart of the mystery that shrouds this movie. It inexplicably contains harsh, strident images conjuring up a mood of anti-Semitism. Oberammergau couldn't top this one. Jew-haters could rub their hands with glee and chortle loudly—maybe go out and get drunk in a combination of bewilderment and delight that somebody else, surely inadvertently, has done their work for them—when they sit down in a theater to see *Jesus Christ Superstar.*

Yet this film was made in Israel with government cooperation, although curiously without its approval. What went wrong? Who is to blame? The problem is a mind-boggler.

The film arrived at a moment in history when there had occurred an official relaxation of traditional, Establishment Jewish-Christian relations. After Vatican II had moved resolutely in this direction, a humorous footnote was offered by Harry Golden. He observed that, inasmuch as the Christians had finally absolved the Jews of collective guilt in the death of Christ, maybe the time had come for Jews to convene a world congress to absolve the Christians of collective guilt for the Crusades. A new age had arrived, ecumenically speaking. One could make a joke, and smile.

Then the Six-Day War, and Christian reactions to it, brought Jews and Christians into an altogether original dialogue that was sometimes painful but broke ground in its candor and creative possibilities. Yet Auschwitz always lurked immediately in the past, eerily and uneasily shadowing the present.

But the movie *Jesus Christ Superstar,* with its G rating, which drew in families and youths, equates Jewishness with villainy. Jewish priests, scowling beneath their grotesque hats that resemble medieval caricatures, peer down from a scaffold at the middle-American Jesus who strides up the road surrounded not by sweaty disciples but—of course!—flower children. Theirs is the kingdom; their enemy is organized religion—and this is Judaism, represented before our eyes by unsmiling, conniving, murderous, unprincipled, unloving, always Machiavellian Jewish priests. Voilà!

The film's dialogue introduces Jewish references that cannot be found in the Bible. Why were they glued onto the script? Pilate addresses the crowd, "Look at me—am I a Jew?" He says, "You Jews produce messiahs by the sackful."

When the Broadway version of *Jesus Christ Superstar* presented a black Judas, I simply accepted this as a producer's decision. However, black Judas is back again in the movie, and this time

I found that I had serious questions about the casting, primarily because of the film's potential impact on a worldwide audience. Let me explain.

There is a scene, for example, where Judas angrily stalks away from Jesus. Dozens of white hands are raised in a praise-and-clapping sequence; superimposed over these is the departing and alienated black figure. This scene will be instantly understood in South Africa or anywhere else—locations are legion—where Manichaeanism still lurks in human minds.

Black Judas, critically standing apart from Jesus and his followers, speaks in a condemnatory manner of their spending money on ointment when there are "people who are hungry, people who are starving"—this, in an explicit modern Israeli film location. His presence unmistakably suggests a Third World identification. Symbolism in juxtaposition with the film's script speaks for itself.

This racial mark takes on bizarre connotations when Judas says to the Jewish priests, "I don't need your blood money"—an exacerbating line in an era of strained Jewish-black relations in the schools and changing neighborhoods of modern American urban life. Black Judas reaches out for the bag of death money. A Jewish priest drops it on the ground. Black Judas kneels down to pick up the Jewish money, a scowl on his face. Uh-uh. If this was done without any awareness of present racial tension amid urban stress, it reflects an incredible human insensitivity.

Black Judas emerges as a white liberal stereotype of a black man. He and three black female dancers (spin-offs from the Supremes) turn on the rhythm in a movie fantasy way that makes more and more black men and women quite legitimately cringe and say that they are frankly sick and tired of the stereotypes in which they find themselves contained. A white liberal view of black male—as hip, groovy, stud—is ultimately claustrophobic and dehumanizing.

Judas, if he were to be black in this film, could have been a quiet, low-key, thoughtful sort of guy—as so many black men are. Indeed, black caricature is carried so far in the movie that, when Judas commits suicide by hanging himself from a tree limb, the scene calls to one's mind a Southern lynching tableau. One cannot help but mentally superimpose on the screen the words *Strange Fruit.*

The most significant aspect of Judas' blackness insofar as *Jesus Christ Superstar* is concerned, however, must be Jesus' white missionary paternalism toward him. Jesus, seen in relation to Judas in this movie, is mockingly his brother's "keeper." Jesus' followers in organized religion have traditionally been sinful racists, while they tried to palm off sin as being sexual.

But for *Jesus Christ Superstar* to suggest personality characteristics in Jesus that delineate feelings of racial superiority, by means of symbol cum non sequitur, raises questions about the film's initial credibility. When Judas asks, in despair, "Why was I chosen?" (for the damning act of Jesus' betrayal), racism looms larger than life. Racists who use biblical fundamentalism as their text for hate traditionally assigned God-given inferiority to the black race.

I have no idea what went awry in the making of this theologically and artistically unsuccessful film. The Herod scene, for example, is so tasteless that a preview audience, seated in a heavy silence where no one seemed to breathe, was left stunned by its fatigued banality.

The ending of the film? Well. A bus prepares to drive off as the various cast members finish climbing aboard. Bravo. Inventive. Refreshing. *Stop there.* But no. We have to go on until a pumpkin-like object (the moon? the sun?) is on the screen. And—you guessed it—standing in front of the object is an empty cross.

Frankly, does it matter in the long run whether a Hollywood screen portrayal of Jesus is good or bad? Does *Jesus Christ Superstar* in Technicolor and Todd–AO 35 make any difference? It does, and I'll tell you why.

Despite its success symbols—real estate, money in the bank, endowments, Establishment connections, and occasional athletic publicity efforts—Christianity does not seem to be on very intimate terms with Jesus Christ.

One is told that the successful preachers in America today offer a practical Christianity directed toward individual needs, because people are more interested in themselves than in society. Such a distorted and partial gospel, in a world that contains South Africa, Vietnam, and El Salvador, readily explains the troubled crisis of Christianity in Western civilization. The habit of churchgoing has not seriously threatened militarism, white racism, institutional persecution of black people and other minorities, and the breakdown in public morality that is partially evidenced by the phenomenon of Watergate.

The tragedy cuts deeper. People call for something in which they can believe. A faith. Computerized nominal Christians— names on a list, bodies in an occasional pew—do not know Jesus Christ as a real person or a personal savior. Take a youth to lunch and find out about the present and the future of contemporary faith.

For Western civilization, the implications of this crisis in belief are staggering. Millions of people are not turning away from the person, example, or teachings of Jesus; they are rejecting church-as-usual. They are turning away from a selfish "help me but not my neighbor" parody of serious biblical religion, cynicism encased in the loss of idealism, faith without practice, and the loss of spiritual vitality and dynamism.

Against the backdrop of this existential religious situation, movie Jesuses come and go. Well-meaning but uninformed clergy, anxious to find a secular handle for the communication of the faith as well as a sharp, quick way to draw a big crowd of otherwise alienated youth, respond with alacrity to the promotion propositions of movie press agentry. So they fill buses with Sunday School kids and cart them off to see Jesus in a new "religious" film.

Evangelism! The kids receive an education by way of movie glamour, stars, color, music, and the big screen. These teach them more about God, Jesus, the Holy Spirit, sin, grace, salvation— well, name it—than all the volunteer Sunday school teachers manage to do in their limited time, drab classrooms, and struggle for secular credibility. However, the big-time glamour teaching is showbiz entertainment. Cosmetic Christianity, in this or other forms, fails because it lacks content and substance. And what, in the end, went wrong? These kids never asked for a stone; they asked for bread.

This is surely not the fault of movie producers. The problem must be placed at the feet of those church leaders who, over the years, have thanked the movie producers for their "relevance," "contributions to the faith," and "religious" pictures.

In 1912, Jesus was portrayed in a film called *From the Manger to the Cross*. Press agents went to work on religious promotion. It was declared inadvisable for theater ushers to be garbed in ecclesiastical vestments. However, exhibitors were advised to burn incense in the theaters shortly before the crowds poured through the doors to see the movie. We need some incense for *Jesus Christ Superstar*.

*Godspell* offered us yet another theatrical and mass media view of Jesus. I saw the first Los Angeles production of this musical based upon the Gospel according to St. Matthew as a guest critic for the Los Angeles *Times*. A youthful actor played Jesus with a clown's red heart on his forehead and blue paint marks on his cheeks. He appeared first in yellow shorts, then changed to striped overalls for the rest of the show.

His followers were clown-like, happy-sad members of what could be a commune of innocent folk. Looking at them, I was reminded of Peter Berger's statement that laughter is the final truth, power the final illusion.

In *Godspell*, Jesus teaches his followers in an utterly unsophisticated, light, often humorous manner; his parables are staged in what is made to appear an improvisational style. The show was luminously "conceived and adapted" by John-Michael Tebelak, with music and new lyrics by Stephen Schwartz.

The young Jesus of *Godspell* sparks his followers to act out their own feelings. He does not "star" or dominate the proceedings, and the result is not only refreshing but convincing. A clown? He is a tragedian, too. But his portrayal is singularly unphony because of his refusal to take himself seriously, become morbid, hold a grudge, or pontificate.

"Did I promise an answer to the question?" he quickly shoots back to a follower who has demanded the neatly packaged literalism of an unpoetic answer.

*Godspell* started slowly for me. I remained skeptical and untouched well into the show. Would this be yet another exploitative Jesus gimmick? Then the gentle tenderness and human quality of the show took hold of me. *Godspell* on stage offered probably the most moving Last Supper I have yet seen, absolutely without posturing or stiff, pious gropings for feeling. The good-bys between Jesus and his followers were bear hugs and warm embraces untouched by devastating despair. Reactions were thoughtful, sensitive, and trusting.

An altogether new dimension was given the betrayal scene. Here, it was not Judas' kiss of ignominy that became central. Instead attention was focused upon Jesus' kiss of forgiveness, marked by an absence of fear or personal betrayal. The Crucifixion was a compelling scene suggestive of rock opera.

"Oh, God, I'm dying," said Jesus in *Godspell* as he stood on a simple set where lights simulated the passion of an electric chair death with its jolts and body thrusts.

The youthful Jesus portrayed on the stage in *Godspell* caught the significance of Christian witness. Does a Christian witness in strength or in weakness? Let me put this question another way: Is the strength of Christian witness found in its own weakness and, at the same time, in the strength of Jesus Christ?

Karl Barth once interpreted witness in this moving way:

> A man may be of value to another man, not because he wishes to be important, not because he possesses some inner wealth of soul, not because of something he is, but because of what he is ... not. His importance may consist in his poverty, in his hopes and fears, in his waiting and hurrying, in the direction of his whole being towards what lies beyond his horizon and beyond his power.
>
> The importance of an apostle is negative rather than positive. In him a void becomes visible. And for this reason he is something to others: he is able to share grace with them, to focus their attention, and to establish them in waiting

and in adoration. The Spirit gives grace through
him.

Jesus, on the stage in *Godspell*, conveyed this meaning to me.
And the portrayal of Jesus' followers somehow caught the mean-
ing of these words written by the American poet Delmore
Schwartz in *The Starlight's Intuition Pierced the Twelve*.

"And I will always stammer, since he spoke,"
One, who had been most eloquent said, stammering.

However, the movie version of *Godspell* shifted gears. It presented us with something totally unexpected, an arresting symbol of the spirituality of the contemporary era in America's and
the world's life. How does one precisely define this? As I wrote
in the Washington *Post,* it is bright packaging of spiritual form,
benign neglect of abrasive truths concerning human needs, with-
drawal from the fervor of social involvement, and the absence of
moral passion.

Only half a gospel is told by the film *Godspell*. Its attractive,
vivacious, and colorful view of life is not balanced by darker hues,
the verities of human savagery, and the depths of loneliness and
despair that are to be found, along with belly laughs and gentle
dreams, in the city's byways and alleys.

This Jesus, played by Victor Garber, wears a clown's red heart
on his forehead, too, along with paint marks on his cheeks, and
he performs a nimble song-and-dance routine. Undeniably it is
a refreshing change of pace from the plastic Christs of too many
Hollywood movies. Yet this Jesus has astonishingly few sharp
words to say in protest against the Establishment. He is ultimately pleasant but characterless, and his nickname could be
Sunny.

The film casts contemporary spirituality with a Jesus who
turns a sad, bland glance at tragedy when he is inescapably confronted by it but would much rather look the other way. Generally he does what he would rather do.

*Godspell* on the screen relentlessly avoids a familiar Gothic look. It eschews cathedral interiors, crucifixes, pulpits, Sunday schools, incense pots, and anything else that spells church. Instead, it utilizes such disparate, and churchly unfamiliar, elements as explosive human exuberance, mime, and the megalopolitan backdrop of contemporary Manhattan.

This, in my opinion, is fine. Traditional methods of telling the Christ story bogged down long ago in hackneyed techniques of simulated pious expression as well as overly familiar details that became idols and therefore obscured the central message. All of this had to be changed, and *Godspell* changed it. Allegory and poetry are employed here to tell the story in a modern urban context with verve and speed.

The film's representation of the Last Supper is excellent. Theology and art come together gently in the final scene of *Godspell*, directed by David Greene from a screenplay that he wrote with John-Michael Tebelak.

A small, vulnerable band of Jesus' followers, dwarfed in juxtaposition against the buildings of New York City, carries Jesus' body in what can best be described as a funeral-Resurrection procession. Before our eyes the handful of disciples is changed into a teeming crowd of contemporary people roaming Fifth Avenue at noon. The primitive church has moved into the modern world.

Yet a major flaw is that the translation of *Godspell* from stage to screen has lost the intimate audience rapport it had for mime-telling the parables. This basic device of the stage presentation now often becomes coyly heavy-handed, resembling an awful Sunday school class. More important, it is unfortunate that millions of filmgoers, who may well be open to a portrayal of the hope of the Christian gospel as it is rooted in sober realities of the human condition, will see this simplistic view of Christ without being offered a fuller dimension.

One wishes to see the meaning of Christ's life placed in the perspective of human captivity, struggle, and even endemic hopelessness that provided the ambiance of his earthly experience. The gospel certainly addressed the wholeness of life that the film curiously lacks the guts, or imagination, to show.

The sheer passion of Christianity must be recovered if the faith is to seriously activate personal life and be a central force in the life of society. The Christian faith teaches that the cross *is* empty. The Resurrection of Jesus Christ enables us to live in hope instead of existing in despair. Yet Christianity is failing to communicate the reality of the Resurrection.

Linked to this failure is an absence of sheer joy, abandon, and passion. A Christian must be prepared to spill his or her blood for the sake of Christ in a bleeding world. Yet Christians' own blood has become more important to them than the blood of Christ—which means not only the shed blood of the crucified but that of Christ alive in the world, especially the persecuted, the suffering, and the poor. Christians today give so many "little things"—a relatively small amount of money, a little bit of time, an ounce of energy, a shudder of passion, a measuring spoon's worth of love. But one looks in vain for the essential gift, that of self and of life's blood.

How can Christian passion be recovered? Not by global conferences, erudite or fiery speeches, public relations efforts, new leaders at the summit, massive fund-raising, a new curriculum for mass education, or reorganization of the structures of church life.

The "solution" may be found only in showing forth the glory of Christ in the very living of a Christian life. Showing forth the glory of Christ means a number of related things. To practice prayer as action, action as prayer. To be really prepared to break one's bones and spill one's blood for Christ—and so, for *the other*. To comprehend that such a faith is not at all playing church, but is indeed a radical, overwhelming, life-changing commitment to Christ that leaves no single part of one's life unchanged. To share in Christ's Resurrection is to find that life—one's own, and the life of society that one indwells—is absolutely transformed.

Christian communication, of whatever kind, has to say this clearly to people. It hasn't. Its work is cut out for it. This is a bread-and-butter issue that is second to none in Christian significance.

# Three Fables

*Be prepared to meet in these fables a strange cast of characters summoned into the community known as a story.*

*In "The Fantasy Worlds of Peter Stone," a charismatic, daring, world-class Italian filmmaker finds himself in adventurous orbit with a youthful, idealistic seminarian who becomes a celebrity.*

*A legendary heiress and art collector comes home to one of the richest, most elitist suburbs in North America in time to witness a sensational disappearance that may be a murder, in "Odor of Espresso."*

*When a Jew runs for president of the United States, he suddenly finds himself locked in the midst of a cynical, evilly engineered "spiritual revival" with political overtones, in "Samuel Joseph for President."*

## The Fantasy Worlds of Peter Stone

He was now Jesus as well as Peter Stone. This warred against his imagination.

Peter had to let it rest. He could not bear to think about the endless images of Jesus, *and* Peter Stone, which were mixed up in millions of people's minds.

"Silent Night." Listening to it, Peter cried. Since he was a child he always had. Now it was Christmas Eve again. In an hour, he would be seen by fifty million Americans on nationwide television. It frightened as well as exhilarated him.

"Holy infant so tender and mild. . . ." Peter thought of his boyhood. He hadn't minded being a minister's son, although it cost him ridicule and limited the number of close friends he had. The Stone household had been a strict one. Peter's father was a Southern Baptist minister who felt it was sinful for a person to smoke, swear, or take a drink.

It was terrible for Peter when his father died. Why, he wondered, had God *done* this? But he decided, even at that early age, never to question God's wisdom. God had done it, and that was that.

Peter remembered the day he had told his mother he would study for the ministry. He was called to this. He must follow in his father's footsteps, and Jesus'.

All through school, *that* was settled and Peter simply prepared for it. He was an exemplary student in every Sunday school, sang in the children's choir until his voice changed, and, during high school, assisted the minister by teaching younger boys about the

Bible and God, the Church and Jesus. Peter loved these activities very much.

When the minister stood in the pulpit on Sunday mornings, the lights in the church dim with just a spot shining on him, and the people waiting expectantly to hear the Word of God, Peter always felt anticipation and exultation. The minister's voice seemed like great sounds coming out of an organ, beginning softly and easily, swelling in feeling, reaching heights of passion, then ending on a positively dramatic note that sustained and fulfilled all that had gone before.

In Peter's small town, Baptists thought Catholics were anti-Christ. Nuns and priests lived in sin in rectory basements—so the stories went. The basements were filled with ammunition and guns, it was rumored; Catholic priests (God forbid) smoked, swore, and drank; Catholic churches were pagan temples; the altar was magic, and unholy candles flickered inside the church day and night. Visions of these things terrified Peter.

In his early teens Peter went away to a big convention in St. Louis. He had never been away from home before. The whole world seemed to open up and make him dizzy. And a new close friend took him to a Catholic church. He shook hands with a priest. The priest laughed and didn't hurt Peter. He met a nun. She was dressed in a long black robe and Peter nearly cried out in fear. But she smiled and put her arm around him. She didn't hurt him, either. Peter slowly walked around the church, running his hands over some stations of the cross. Gradually the numbing fright left him. To his amazement, he found the church the most beautiful place he had ever seen. He lighted a votive candle for his father.

When he returned home, Peter could not mention this experience to anyone. He knew that he could never hurt his mother by telling her about it. However, when Peter was sent off to college, he found himself in the midst of a great state university. He could lose himself in new experiences and feel free.

He often became angry. Christianity was true and had to be believed and accepted by faith alone. Why did his professors attack faith, ridiculing it and extolling logical proofs? There could be no proofs of God! Yet he sometimes felt himself losing God. At such times he hated himself.

Peter found the Catholic chapel. No one from the Southern Baptist group ever visited it. This provided necessary secrecy for Peter's daily visit to early Mass. The altar. *God's* altar. It was so high—up, up there with the six blinding candles on candelabra and great bronze vases of holy flowers. In front of the altar Peter could scarcely get his breath. *This was holy.* One day he went with everybody else up to the altar to receive the *holy* communion. He closed his eyes. A priest placed the bread, the spiritual body of Jesus, *in his mouth and he ate it.* For a moment, until he swallowed it, he was holy, too. It burned in his throat. He did not dare taste it, for what if a miracle occurred and it were real flesh and not only spiritual? He feared that he would vomit or faint, and maybe be struck dead by God.

Not able to bear the awful intensity of this, Peter was relieved, yet sad, to leave the presence of God. He knew he would be back again the next morning. Meanwhile there was life to be endured and lived.

He wrestled with things of the flesh. He knew that he must put sex, with Satan, away from him. Once, after a period of weakness when he had had sexual relations with a woman he dated on campus, he felt fallen from grace. He was stained by filth. He was unworthy to stand in the holy presence of God.

That night he stayed in the church, prostrated on the stone floor before the altar, his arms outstretched as Jesus' arms had been on the cross. Only, Jesus had been nailed to the holy wood when Jesus died for all, including Peter, on the cross. Jesus died for him and he was ungrateful, faithless, and impure. Peter thought of St. Peter trying to walk on the water. Oh, Lord, sustain me, he cried within himself. "The devil, as a roaring lion, walketh about, seeking whom he may devour." Tears ran down Peter's face as he lay on the cold stone floor.

After that Peter stood firmly against Satan. He did not kiss again in college. He would be a Southern Baptist minister with the celibate fervor of a Catholic priest. Peter would be *God's* man.

And on Sunday morning, during the Baptist service, as the mighty hymns of the church sounded triumphantly, he felt he could not wait for his service in the Kingdom to begin.

At last it did. Peter entered the seminary to immerse himself in the religious life. Thank God, Peter thought, the world was *out there*, with its filth, temptations, and false values. Peter was grateful to be always with God inside the very high stone walls, theological structures, and devotional practices of the seminary.

There was a brief period of protest and revolt when Peter was in the seminary. Two young assistant professors, who had got mixed up in civil rights and peace, stirred up nine students to fight for "academic freedom" and "seminary power." Peter was glad he could play a leading role in defeating the movement that led to the expulsion of everybody involved. They had not apparently realized that Christianity is concerned with spiritual, not temporal, matters; the soul, not the body; the Reign of God, not the world.

Then, in Peter's third year of theological training in the seminary, his whole life changed abruptly. He would never again be the same.

Aldono Forminelli planned to make a $20,000,000 film entitled *Jesus*. A worldwide search was announced to find an "unknown actor" for the role of Jesus. Lately, the search had centered on seminaries.

At the time of his first interview with a talent scout from Hollywood who visited the seminary, Peter had scarcely given the matter a second thought. In fact, he considered it altogether remote and utterly impossible.

Later Forminelli himself flew to the seminary to interview Peter.

"It's remarkable," Forminelli told him. "You *look* like Jesus. Did anyone ever tell you you did?"

"How do you know, sir, how Jesus looked?" Peter asked him, not without indignation tinged with pity.

Forminelli laughed, throwing his head back with the earthy insolence of a successful peasant.

"Have you ever thought, Mr. Stone, how Jesus acted as a man in everyday life?" Forminelli asked him.

"Don't forget, Mr. Forminelli," Peter said, "that Jesus was not only a man in everyday life. He was also completely divine."

Forminelli liked Peter's earnest sincerity, even his apparent lack of a sense of humor. There seemed to be no guile or taint of opportunism in the young seminarian. Success should not spoil him.

The choice had narrowed to a competition between a young Yugoslavian actor, a seminarian in Rome, and Peter. When Peter was finally offered the role, church leaders were drawn into negotiations. Along with the head of the seminary, they were unanimous in urging Peter to accept. "It is an unprecedented opportunity to preach the gospel by portraying Jesus Christ before millions of people throughout the world," a church leader said. "Think of it. Jews and Moslems, Hindus and Buddhists, atheists and mere humanists, will all be confronted by Christ. And a Southern Baptist seminarian will portray him! This is truly a blessing from God. I have prayed about this and feel it is surely God's will that you accept."

When Peter did, there was a service of leavetaking, to ask God's guidance for him, in the seminary chapel.

"Go in faith," the preacher said in the service. "Go out from this place in pure Abrahamitic faith. You will portray our Lord on the screen. Go in the faith of Him who always moved in faith."

Peter was to catch a plane for Hollywood. His fellow seminarians lined up to say good-by. In his heart, Peter swore that he would not be corrupted, but would return. After the plane took off, he wanted to read the New Testament. Yet he had his script to learn.

Initial shooting of the film would take place in Hollywood before it shifted to locations in various parts of the world. Significantly, only half of *Jesus* would be filmed in a historic and biblical context. The second half would be shot in modern dress and contemporary locations. The screenplay depicted Jesus, during the latter part of the picture, as being present in nine different situations involving people and their problems. In one, Jesus would be seen as a member of a labor union; in others, a Peace Corps volunteer, a stockbroker, a black militant, a Latino poet, a French artist, a schoolteacher, a vice-president of the United States, and a priest.

Aldono Forminelli fascinated Peter almost as much as Peter fascinated Forminelli. At first they could only reach out to one another quite tentatively. Each wondered what really motivated the other. Peter felt Forminelli was being used as God's instrument to make the picture, yet he felt confident that the producer was unaware of providence. Forminelli was convinced that Peter felt called by God to portray Jesus in the film, and seriously pondered if Peter were half-mad or lost in sexually activated religious hallucinations. Underneath such feelings, each liked the other.

Forminelli, the son of an Italian peasant, had forced his way to wealth and international prestige. Now married to Lucia Perizzi, he had established her as a ranking box-office star (she would play a cameo role as Magdalene in *Jesus*). He had amassed a vast personal fortune, accumulating two castles—one in Bavaria, the other in Ireland—along with a Greek yacht well known to the Jet Set, a skiing haven in Gstaad, a New York town house, and a place in Palm Springs where he had acted as host to two U.S. presidents. He was living in a bungalow at a Beverly Hills hotel during the shooting of *Jesus*.

Peter occupied another bungalow at the same hotel. His meals were with people also working on the film and were catered by hotel room service, to be eaten in his bungalow or Forminelli's. Peter needed a car; he was given a new Mercedes. It was generally assumed that, after the film had been completed, he would return to seminary and continue his theological studies. Meanwhile, his salary ($2,000 a week) was deposited for him in a bank account and his living expenses paid by the studio.

"Don't misunderstand what I am doing," Forminelli told his publicity director. "This *is*, despite appearances, a biblical spectacular. I'm deliberately throwing the critics and public off guard by utilizing modern situations and locations in half the picture.

But, from beginning to end, the production itself will be that of a biblical spectacular.

"Peter Stone will be permitted to grant, at the most, a half-dozen press interviews during the shooting. When that's finished, we'll send him on a three-month world-wide publicity tour.

"While we're in production, he will live, eat, and sleep either on the set itself or in his hotel bungalow near me. When we're on location, it will be the same. Your main job will be to keep a close watch over him at all times. Don't let people get to him. We want to build up almost a feeling of holiness and transcendent aloofness about him. No one must ever forget that he is playing *Jesus Christ*.

"Then, when the movie is released, the shock of a modern, human Jesus will be all the more pronounced because of our earlier secrecy and mystery. Then we'll really spring Peter Stone on the world. I've got him tied up for his next three pictures. Don't ever, *ever*, mention this to him or anybody else.

"I personally selected you because I noticed the press job you did on the Moses spectacular two years ago. I liked it. Only this job is going to be more sophisticated and challenging for you. Trickier. Tougher. We don't want newspaper and magazine space *first*, remember. The same applies to TV or radio exploitation. We want mystery. We want the creation of illusion. We want the whole world to care about this film. I expect the highest grosses in the history of motion pictures."

The first scene to be photographed on the Hollywood set in which Peter appeared was one depicting Jesus walking with a group of his disciples. Looking at the rushes, Forminelli observed a strength he had not previously acknowledged in Peter. To the portrayal of Jesus he brought a sense of motivation and inner power. The word was out that Peter Stone would be an important star when *Jesus* was released.

Tyle Alcott was directing *Jesus*. His relationship with Peter was very tenuous for the first three weeks of shooting. Part of the time Peter passively accepted direction. Then, without warning, he would flare up on the set, rejecting Alcott's interpretation.

After this he would sometimes remain hidden in his feelings for days. At these times filming was a tedious, edgy process and communication was fragmented.

Tension had built up unbearably when the Lazarus sequence was to be filmed.

"Now, Peter, I want you to play this with dignity and power," Alcott told him. "I see real majesty here. You're going to perform the greatest miracle of your life."

Peter didn't answer. He seemed tied up in knots of silence within himself.

"Damn it, Peter, give a little," Alcott shouted at him. "Give. Aren't you human, man? Talk to me. Talk. Give. If you can't talk to me, Peter, I'm walking off this picture and I'll never come back. I can't work with some kind of a divine machine, man."

A hush had fallen on the set. Peter looked at Alcott for a moment. Then he spoke very quietly and there did not seem to be any anger or hostility in his manner.

"Tyle, I know how you feel and I'm sorry. This is tough for me, too, Tyle." A look of relaxation came into Alcott's eyes. "Let me try it my way first, will you, Tyle?"

"Sure, Peter. Sure. How do you want to do it?"

"I'll show you, Tyle. I want to do it quietly. Very slow and easy, Tyle, without any phony dignity or anything like that."

As the Lazarus sequence was filmed, tough members of the crew were seen to have wet eyes. After this, Alcott trusted Peter. He didn't give Peter all the rope, but he let him lead. Portraying Jesus seemed, to Peter, a natural and easy thing to do. He had a definite sense about it. He was happiest when the cameras were rolling and he was involved, as Jesus, in historical or modern-life situations. The hardest times were when he had to be Peter Stone again. Forminelli was the first to spot this, although it was only intuitively. Considerably later Tyle Alcott came to realize it.

Peter loved the episode with Mary Magdalene. Lucia Perizzi played the part very well, he thought. She came to him in her beauty and pride, also her degradation and overwhelming sin, and he forgave her. He healed her. No longer would she cast away her life on corruptible things of the flesh world.

Peter dined that night with Forminelli and Lucia. One of the world's reigning beauties, she was in a relaxed and generous mood.

"Peter, darling, you were fabulous," she said.

"This was one of my favorite scenes in the film," he told her.

"Sweet. You're sweet. You were positively sexy, darling, I don't know how else to say it. You played this with tenderness and compassion, Peter, but you also came through as a very sexy man. I loved it, darling. You gave strength and love and sex to *me.*"

Peter excused himself soon after dinner. Lucia flew to Rome in a day or so to start her new film there. Forminelli and Peter never mentioned the incident. Instead of giving Peter confidence, it shattered him. However, after several days Peter's composure returned and soon afterward his apparent inner strength. Forminelli marveled.

Peter felt great camaraderie playing Jesus with the disciples. They followed, obeyed, and *loved* him. Peter interpreted the miracles with exceptional grace and charm, the crew thought. He was not heavy-handed and somehow took them for granted. And, in the scenes depicting Jesus on the cross, an unnatural, chilling stillness spread across the set. The words uttered from the cross caught fire, came to real life, and seemed to cut their way through religious cant.

Forminelli's secrecy began paying off for him in publicity. Headlines stressed it. "Why Secrecy on $20,000,000 *Jesus*?" "*Jesus* Set Tighter Than Drum." "Controversy Rages over *Jesus* Film." Two hundred thousand photographs of Peter in the role of Jesus (in historical costume) were requested by the Youth Department of a major U.S. denomination for distribution to youth throughout the country. However, in instance after instance, requests for press interviews with Peter were turned down by Forminelli's publicity staff. Every precaution was taken to avoid overexposure of Peter before the film's release.

A brilliant woman journalist was made an exception by being granted an interview. It was an assignment from one of the leading magazines. The interview took place on the site of a reconstructed Jerusalem street. Accompanied by a press agent (who had formerly worked as executive secretary for a bishop), they sat on the stone steps. The journalist asked permission to smoke and it was given.

"Have you been more influenced by the Synoptics or by the Fourth Gospel?" she asked.

"Oh, the Synoptics," Peter replied. "I suppose more by Luke than the other gospels."

"Do you think Jesus was homosexual, Mr. Stone?"

"I feel that Jesus' sexuality transcended all human categories," he replied. "Yet it encompassed an awareness and understanding —even something deeper, an involvement with the whole spectrum of what we call sex. And without sin. He remained sinless."

"I know this sounds like a terribly academic question, Mr. Stone," she continued, smiling and shaking her famous tawny hair, "but what *is* sin?" She coughed her celebrated cough, known to the nation because she was seen widely on the television program *Press Conference.* She fixed him in her gaze. "I mean, *really,* you know, what is it?"

"Sin is separation from God."

"*Can* one be, well, *separated* from God, Mr. Stone, if indeed God is everywhere?"

"Oh, yes, because of one's free will. One may reject or accept God."

"Fascinating." She flipped through her pages of notes. "And are you returning to seminary, after this?"—she gestured with her hand to the set—"or will you become a star, Mr. Stone?"

"I expect to return to the seminary."

"Forgive my candor, I don't in any sense wish to appear to be rude, but I'm sure you realize you give the figure of Jesus a contemporaneity, even, one might say, a definition of bold human masculinity. You're sexy to women, Mr. Stone. Do you feel you *ought* to be? Your face, your body, *shouldn't* they be less *attractive?*"

"Jesus was completely human as well as completely divine. He was a real man. A total man. Surely he neither exaggerated nor diminished his manhood. He was, I should think, unself-conscious about it."

"I *see.*" She was hurriedly jutting down his words in her note pad. "And I do want to *thank* you, Mr. Stone. You've been absolutely charming."

Protected for the most part from press and public, Peter maintained a very simple existence between the hotel and the set. He met an early-morning makeup call, worked hard all day, then studied the next day's script in the evenings, and went to bed right after looking at the II P.M. television news. When the film went on location, Peter's life still remained simple and functional. Location shooting started in Israel, then moved to Spain, England, France, and Italy. Already Peter was a celebrity. A full-time secretary was required to handle his fan mail, even though the public had not yet seen him on the screen.

As he grew in the role, Peter matured. He grew as a man before other people's eyes. Forminelli saw that the humanness he possessed was warm, compassionate, and marked by an inner authority he seemed to have no need of justifying. Yet Forminelli sensed that at the core Peter was flawed by inner insecurity and a curious lack of self-identity.

In foreign countries Peter became something of a hero. Yet, to Forminelli's amazement, Peter refused to capitalize on it. Forminelli had become quite fond of Peter, but Peter was increasingly a mystery to him. He knew that Peter lived the private life of a recluse. What did Peter *want?* In fact, who was this man, Peter?

The final scene was photographed late one night on a near-empty Hollywood set. People shook Peter's hand, assured him that he had been magnificent, drank cups of coffee, and went home to their families. It was finished.

Between the time he finished dubbing and reshooting, and the release of the film, Peter was at loose ends. He returned to Europe, traveling to Chartres, St. Peter's, St. Mark's in Venice, Westminster Abbey, Fatima, the Patriarchate in Constantinople (he refused to call it Istanbul), Mount Athos, and thence to

Jerusalem. Later, back in the United States, he visited his seminary for a week. Then he made an ecumenical tour of some sixty seminaries. Soon there were magazine interviews to give, appearances to be made at church conventions, and a head-on confrontation with celebrity.

When *Jesus* opened in New York, church leaders mixed with the world of society, fashion, and communications for the gala benefit world premiere. Peter attended it with Forminelli. When the film ended Peter received an ovation. People wept openly and a spirit of adulation seized the audience, which seemed to take Peter into its collective arms.

During the showing of the picture, Peter felt a sense of well-being and security. Life was happening *up there* and he was a part of it. But when the lights came up inside the theater, that life abruptly ended, and his own was suddenly reduced to people in a mob smiling at him and trying to grab his hands. He felt dead.

That night, he sat up late with Forminelli.

"I don't know what to say to you, Peter. I'm proud of you. I'm proud of you, Peter."

Peter fingered his glass and didn't reply.

"Peter, the whole world's at your feet, boy," Forminelli went on. "Don't you want this? Isn't this what you wanted?"

"I don't know what to say or do, Aldo," Peter told him. "I wish I could see ahead."

"I'll do anything you want, Peter," Forminelli said. "You can go straight back to seminary if you want. I don't care. I want to do whatever will make you happy."

"Happy?" Peter laughed, then grew quiet again. "Seminary is a fantasy world in the past, Aldo. It seems like a nice religious drama that I remember seeing in a church a long time ago. I can't ever go back to it. I have to be me and live my life."

"Who are you, Peter?"

"Good, Aldo," Peter said, laughing again. "I might as well say, who are you, Aldo? And you don't see anything funny about that."

A silence fell between them.

"Yes. Yes, Peter," Forminelli replied. "I see what is both funny and unfunny about that."

"You see, Aldo, I am simply myself. You brought me into this situation. It made me happy and gave me a sense of fulfillment on the basis of the self I was. Now the present, the immediacy, you gave me is ended. I can't go back. I can't stand still. And I don't know where to go."

"What makes you so different, then, Peter?"

"Ah, Aldo. I can't win with you. All right. I accept the universality of problems, but my own remains."

"Doesn't your Jesus Christ help you, Peter? I have never discussed this with you. Now I feel I have the right or at least I must, for I care about you. What about your Jesus? Where is he? Is he with you, Peter?"

"Aldo, I can't talk about it."

"Why can't you talk about it?"

"I have a lot to unlearn, Aldo. I am close to Jesus, but not to religion now. I have searching to do. Maybe one doesn't need to bring Jesus anywhere. Maybe Jesus is already there. I don't know, Aldo. I'm trying to sort things out."

Peter still had a three-month promotional tour, which would take him around the world. Forminelli assigned three press representatives to accompany him, warning them to preserve Peter's privacy wherever possible. Yet it was an occasion of almost total exposure. Peter flew to Boston, then Washington, Detroit, Chicago, St. Louis, Denver, San Francisco, and Los Angeles. After this he set out on his flying trip circling the world. Everywhere he met the press, spoke with church leaders, and appeared on television and radio.

"When I see you I *feel* Jesus is near me," an English duchess told him. "You have made Jesus a man I can relate to as a human being," said a member of the Ghanaian government. "I believe you must truly understand Jesus as no one else can," a journalist in Buenos Aires told Peter. "I mistrust Hollywood and America and the movie and you, but somehow your Jesus is real," said a student leader in India. Peter's face was as well known as the queen's, his voice as Ella Fitzgerald's. He was asked to write books on theology. He had preached in the great cathedrals of the world. People wrote to him for advice about prayer, marriage problems, politics, race, poverty, and war.

Now, the tour had nearly come to an end. Back in New York, it was Christmas Eve. Peter was seated in a dressing room in a television studio. In an hour he would portray Jesus in a short scene for fifty million Americans across the country.

Instead of appearing on the television program he wanted to go away with Jesus, now, in this moment. Somehow he knew he had instead to stay with Jesus here. But he couldn't play Jesus anymore. He would have to be Peter. Someone was singing "Silent Night."

## Odor of Espresso

Father Art had decided years ago to be avant-garde, but it had been necessary for him to repress his feelings. In the first place, he was an Irish priest and nobody expected him to have a vast, hidden life that cut against his outward actions. His image seemed all of a piece and secure.

As a curate and later the pastor of a sprawling, successful Bingo parish in a big city, he had been dutifully jovial, telling his Irish Catholic stories, attending ball games with the kids, preaching sage and patriotic sermons.

He had been jolted out of his wits when he was assigned to ministering to the very rich. At first he had been defensive and careful, always being conscious of his own background of poverty and earthiness. But then he had begun smelling the possibilities.

Rolling Hills was one of the most distinguished and rich suburbs in America. St. Cyprian's was a gem. It had cost a million dollars and could hold only two hundred people. The eucharistic vestments were medieval French and the chalice had a star sapphire in it.

It was a tight, happy Christian family at St. Cyprian's. Social climbers in the holy of holies were few and soon learned that though they could have communion, they would choke on it later when no one spoke to them or apparently even saw their brightly eager middle-class faces.

Father Art could hold his gin, learned to spot the difference in vintage wines, and won the confidence not only of his parishioners, but also of the Rolling Hills community. "Father Art's a nice guy" was the consensus. Actually, Father Art developed an ulcer as he stepped lightly among his flock, never rocking the boat nor stirring deep waters. For the past several years he had wanted to stand for something other than equanimity, but there seemed to be no issues in Rolling Hills—or, to put it more precisely, the only issues he could find wouldn't permit him to take a stand on them. If he had opened his mouth, he would have been sent packing by nightfall. He didn't see what good he could accomplish in Rolling Hills if he were sent precipitously into exile, so he kept silent (except for preaching the gospel on Sunday mornings, of course) and stayed on.

He baptized babies extraordinarily well. They never cried, the story went, even when he was slopping their faces with cold water. He married people beautifully, thereby joining grace to the highest social prestige. His burials moved observers to tears, quite aside from who the deceased might happen to be. It was partly due to his deep, ringing voice and his spectacularly clean-cut, sincere, handsome appearance. Yet, if he had lacked these, Father Art would still have possessed his magical quality, his "style." It set him apart from other men whether he was at a cocktail party or the altar, in the Country Club or the pulpit.

Father Art was, simply, a resounding success. Pledging was up to inflationary levels in the parish, a new half-million-dollar educational building was about to begin construction, and word was honeycombing the Eastern establishment that a new bishop was being made. A shrewd religious publishing house had, in fact, recently asked Father Art to write a book, to be entitled modestly *Memoirs and Chasubles: The Early Years.*

Yet Father Art began to feel as if he were suffocated at St. Cyprian's. He longed for the moment when he might openly express his avant-garde feelings. Noting that students were disinterested in the church, he wanted to bring them back, and arouse their sleeping parents, by sharply relevant developments. The church must be revolutionary, he felt, but how to bring this about in Rolling Hills escaped him.

At that moment in Father Art's life, Agnes DuLuth came back to Rolling Hills. The DuLuths were unquestionably the leading family. They had made about a billion dollars in railroads, ships, planes, copper, steel, and tires. Agnes was their only child. She had been a debutante, and, after graduating from Radcliffe, went off to Paris. She dabbled in existentialism, bought paintings, wrote poetry, and married a Portuguese revolutionary-in-exile. In Paris and later in Rolling Hills, he was known as Juan.

Agnes and Juan met Father Art at a party that the DuLuths gave for the French consul.

"We're back to settle down," Agnes told Father Art. "Europe was absolutely thrilling, but one can't just keep running all the time."

"We plan to carve out a life for ourselves, if I might put it that way, back here in Rolling Hills, Father," Juan said.

"You can help me," Father Art told them. After that night he was in touch with them every day. They would have lunch or talk endlessly over the phone, meet for a drink or make plans over dinner.

"We're not going to belong to the church," Agnes told him, "but we want to help you. Is that all right? It's just too late for us to get mixed up in church things again, but being mixed up with you will be amusing and terribly stimulating."

Through their eyes, Father Art saw the world in a startlingly new light. He felt that he must be involved in *it* rather than merely in church matters. Agnes and Juan took him to concerts, art shows, the theater, the best foreign films and lectures. Where there had previously been an obstructive wall within his life, now there was an altogether new dimension of freedom and discovery.

"It's time for change in Rolling Hills," Juan remarked one night after the three of them had been to a concert.

"That's the way I feel," Father Art said. "I want the church to lead the way. But first the church has to be changed from merely an expensive and prestigious social club."

"I don't agree," Agnes replied. "The church can only be changed itself as it becomes a part of the entire process of change in the community."

Agnes and Juan felt that Rolling Hills must become culturally activated. An emphasis on art, music, and drama should replace the round of parties, life at the Country Club, and in-fighting gossip. All the power alignments in the community were terrified because Agnes could pull them apart as putty in her hands. She decided to do battle for her cause and got underway by throwing her own collection of modern art into the balance of power. It was one of the important collections in the country.

Wanting to make the church dramatically contemporary, Father Art asked Agnes if he might show the collection for the first time publicly in St. Cyprian's. It would be on a Sunday morning during regular worship services. Juan was amused, but Agnes took the invitation with deep seriousness and agreed.

A total cultural assault was Father Art's plan. The first Sunday in Advent, when Rolling Hills society walked into St. Cyprian's for divine worship, it experienced a head-on collision with the world of art. The night before, moving vans had transplanted Agnes' collection of modern art to the church. Abstract designs were at eye-level with steel executives. A jazz combo, imported from an avant-garde downtown hot spot, struck up the processional hymn. The president of the Junior League did an interpretive dance, accompanied by an Indian student playing the sitar, for the offertory. Instead of the sermon, the Rolling Hills New Ideas Theater presented a reading of the story of Jerry and the Dog from *The Zoo Story* as a sanctuary drama. High school students dressed in clown costumes acted as ushers, wearing buttons reading: "All the World's a Stage: Are *You* Playing *Your* Part?"

Rolling Hills decided, quite spontaneously and without collusion, not to become disturbed. The immediate reaction, therefore, took the form of no reaction. At the church door when he greeted parishioners leaving St. Cyprian's after the service, Father Art met only pleasant smiles and platitudes. "Wasn't the choir marvelous today?" "It was a wonderful sermon." "We enjoyed it." Back in their homes, people did not discuss church that Sunday.

Agnes and Juan wrote off the church and pursued their cultural program with renewed zeal and new conclusion. Father Art realized, however, that he was faced with a terrible problem. He could give up and accommodate the people of St. Cyprian's in their clear desire to be left alone, or he could persist against great odds in his desire to make St. Cyprian's relevant and revolutionary. He chose the latter course. Yet how could Rolling Hills be *reached*? He wanted a clear response from the community, even if it must be anger. If the art world could not deeply stir Rolling Hills, then he must turn to social issues.

Poverty was, of course, not an issue understood in Rolling Hills. War seemed remote—one observed it on TV while drinking Beefeater-on-the-rocks. Anti-Semitism was not a problem because there were no Jews.

One met Jews downtown in the bustling arena of finance, and at great civic luncheons related to brotherhood, but the community itself remained gentile as well as white. There *was* an exception to its whiteness: the young scion of a leading family, related to the DuLuths, had married an Oriental princess. This was always mentioned as an example of the community's complete openness and liberalism when the racial question was raised. Many blacks worked in Rolling Hills as butlers, maids, chauffeurs, and cooks. Lunching at the club (known affectionately as the Big Club), the community's matrons deplored violence in the streets. They were certain black militancy was directly attributable to communist infiltration. After all, they "knew their Negroes," who had solemnly assured them of their opposition to black power and "uppity niggers."

Rolling Hills remembered the brief shadow that civil rights had, in the mid-sixties, cast over the community. A young Presbyterian assistant minister had, in fact, in a hysterical and frenzied moment, opted to march in Selma. Upon his return he was quietly and immediately disposed of. Father Art vaguely recalled that he either became a missionary in the Philippines or else took a church in southwest Montana. But the young Presbyterian's emotional action was the only example of religious frenzy within the area's recorded history.

It was clearly time, Father Art decided, to have more religious frenzy in Rolling Hills. This could serve to jolt people into bona fide involvement. After all, the apostolic early church had been in and out of jails, was led by social undesirables, and speckled with civil disobedience, political malcontents, and violence.

Father Art spent more and more time away from Rolling Hills. He made contacts within the inner city of the adjoining metropolis, in relation to which Rolling Hills was a mythical and royal suburb. He had decided that St. Cyprian's must be forced into a confrontation with social issues. He gave priority to black power. Now he was looking within the inner city for just one thing: black nationalists. He felt he must become informed firsthand if he were to be the moral leader that his ordination as a priest seemed to signify.

His search was slow and painstaking. He established the essential beachhead of his operation when, at an inner-city art museum evening seminar on African sculpture, he met a young, very black man who looked angry and refused to engage in the social amenities of politeness or mere forms, such as shaking hands when introduced to whites. The young man's name was Henry Brown. Father Art knew immediately that Brown represented his breakthrough. He was amazed to discover that Brown was the son of a maid, Thelma Brown, who worked in a Rolling Hills home.

Henry Brown, while opposed to white involvement in the black revolution, was intrigued by Father Art's strange naiveté and earnest resolve for St. Cyprian's. He came to agree with Father Art that the strategy of confronting St. Cyprian's with black power could be mutually beneficial. It would assist Father Art to do *his* job, as a white man working in the white community, to awaken whites to political and social reality. It could represent an unusual opportunity to make the white power structure aware of black power in an intensely direct way.

Within a short time, Father Art was catapulted into a whole new world of ghetto blackness. He ate soul food. He heard soul music. Regarded with suspicion, he was partly accepted as a friend of Henry Brown. Seesawing between the two worlds, one in Rolling Hills and another in the black ghetto, he sometimes felt as if he were losing all sense of his own identity. One evening he was present at a dinner party at the Big Club, the next he was engaged in a new kind of naked dialogue with angry young revolutionaries. He could not see bridging the separate worlds, but simply felt he must make St. Cyprian's aware of their existence.

Father Art embarrassed Henry Brown's mother by seeking her out in the home where she worked.

"Mrs. Brown, I know your son Henry and I promised him I'd come to see you."

"Thank you, Father."

"He seems to be getting along well. He's taking classes at night school at the university and has a job. I guess you know this."

"I'm glad. Yes, I talked to his sister last week and heard about him. I'm certainly glad."

"Can I give him a message from you, Mrs. Brown?"

"Why, I can't think of anything in particular, Father. Just tell him I'm glad he's fine and getting along well."

"All right, Mrs. Brown, I'll do that."

She had never changed her expression or her voice, but he knew she didn't like his intrusion into her life. Henry Brown continued to help him make plans for an assault on St. Cyprian's conscience.

One night he met Henry Brown late in a bar near the university where he took night courses. The juke box was loud as they drank beer and talked.

"White priest, what in hell are you doing in here?" a young black man, suddenly at his elbow, asked Father Art.

"It's okay, Archie, he's my friend," said Brown. "He's with me."

"I don't care, man, who he's with. I just want Whitey to answer my question. Whitey, white priest, what in hell are you doing in here?"

"I'm with my friend, Henry Brown, and I'm drinking a beer and talking," Father Art replied.

"You come in here to save me, white priest? *You* come in here to save *me* with your white God and your white Jesus, Whitey?"

"No, I'm just with my friend, Henry Brown."

"This is a black man's hole. Can't you leave a black man his own hole, Whitey?"

"I'm sorry. This is Henry Brown and I'm just drinking a beer with him and talking."

"White priest, I'm for *black* religion. My God is black, man. My God isn't your God, man."

After this, Father Art felt more strongly than ever that time was running out. The people of Rolling Hills who attended St. Cyprian's must be told about life outside their rich, white ghetto. As a matter of fact, Father Art got to know Archie, who helped Henry Brown make the plans for St. Cyprian's that were in motion.

Father Art did not give Rolling Hills even a slight warning as to what would shortly transpire. Lent was now drawing to a close, with Easter just around the corner. The time seemed propitious. Perhaps Easter could indeed mean resurrection, renewal, and new life this year for the parish and community.

Good Friday went quietly. There was the traditional observance of the afternoon three-hour service. This was, as always, solidly attended by the women of Rolling Hills. It had, over the years, become a very "in" thing. On Easter Eve, Father Art baptized a dozen babies in the church. The community found this as inspiring as always. Later afternoon shadows filled the gemlike church, deepening its always intrinsic drama. Candlelight flickered against Father Art's handsome, clean face as he sprinkled water on the babies' bright young faces and baptized them in the name of the Trinity. A grande-dame grandmother was moved to gentle tears by the spectacle. Afterward, there were cocktails at the Big Club. Then Rolling Hills slowly unwound. Tomorrow would be the High Day of the social year— Easter at St. Cyprian's.

It was almost like rolling away the huge stone from the empty tomb as the first parishioners opened the heavy door of St. Cyprian's the next morning. They wanted to flee, but stood transfixed, gazing at the life-size jet black figure of Jesus, garbed in a black loincloth, hanging over the altar.

A black choir, bused from the inner city, sang the processional
hymn, "Swing Low, Sweet Chariot." The church bulletin contained the announcement that, on Tuesday evenings at 8:30, there
would be a fifteen-session course on Afro-American History and
Culture, conducted by a well-known black militant who was a
social worker in a settlement house. The Easter sermon was
preached by a militant black preacher and freedom fighter, a
Baptist, who had been flown to Rolling Hills from Birmingham,
Alabama.

The Easter collection, it was explained in the bulletin, would
not go to the building fund for the new educational building, but
instead would be given to the Negro College Fund. Sunday
school classes were dispensed with, and the youth of St. Cyprian's heard an address by a young black nationalist out on bail
following a recent civil disorder in the city.

Paintings by black artists filled the sanctuary. A performance
in Rolling Hills of Genet's *The Blacks*, as a sanctuary drama in St.
Cyprian's to be performed by Afro-American actors from an
inner-city coffeehouse theater, was announced for the following
weekend.

Rolling Hills responded with *noblesse oblige*. The preacher, before catching a plane back to Alabama, was feted at a dinner party
at the Big Club. The series of classes on Afro-American History
and Culture was immediately oversubscribed. The offering hit a
new high level. The young militant who addressed the Sunday
school was enthusiastically asked to return in order to speak at
a high school assembly. Tickets to *The Blacks* were unobtainable
within three days. The Altar Guild wondered if a picture of the
new *Christus* over the altar might not appear on the next year's
church calendar.

Shortly thereafter, a black millionaire wished to buy a home
for his family in Rolling Hills. His son attended graduate school
at Harvard, his daughter was a sophomore at Sarah Lawrence,
and he was a principal benefactor of the symphony. His request
was granted and the new family moved into the community.
Rolling Hills now felt more liberal than it had even when the
local scion married the Oriental princess.

Father Art, outwardly poised, was a churning, mad charade inside himself. Henry Brown had been more than satisfied with the success of black power's confrontation with St. Cyprian's, and was back in the city's ghetto. Unruffled by events, St. Cyprian's was unchanged except that it felt somewhat more self-righteous than before. It knew now that its capacity for resistance to change was a mastered art.

Continuing to spend time outside Rolling Hills, Father Art tried to keep very close to changing political and social currents of thought. He had established contact with students at the great inner-city university not far away. He refused to relax his efforts to awaken St. Cyprian's to revolutionary change. The peace movement was of major importance to students, Father Art knew, and he thought he might somehow be able to make St. Cyprian's deeply sensitive to it.

He announced a week's fast in the interests of world peace, with prayers for a cessation of fighting. It began with an all-night vigil in the church. The crowd exceeded Easter's in size. Everybody fasted. One matron lost eight pounds and canceled her scheduled semi-annual visit to The Golden Door. Several parishioners commented that this beat giving up liquor for Lent.

As a concentrated "crash" diet it worked, and spiritually one felt one had *done* something.

Feeling the ground give way beneath him, Father Art decided he must summon final resources of strength in order to awaken the community to authentic involvement. His weapons would be his new, deepening contacts within the student world. Already youth comprised approximately half the national population. If youth could not be interested in Christianity in an honest and compelling way, then the church would probably not even be alive in fifty years.

Father Art came to grips with his new apostolate. He shared his problems at St. Cyprian's with new friends among students at the two universities. They offered to help him. After visiting the church, and quietly meeting some of the parishioners, they offered Father Art their idea.

He should, they said, open a coffeehouse in the basement of St.

Cyprian's. It would provide a touch of authentic scandal to needle people into expressing their true feelings. Then Father Art could, for the first time, engage them as human beings in honest controversy. They would no longer be role-playing on their terms of status quo and polite dismissal of real issues.

No one in the church opposed the idea of the coffeehouse. Students painted the walls in a combination of religious and secular motifs. An espresso machine sent from Italy was on hand for the lively opening. The coffeehouse was called "The Appian Way." Immediately it became fashionable and was featured on the society page of the city's leading newspaper. On the opening night, underground films were shown, and a young Cuban poet recited revolutionary verse. Parents were delighted with the project. A virtual Social Register of women signed up to make coffee, wash cups and saucers, and mop the floor in shifts.

The students were as appalled as Father Art. Rolling Hills had no mortal flesh to needle, no conscience to be stirred. Father Art was taking steps to seek a transfer when, overnight, the picture changed. Unplanned, genuine controversy finally came to St. Cyprian's.

A student at "The Appian Way" was arrested by a police officer for smoking pot. Most students insisted that the police officer planted marijuana on the young man. Whatever the facts might be, a veritable emotional maelstrom ensued. Debate raged within family circles, the Big Club was split right down the middle on the issue (the arrested student was related to a leading family), there were cries alike of "moral decency" and "police brutality," and "The Appian Way" was photographed in *Time*, *Newsweek*, and *Life*. Rolling Hills was outraged, considering publicity the only essential vulgarity.

Clergy in every part of America gave sermons alluding to "moral degeneracy" as found in a church-related coffeehouse that seemed to be a dope den. A former child actress in California, now a respectable matron, declared she would not drink another cup of coffee until "the dirty coffeehouse in the underground church" had been closed and padlocked. The White House made an indirect but immediately identifiable reference to the incident in the course of remarks at a presidential prayer breakfast.

Father Art gathered with some students to discuss the incident and determine future action.

"That church bag doesn't seem right for you, Father," one student said. "They're all hypocrites and it's hopeless. Why don't you get out and try to land a job with the Peace Corps or a poverty program?"

"I'm not questioning at all what you're saying," Father Art replied. "But I believe in the church beneath the church. Under the organization, you see, and all the forms, is a reality for me. I think my place is to stay."

"But you can't stay, can you?" another student asked. "They seem to want your hide, Father. I mean, you keep trying to wake them up and they'll bomb you before they let you really get to them in a nitty-gritty sense."

"Well, I didn't take this church for popularity," Father Art said. "Being a priest isn't being a worldly success. I'm not a masochist, but I think I've got to stand my ground."

"You're a nice guy, Father, but I'm sure through with the church after this," another student said. "Pardon me, but I'm fed up. I want to get away from double-standard morality and I feel the church lives that way. You're okay up to now, but so what does that mean? It doesn't change the institution."

Runaway children, Ivy League students with pot, and some hardened addicts began arriving in Rolling Hills. Since there was no hotel, they slept in the completed basement of St. Cyprian's new educational building. Rumors about sex orgies spread quickly.

Publicity mounted. The *Wall Street Journal* ran a front-page depth report on the developing affair. TV camera crews from New York interviewed matrons outside the Big Club. (They were barred from setting foot in it.) *Vanity Fair* canceled a story about Rolling Hills pending the outcome of events.

Father Art hadn't had a real talk with Agnes DuLuth and Juan for a long time. He called them and they invited him to dinner.

"We feel guilty we haven't seen you," Agnes said. "My God, what are they doing to you?"

"What are you going to do?" asked Juan.

"I suppose just stay until I'm kicked out or this blows over," Father Art told them.

"It's absolutely incredible," Agnes responded. "I feel so sorry for you. No. Don't tell me not to say that. I don't mean to be demeaning. I'm not patronizing. I'm just so sorry for you, not as a priest, but as a man. Can we do anything to help?"

"We'd like to help if we can," Juan interjected. "This is really all so ridiculous. You're trapped in a lot of nonsense. You can't let yourself be destroyed."

"I appreciate your friendship," Father Art told them. "I don't think you can help in any other way right now but just to let me talk and know my friends are listening."

A few days later, Father Art made his tragic and irremediable move. He grew a beard.

No one ever knew why he did it. Young Archie and Henry Brown and other black nationalists grew beards, and it was known that Father Art admired them. A number of university students whom he knew also grew beards. But no clear line of connection between anyone else's beard and his was ever drawn.

However, his growing a beard caused communication to break down at every level within the community. Some saw him as a saint, even a modern Jesus figure, while others flatly claimed he was a communist or a fanatic. When a guru representing Eastern mysticism flew from India and was photographed with Father Art, all hell simply broke loose. The Big Club closed "for alterations," but, in fact, it was dangerous to congregate in Rolling Hills, and best friends had ceased speaking to one another.

As Father Art's beard grew bushier and heavier, so attendance at St. Cyprian's diminished in alarming proportions.

There has been endless speculation about the last night. It is a known fact that Henry Brown and some five other black nationalists met with Father Art in the rectory for approximately one hour. It is also documented that Agnes and Juan were with him for forty minutes. Two or more students from the inner-city

university dropped in for a chat with him shortly after ten
o'clock.

After that, nothing is known. The next morning he was gone.
Father Art seemingly vanished from the face of the earth. Rumors have placed him everywhere. One school of thought
claimed he had been murdered, and his body cremated in the
basement of the Big Club. A Chicago *Sun-Times* dispatch circulated the report he was a guru in Nepal. A religion writer for
the St. Louis *Post-Dispatch* suspected his presence among Latin
American revolutionaries, while the Cleveland *Plain Dealer*
hinted he was active as a guerrilla priest. From London came
reports that he had joined a celebrated singing group to open a
clandestine meditation center in Tonga.

To the horror of the parishioners, St. Cyprian's was never able
to lock its doors again, at any hour of the day or night. Thousands
of people flocked there to meditate, with the number increasing
each year.

Father Preston-Armistead, who followed Father Art at St.
Cyprian's, was a gray, conciliatory figure. The parish flourished
economically, but the spark had gone. Of course, "The Appian
Way" was discontinued. In fact, the basement of St. Cyprian's,
following a short but respectable period of disuse, was turned
over to the Altar Guild for its meetings. There was an unwritten
law, preserved by oral tradition, that coffee was strictly banished.
Inside the site of the former coffeehouse, only tea could now be
served.

Despite repeated scrubbing and fumigation, and outcries of
indignation from the Altar Guild, the odor of espresso coffee
clung resolutely to that hallowed room. Lately, rumors have been
circulated wildly in Rolling Hills that the curious odor grows
stronger with each passing year.

# Samuel Joseph for President

The presidential jet was flying from Washington, D.C., to Los Angeles. Inside it, his coat off and sleeves rolled up, the president of the United States was in conference with a group of key advisers.

"It looks far worse than I had any idea it could, Ron," the president said to one of his intimate aides. "What can we do?"

"I don't know, Mr. President," Ron Dixon replied. "It looks very bad indeed. I'm stumped. If I could have a day or so to think about it, I might be able to come up with something."

"Unfortunately, I've got to know exactly what to do the minute I get off the plane in Los Angeles," the president said. "I'll be riding with Wilson in the car from the airport to my hotel. That's when I've got to talk with him about it."

The presidential advisers looked at one another uneasily. Two of them put out their cigarettes, two others lit cigarettes, and one stroked his pipe. Fresh coffee was poured.

One of the younger aides in the group spoke up.

"Mr. President, it's no secret now that Vice-President Wilson is losing the election." He pulled out sheafs of paper. "Look. Here are breakdowns on all the latest polls. You've seen them. Unless something drastic can be done in the next three weeks, he hasn't got a chance."

This direct confrontation with the commonly known, but forbidden, subject took the lid off a growing and unbearable tension.

"If that's true, then my eight years as president will be repudiated when my party goes down to defeat with Wilson in November." The president shifted in his chair. He brought down his fist on the table. "I'll fight. I'm willing to fight, do anything to prevent that from happening."

The young aide persisted in his line of reasoning, looking the president squarely in the eye.

"We've checked and rechecked every conceivable angle in this election, sir," he continued. "There doesn't seem to be any area of flexibility where we can safely introduce a new angle or exploit an old one. We're stalemated on peace, race, poverty, health, urban development, air pollution, the space program." He held up a finger of his hand to emphasize each item he was ticking off. "Mr. President, we're in the worst possible position."

Blocked by frustration, the president was visibly growing angry.

"I think I've got an idea," Ron Dixon said.

He leaned forward in his chair, holding in check his excitement.

"There's one area we might be able to maneuver in. I'm not saying it would be easy. It's difficult and explosive. But religion could make the difference and throw the election to Wilson if we handle it right and keep our heads."

The president was displeased.

"Damn it, Ron, you never mix religion and politics. Rule one. Have you lost your mind? This situation is serious. Can't we be serious, too?"

Ron Dixon smiled.

"You mix oil and water if you have to, to survive, Mr. President." He was cool and seemed quite confident of himself. "Religion is an untapped political resource in this election. The church is unpopular, but God isn't. Nobody knows how to define God but most people believe in a God. Now, as to this election. Wilson is running against a Jew. The first Jew to run for president. Samuel Joseph."

A sudden interest gripped everybody seated around the table.

"Anti-Semitism seems to be over, at least on the surface. Nobody in his right mind would dig it up. In fact, you have to appear liberal about a Jew running for president. Wilson has been very good about that. So have you, Mr. President. And

America is saying we've-had-our-Catholic, now-let's-have-our-Jew. Okay. But now I come to my point. Samuel Joseph isn't mentioning religion. He's a Jew, and that's that, but Jewishness is not being brought up by anybody. This leaves a vacuum in the election for religion. Why doesn't Wilson bring up religion? Not negatively. Not in any sense against, or related to, Joseph. But positively. Positively for Wilson."

The others could tell the president was excited by the power of this new idea. "You may have something, Dixon," he said, leaning back and lighting his pipe. "You may really have something. What you seem to be saying is, Wilson should get religion. God is not dead, he's in conference with Stephen Wilson."

Everybody laughed.

"All right. How do we implant this? You tell me we've got three weeks at the most to change the course of this election. Wouldn't you think we should get started on it today?"

Ideas were shot back and forth across the table.

"I think it might work," one advisor said. "But the public must be told Wilson isn't discovering religion three weeks before the election. He's had it all along. He didn't want to exploit it. That cut against the grain of his integrity and humility. But something must happen to force him to open up on religion. You know, he must do this according to the dictates of his conscience."

"Couldn't Wilson have prayed about this for a long time?" Dixon asked. "Now he believes it is God's will for him to speak about religion because of the immorality of the nation."

"People cannot cope with the problem by themselves," another aide suggested. "Steve Wilson suddenly realizes the peril in which the nation stands. Only God can make the difference. You know, between disaster and what might be called a new morality."

"I like it," said the president. "Put your heads together. Come up with some kind of a definite program. I can give it to Wilson when I'm riding in the car with him from the airport. There's just no time to lose."

At the airport, the president spoke briefly to an army of TV, radio, and press correspondents. Wilson, bareheaded and smiling, stood next to the president. Then the two men got into a limousine and a police escort started them on their way to the gigantic political rally.

"I'm worried," Wilson told the president. "I seem to have hit a slump and can't pull myself up again."

"Don't worry, Steve." The president laughed. Wilson sensed his confidence. "I've got an idea. If you agree, I think it might just do the job."

That night Ron Dixon put in a long-distance call to Ellsworth Pinkney, who agreed to meet Wilson and Dixon the next day in Kansas City. Pinkney was one of the most influential magazine editors in the country, an elder statesman of contemporary Protestantism and a party stalwart. He would be told nothing about political strategy, only that Wilson's conscience made it necessary for him to speak out boldly concerning the state of the nation's morality and how God must be given the reins of action.

At noon the next day, Pinkney had lunch with Wilson and Dixon in Kansas City, where Wilson was to speak in the evening at a political rally.

"Of course, I'm delighted, even, I must say, quite thrilled, Mr. Wilson, to find out your real feelings," Pinkney said. "But I also must confess that I'm puzzled by your previous silence on the subject of religion. You haven't, to my knowledge, said anything at all about it. Nor have I been aware that you even attended church services on Sundays during the campaign."

"You see, Dr. Pinkney, I feel very strongly about the separation of church and state," Wilson replied. "And, too, I've leaned over backward, I can tell you confidentially, not to raise the subject of religion because I thought it might prove to be politically embarrassing for Mr. Joseph."

Pinkney sipped his glass of milk.

"I see," he commented. "I see. Well, Mr. Wilson, I certainly respect you deeply for what you have done."

Wilson folded his hands together on the table.

"But I can't keep religion out anymore," Wilson announced. "I can't try to keep God out of the election anymore, Dr. Pinkney. And, frankly, I just don't care if it hurts me or not, even if it should cost me the election, because the issue is basic now for our very survival as a Christian nation. I suppose I should say as a religious nation."

"No, I see nothing wrong with acknowledging our destiny under God as a Christian nation, Mr. Wilson." Pinkney paused. "How can I be of immediate help to you? I'm quite aware that our time is fast running out."

"We need your thinking, Dr. Pinkney," Ron Dixon replied. "Your ideas on how we can best communicate Mr. Wilson's deep feelings to the nation as rapidly as possible."

Pinkney took a small black leather notebook out of his coat pocket and started to make some notations in it.

"First, you must make a major statement of your viewpoint. Where will you be speaking tomorrow night?"

"In Cleveland."

"Excellent. I'll work with you on drafting your statement. It should be made tomorrow night in Cleveland. In addition, I'll see if something can't be worked out on the television over the weekend. There's to be an important TV special on religion in America. Perhaps you've heard about it. I just might be able to get you a spot on that. And, of course, I'll have to get you and Bruce Whippick together as quickly as possible."

Ron Dixon relaxed inside. It was going to be all right. Bruce Whippick was known as "the patriot's revivalist" and was one of the most loved and trusted men in American life. If these new plans could get rolling quickly enough, Dixon thought, Wilson might damned well have an excellent chance of reversing the tide.

Cleveland, the next day, was friendly to Wilson. The largest crowd of the campaign greeted his motorcade. The networks planned to cover his address that night.

The auditorium was packed to the rafters when Wilson mounted the podium to speak. After deafening applause, there was suddenly total stillness inside the great hall.

"My fellow Americans," Wilson began, "I have reached a momentous decision after considerable soul-searching and spiritual anguish." It seemed that nobody breathed among the thousands seated before him. "Up to this time I have painstakingly endeavored to eliminate a great factor, indeed, the greatest factor of all, from my campaign. I can do so no longer.

"Our great and beloved nation is pressed on all sides by forces of godless communism abroad and by the decadent and godless forces of pagan immorality at home. As men and women, we cannot win our battles against these enemies alone. We must humbly and prayerfully turn to our great Father. We must now, as faithful children, ask God to bring us through to victory abroad and morality and love at home."

For a long, sustained moment there was only silence. Dixon counted to three, wondering what might happen. Then a groundswell of applause started on the auditorium floor. Like fire, it spread to the balconies. On all sides, people seemed to respond to a primordial vision embedded deep within themselves. Now the crowd was on its feet, shouting and swaying. Someone started an old gospel hymn. Men and women were openly and unabashedly crying. Underneath layers of sophistication and cynicism, a terrible need had been touched.

For twenty full minutes, Wilson could not go on with his prepared address as the people inside the auditorium were unrestrained in their emotional response. Finally he was able to continue.

"I was ashamed of my religion. I thought that politics required of me that I should not speak about my God. I am ashamed no longer. We are one nation, indivisible, under God. In God we trust. America is the most Christian, the most religious nation in the history of the world.

"We have a destiny. It is a holy destiny and we are a holy people. We are truly called by God to be his instruments of peace, love, and morality in the world. We must cast down the pagan idols of immorality. We must burn those things that are filthy and degrading to our holiness. We must oppose all things, all ideologies, that are godless. My fellow Americans, I pledge myself to the task of setting this nation on a mighty forward march with God."

Again and again, his speech was interrupted by applause,

shouts, and cries of encouragement and support. When he left the podium, tears in his eyes, the thousands stood in an ovation that stirred the nation. And then, at just this moment, Bruce Whippick, the revivalist who had become a folk hero in his own time, walked on the stage and to the podium. The crowd went wild once again. "God! God! God!" the people shouted, starting slowly and ending with a fast locomotive yell.

Whippick spoke very briefly. He promised to be a part of Wilson's campaign until the election.

"I support Stephen Wilson as the candidate for president who promises to put God back into politics. He will place God in the center of American life, my fellow citizens. God will fight for us against communism. God will wage our war against the forces of filth and immorality. God will be our leader, at home and abroad, and Stephen Wilson will be his faithful servant in the White House and the hearts of his people."

When he had concluded his remarks, Whippick asked a rabbi, who had been flown in from Detroit, to offer the benediction. The people were requested, after that, to file out of the auditorium in silence, offering prayers to God instead of speaking. As the thousands departed, only the sound of shuffling feet could be heard along with old-fashioned hymns played on an organ.

Pinkney was able to get Stephen Wilson a major spot on the weekend TV special about religion in America. The network also offered a place on the program to Samuel Joseph, but Joseph declined.

In prime time Sunday night, the television program opened with a cathedral choir singing "The Star-Spangled Banner." During this music, there were camera stills of the American Revolutionary War, mixed with present-day films of Hawaii beaches, Midwest fields of grain, the Rockies, the nation's Capitol, the metropolis of New York, blooming flowers in the deep South, Los Angeles freeways, and the sea off the New England coast.

Pilgrims were shown, fleeing the religious persecution in England to settle in America. There were location scenes in some famous early churches, with local choirs and clergy singing and speaking. European persecution of Jews was depicted, along with their exodus to the land of the free and the home of the brave. There were no shots of early American blacks. However, later in the program, two famed black singers were featured in traditional Christmas carols.

After the program showed films depicting drug addiction, urban crime, racial unrest, ghetto poverty, and a home for unwed mothers, Stephen Wilson spoke about God and morality. He was televised live, making his remarks from the pulpit of a leading Fifth Avenue church.

"America was founded on obedience to God's laws," he declared. "Just as God freed the people of Israel from the bondage of Egypt only to have them turn their backs on him, so Americans have forgotten the God who fashioned their nation and have likewise turned away. It is our national salvation to return to the great Father who makes all of us brothers to one another. This nation was called into existence by God. In God we trust."

Immediately following Wilson's remarks, a children's choir of a West Coast cathedral sang "God Bless America." The closing shot was of ten national religious leaders, representing Catholicism, Protestantism, and Judaism, standing in a single line. A cross and a Star of David were revealed behind them and, over their heads, an American flag fluttered in a breeze mechanically induced by electric fans outside camera range.

Attacks followed immediately.

Liberal Catholic and Protestant journals, with very limited circulations, attacked Wilson for indulging in political opportunism and religious huckstering. Segments of the press joined in the attack on "outrageous chauvinism." When Samuel Joseph replied to Wilson, in his next political address, calling for a return to the separation of church and state as an honored American tradition, he was booed. His remarks led to swastikas being painted on synagogues throughout the United States.

Wilson promptly denounced theses "acts of political demagoguery."

"God is love," he said in a press statement after a New Jersey synagogue was bombed and the word "God" was scrawled in red paint on a nearby stone wall. "God calls on us to love our enemies as ourselves." He said that his political followers must "obey the law of love."

The campaign was now in a state of chaos. The president had not foreseen these subsequent events and was distressed by them. At the same time, he was pleased to note that the polls, in an abrupt shift, now clearly favored Wilson. When a Supreme Court justice unexpectedly died, the president swiftly replaced him with a Jewish law professor from Seattle.

Reporters delved into Wilson's religious past. He had been confirmed by an Episcopalian bishop at the age of thirteen. After that, his institutional religious ties were vague. As Wilson's press conferences leaned more and more to the subject of religion, he supported public prayer in the schools, affirmed the active presence of God on America's side in international relations, and called on ghetto blacks in U.S. cities to "follow Jesus' way of love and peace instead of the devil's way of hate and violence."

During a nationally televised debate, both Wilson and Joseph were asked to discuss their religious beliefs. Joseph indicated that he was a practicing adherent of Conservative Judaism, with his social ethic based on the teachings of the Torah. Wilson explained that he was "simply ecumenical," believing that God is "the Father of us all." When pressed by Samuel Joseph, he confessed that he personally rejected the long-accepted categories of American religion as Protestant, Catholic, and Jewish. "But I do not wish to impose my views on anyone else. A person's religion is sacred to one and must be so respected by others. It is just that, for me personally, I believe and practice one God, one religion, one Father, and one people."

As anti-Semitism sharply increased, and religious controversy replaced political campaigning, the president called an emergency meeting at the White House. Stephen Wilson was present, along with Ellsworth Pinkney and Bruce Whippick.

"I respect your views, Wilson," the president said, "but we're caught in a hornet's nest. Stability must be restored, at whatever cost. Some latent and dangerous feelings have been stirred in the public, I fear, and the situation must be set aright."

"What can I do, Mr. President?" asked Wilson.

"I don't know, Wilson. That's why I've asked you to come here to meet with Dr. Pinkney, Mr. Whippick, and my aides. We must devise a strategy to lead us out of this dilemma."

Pinkney was the first to speak.

"Mr. President, I deplore the controversy and violence as much as you do, sir. But I do not regret the explicit inclusion of God and religion in this political campaign. It has shown me that we are, truly, a godless people headed for destruction unless we are able to come to grips with the presence and sovereignty of God in our lives."

Ron Dixon leaned forward and addressed Pinkney.

"But when you say 'God' in today's American society, what have you said? It seems to mean whatever an individual person wants it to mean. So, for example, if someone says 'In God we trust,' what specifically does he mean by 'God'? I think we're lost in a jungle of conflicting words and images, and it's—pardon me, sir—damned dangerous."

Bruce Whippick spoke next.

"We've always been taught, Mr. President, that things must get worse before they can get better. So, in this case, we find ourselves in the midst of a lot of trouble at present because, without it, we cannot grow. It seems to me, Mr. President, it is God's will for us to suffer as we are presently doing. Jesus, in Gethsemane, asked the Father to take the cup from him, if it was the Father's will. But the Father asked Jesus to accept being nailed to the cross. If we will not accept the pain and suffering and misunderstanding of this moment, how can we think of pleasing God or doing his will?"

The president didn't speak. His displeasure was evident to all his aides.

The meeting was terminated without any conclusions having been reached for a positive line of action.

In Detroit, the next day, an ugly crowd gathered to hear Samuel Joseph deliver a major campaign address. At one point he was drowned out by their singing "Rock of Ages." Crucifixes were plainly visible throughout the hall. A militant from Dearborn, carrying a gun, stood up and shouted at him, "Do you accept Jesus Christ as your personal lord and savior?" Immediately, fistfights broke out. The police stormed the hall. No one could say precisely what happened next. Mass pandemonium and then, without warning, all the lights went out.

The 26 dead and 690 injured persons provided a desperately sobering statistic to a divided nation.

The president, appearing on television, looked more drawn and harried than the public had ever seen him before. He had engaged in an all-night meeting with Ron Dixon and other aides.

"The forms of divisiveness must be overwhelmingly repudiated," he told the nation. "America is founded on principles of religious toleration, social justice, and human compassion. Religion must be a unifying force, not a destructive one. People's approaches to God must heal old wounds, not inflict new ones. I call upon the American people, in this tragic hour, to pray for peace in the stead of conflict, for community in the place of strife, and for national unity of many men, women, and children under one God."

Reaction to the president's speech was violent. Fifteen thousand hymn-singing protesters, carrying guns, marched angrily on the White House. The mob's head-on confrontation with the National Guard was bloody.

That night, Stephen Wilson spoke in San Francisco. The invocation opening the meeting was given by Ellsworth Pinkney. Bruce Whippick led the 30,000 assembled people in singing "What a Friend We Have in Jesus."

At first, the crowd did not sense what was happening. Gripped in the frenzy of religious fervor, their bodies swaying and close together, the people remained unaware of the building rhythm of a movement undergirding their own. The ground rolled beneath them, seeming to move in concert with their pitched cries and muscular thrusts.

When the earthquake sustained its five-minute uninterrupted peak, as the West Coast of the United States split asunder, the crowd disappeared, screaming and writhing, into the belly of the earth. The ensuing tidal wave swallowed it up.

The nation was caught in the greatest catastrophe and emergency in its history. Raging waters swept inland, submerging San Diego, Los Angeles, San Francisco, Portland, and Seattle. Movie stars were now rarer than imperial gems. Cable cars had vanished from the face of the continent.

Led by the president, the country embarked upon a period of penitence and self-examination. The president himself endorsed Samuel Joseph, who was elected the first Jewish chief executive by receiving 97 percent of the vote.

Pulpits were strangely silent when it came to offering theological interpretations of the disaster. The Ellsworth Pinkney Foundation for Judeo-Christian Dialogues was opened in Washington, D.C. A new song, "Jesus, Jewish Boy and Jewish Man," became an overnight American classic, in both a religious and a secular sense.

Within one year, there were more Jews in America than Baptists, Methodists, and Catholics combined.

# A Parable: The Alleluia Affair

*The following parable is close to my heart because I believe strongly in the theme of hope.*

*The parable's unmasking of hypocrisy—especially in a central scene that takes place beneath a gigantic new stained-glass window inside an outrageously expensive cathedral—was a particular pleasure to write.*

*In the parable, a reader may come face to face with Jesus as I know him, moving in ordinary life with ordinary people.*

## 1

Jesus pulled his legs free.

The rusty nails that had held his feet captive fell clanking below the cross.

It was not difficult now to free his left hand, then the right one. He slid easily down from the full-size wooden cross in the sanctuary of an inner-city church in Indianapolis.

Next he walked into the adjoining parish hall. He passed by Catherine Coombs of the Altar Guild, who fainted. Jesus washed in the men's room—he got the blood off his body—and left the building, walking toward the city's hub, Monument Circle.

It was a hot day, so he felt okay in his loincloth.

Jesus had a bit more difficulty disengaging himself from a gold processional cross in an East Side church in Manhattan, yet within just a few moments he was free.

After he had borrowed a soiled vestment to wear, he headed south toward Rockefeller Center.

A cab driver moving along Madison Avenue in the seventies saw Jesus, who was still wearing his crown of thorns. Before he knew what he was doing, the driver had smashed the cab into the plate-glass window of an art gallery.

Moments later when a distinguished actress saw Jesus, she lost her composure.

However, a dog standing on the corner wagged his tail and walked up to Jesus to get acquainted.


In Paris, sixty Jesuses freed from crosses walked toward the Arc de Triomphe.

A number wore loincloths and crowns of thorns, while others were attired in the majestic robes of *Christus Rex* and had royal crowns on their heads.

Jesus was visible on the streets of São Paulo, San Francisco, Barcelona, New Delhi, Johannesburg, Sydney, Saigon, Kyoto, Prague, Boston, Stockholm, Peking, and towns and hamlets everywhere.


People came up to talk to Jesus.

If he wore only a loincloth, he was offered a shirt or a coat. If he wore royal robes, others often asked him for a robe to cover their own poverty and need.

Jesus went bareheaded now, without any kind of a crown upon his head. He was offered a haircut, a meal, a place to stay, clothing, help to find a job, or simply companionship as he walked along the street.


The crucified became one of the best-known and most widely discussed matters in the whole world.

"What do you think of when you hear the words 'the crucified'?" a French journalist asked a distinguished professor.

"I think of you and me," replied the professor.

A new sense of compassion was felt by millions of people for
the poor, the downtrodden, the hungry or starving, the sick, the
prisoners, indeed, the victims of life.

Yet it was feared that this would become a mere passing fancy,
a new form of chic, and would not seriously alter the condition
of people who were in great need.

Religious leaders throughout the world reacted in press interviews.

Consternation seemed to have taken control of these leaders,
for their response was verbose and tended not to be understood
by the people.

An archbishop in England said that "perhaps the church has
sinned by overemphasizing the crucifixion of Jesus Christ while
not making relevant the fact of the resurrection to the common
man."

A cardinal in Europe attacked "theological sensationalism"
and issued a call for "pastoral control, intellectual discipline,
existential soberness, and faithfulness at the foot of the cross."

People ignored the religious leaders, preferring to confront
Jesus in the streets and talk to him face-to-face.

On this day in the most powerful nation in all the world, there
was the usual number of suicides, serious crimes, and sales of
hard drugs; more people continued to die in automobile accidents
than in foreign wars; and more money was spent for military
purposes than for food, housing, and education.

The nation had drive-in restaurants and churches; massage
parlors for the living and show-biz burial parlors for the dead; ice
cream in a hundred varieties for the kiddies and unlimited drinks
for everybody else.

It had wealth. It had size. It had glamour.

This country had indeed gained the world. Yet a few Cassandras (who were never very popular, in any event) warned that the nation was losing its soul.

## 2

A couple of years earlier
a very, very rich church—
one that had been built
alongside oil wells and near an
ever sunny ocean—had made a decision.
There must be public signs of faith
for the sake of world-wide evangelism,
it had announced to the press.

The very, very rich church
would make a costly witness to its faith
in Jesus Christ.

The church would rip out its rear wall
and pay great artists
to make a gigantic stained-glass window
to be placed there.
This would be the biggest
and most expensive
stained-glass window in the history
of humankind.
It would be taller than many buildings.
It would show Jesus Christ
on the cross at Golgotha,
crucified between two thieves.

Work on the window
had been pursued vigorously
as if everybody's life
depended on it.

Great artists
were flown in from everywhere.
Soon it became apparent
that the stained-glass window
would be gorgeous.
The window, as executed,
would be a mélange of rich colors.
The thief nailed to the cross
at the left of Jesus
would be swarthy and deep brown;
the thief nailed to the cross
at the right of Jesus would be jet black.
Jesus himself
would be white as ivory or pearl.

The nails piercing Jesus' body
would be of gold;
the blood of Jesus—
a bit on his hands and feet,
and flowing gently from his side—
would be a rich red;
trees in the background
would be a spring green
such as to make even Vivaldi
exclaim in rapture;
the crosses
were to be a memorable mahogany;
and figures of people milling about
in front of the crosses would be portrayed
in vivid colors
reminiscent of a doge's court.

Jesus' loincloth and crown of thorns
would be of burnt gold,
and the sky the same color,
but with an encroaching turbulence
to be suggested by rich purple
and dark reds.

Today the window was finally completed.
Its cost was astronomical
but understood to be a sacrifice
to the glory of God
and a witness to Jesus Christ.
The amount was paid in full
out of the church's endowments.
Now the dedication ceremony
was being held
on this glorious sunny day.
Bishops were present in droves.
The most important one in the assemblage
blessed the window.

TV cameras turned,
reporters spoke into microphones
and jotted down notes,
and the whole world took notice of the
biggest stained-glass window ever made.
There was even a letter of congratulation
sent by the president
of the most powerful nation
in all the world.
"May God bless you," he wrote.
"And may God continue to bless
the most powerful nation
in all the world."

The church was extraordinarily proud
of its stained-glass window.
It had been written up
in all of the national magazines.
Pictures of the window
were seen by people everywhere.
Already mass pop-culture had been
directly affected by the window.
"Stained Glass" was a new rock hit.

"Love in a Stained-Glass World"
had been announced
as a new high-budgeted film.

There were more serious ramifications
of the stained-glass window
in the socio-political sphere.
"It is not a melting pot that we seek,
but a stained-glass-window mosaic,
where everything is together
but maintains its own
peculiar distinctive quality,"
a speaker on race relations had said
a week earlier on national TV.

"We are *all* of us in a moral-ethical
jungle now," a U.S. senator
had said in a recent major speech.
"Yet there can be clean lines
and high purpose
if we will accept the disciplines,
the order, and yes, the grandeur
of living in a stained-glass jungle."

Seats at the dedication ceremony
had been reserved long in advance.
Members of the congregation,
a distinguished cross-section
of the prestigious
and the elite, got in.
So did city officials
and an ecumenical sprinkling
of senior clergy representing
main-line churches and synagogues.
Out-of-town guests
were meticulously drawn from the worlds
of politics, religion,

fashion, entertainment,
the military, the arts, and the media.
No one poor was present.
The only blacks
at the ceremony were famous.
"Father, forgive them;
for they know not what they do,"
exclaimed the preacher
who had been flown in from London
for the occasion.

The preacher's sermon
was based on Jesus' last words
from the cross.

"Truly, I say to you,
today you will be with me in paradise,"
continued the preacher.

The two thieves
in the stained-glass window
looked at Jesus on the cross.

The wife of an industrial tycoon
started perspiring,
and let her mink stole
slide back on the pew.

"Woman,
behold your son!—Behold your mother,"
said the preacher,
continuing Jesus' last words
from the cross.

Constance Perregrine,
seated in the fourteenth row,
thought of her son
who was next to her in the pew.

Did he understand her long sacrifice
in holding the family together?
Was he grateful that she had postponed
getting the divorce
until the time came for him
to go away to college?


Don Perregrine, seated next to his mother,
looked at the preacher
but did not hear him.
He wondered whether he should enroll
next year at Nebraska U.
or Colorado State.


The sun
streamed through the stained-glass window.
"I thirst," said the preacher,
quoting another of Jesus' last words
on the cross.


So do I, thought the president
of the chamber of commerce.
Yet it was extremely comfortable
inside the building,
for the air conditioning
was operating perfectly.


"My God, my God, why hast thou forsaken me?"
continued the preacher.


I think
the color of Christ's blood in the window
is absolutely too red,
altogether too jarring,
the president of an ad agency said to himself.

It *is* a gorgeous window,
thought a well-known author
who had been commissioned to write a prayer
for the occasion.

The well-known author's prayer,
a copy of which had been inserted
in the printed program that was given
to everybody present at the service, said:
"O Thou Who wast nailed to the cross
and hast borne there the sins of the world,
reach out to us wretched sinners,
lift us up to Thee,
refresh us who thirst,
bestow upon us what Thou dost desire,
nail us to our own crosses,
then take out the nails
at Thine own discretion,
and reward us with the gift of paradise
spent with Thee,
O Crucified One Who dost reign
forever and ever. Amen."

The preacher had a mane of white hair
that grew long down the back of his neck,
around which hung an amethyst cross.
"It is finished," he exclaimed,
quoting from Jesus' words on the cross.

People started to think
of the lavish buffet
which would shortly follow
in the baronial parish hall.
The buffet had been catered by Messolini,
who was a new restaurateur
in the community,
both chic and expensive.

"Father,
into thy hands I commit my spirit,"
the preacher said,
completing the words
of Jesus from the cross.

A frail woman
in the sixth row wept silently.
A fat man in the twenty-third row
tried to wipe away a tear
that had run down
his cheek into his mouth, tasting salty.

I wonder whom we will elect
as the next bishop,
thought a robed clergyman.

The organ sounded triumphant
in this moment of glory.

The dedication was finished.

People began to fidget in their pews,
women handling their purses,
men folding the printed programs
and placing these in their coat pockets.
Myrtle Epps, who had made ready
the linens and flowers on the altar
for today's event,
gazed at the stained-glass window.
There was no warning before it happened.
When the window seemed to explode
before her very eyes,
she let out a clear scream.

Jesus, the crucified figure in the center
of the vast window,
simply leapt from the cross
and was gone in the same moment.

All that could be seen
in place of the window was blue sky
and jagged fragments of glass.
In the aisles and pews of the church,
hysteria grew around Myrtle Epps.

When all the people had fled the church,
a scroll was found near the altar
that stood below the demolished
stained-glass window.
On the scroll were written these words:

*"When you give a feast, invite the poor,*
*the maimed, the lame, the blind."*

In the choir loft a second scroll
was shortly discovered
by a member of the choir
who had left behind a small purse,
and came back to retrieve it.

*"Do not lay up for yourselves treasures*
*on earth, where moth and rust consume*
*and where thieves break in and steal,*
*but lay up for yourselves*
*treasures in heaven,*
*where neither moth nor rust consumes*
*and where thieves*
*do not break in and steal,"*
the scroll announced.

*"For where your treasure is,*
*there will your heart be also."*

*3*

Jesus, who had escaped from the stained-glass window, was seen hitch-hiking the next day on Highway 23 not far from the church.

Someone said that he was going to join the migrant farm workers.


The thousands of Jesuses who had come down from crosses and leapt out of church windows all over the world now stayed at YMCAs while they sought temporary employment as laborers.

All the crosses in all of the churches were empty.

Thousands of stained-glass windows were shattered.

"The church preached the resurrection," said an old priest. "Now it is confronted by it."


People were confronted everywhere by a Jesus who broke bread in the form of a hamburger bun and drank coffee at counters alongside them. They saw a Jesus who smiled, told a story, and listened to someone else's.

Instead of being nailed to a cross eternally, Jesus did a hard day's work.

He helped to repair a subway, carried trays of dishes, washed floors of office buildings late at night, and cooked meals in steamy kitchens.

Jesus sold tickets in a bus terminal, repaired leaking roofs on houses, collected garbage, and even enrolled for night courses in order to obtain a high school diploma.


It was inside a church in Moscow that an altogether new phenomenon—one that would come to be known by women, men, and children in every corner of the globe—was first observed.


Katerina Palov had been absorbed in her private devotions inside the Moscow church.

Now she looked toward a cross that had once borne Jesus. But to her amazement she saw a body on the cross.

Katerina noticed something very unfamiliar about the body.

When she drew close to the cross, Katerina discovered that a young black man was firmly nailed to the wood.

He did not look like Jesus. He was fully dressed in some kind of a striped uniform.

Investigators discovered that the young black man on the cross was a convict who was serving forty years in a South African prison because he had stolen food from a store in order to feed his starving family.

He did not have a passport. Soviet authorities moved for his immediate extradition.

A handwritten scroll found at the foot of the cross inside the Moscow church contained these words:

> *"Truly, I say to you, as you did it to one of the least of these, my brethren, you did it to me.*

The scroll continued:

> *"I was hungry and you gave me no food, I was thirsty and you gave me no drink, I was a stranger and you did not welcome me, naked and you did not clothe me, sick and in prison and you did not visit me."*

It was 3:45 P.M. when Clara Morris stopped off for a moment of prayer in a church on Wilshire Boulevard in Los Angeles.

She was startled to see a body upon a cross, for she was aware that now all crosses were empty.

Drawing close, she saw a brown woman and heard her crying.

The woman was identified as an "Untouchable" who lived in Bombay.

Twelve hours later inside a church in Addis Ababa, a white youth was found nailed to an altar cross that had previously borne Jesus.

The youth told the Ethiopian Red Cross that he lived in Evanston, Illinois. His parents beat him very badly when they had had too much to drink.

There were scars of beatings on his body and his left eye was swollen shut.

So, people began to see that they crucified one another.

Could they stop visiting agonies and terrors upon each other's lives? It dawned upon them that when they placed Jesus on the cross, they also placed one another on it.

Could they let the cross be empty?

Hubert Lacey stopped inside a church near Fleet Street in London.

He wanted to say a prayer for his wife who was dying of cancer. Lacey had only a few moments to spare from his job. Indeed, he was out on assignment to interview a Hollywood actress for the newspaper where he worked as a reporter.

But a cross inside the church held a body.

It was that of a young woman from Dallas who was pregnant.

Lacey learned from Susan, the young woman, that her family had angrily kicked her out when they found that she was going to have a baby although she was unmarried.

They told Susan that her condition deeply offended their religious beliefs, and they felt that she was damned and therefore no more a member of their family whom they could love.

The reporter picked up a scroll near the cross and read its words:

> *Judge not, that you be not judged. For with the judgment you pronounce you will be judged, and the measure you give will be the measure you get.*

Nancy Fitzhugh had decided when she got up this morning to spend an hour or so alone in one of her favorite places, the Museum of Art.

Now she was walking slowly through the gallery, absorbed in her thoughts.

She would go up to the third floor and visit one of her most prized exhibits. It was a medieval processional cross designed in tempera and gold on wood. The Italian artist had lived in the fifteenth century.

Once Jesus had been crucified on the cross, his arms stretched out upon the wood, his hands nailed down. Of course, Jesus had recently left the cross, so Nancy would miss seeing him, but she would still have a feeling of spiritual uplift from looking at the old cross itself.

She climbed the stairs to the gallery on the third floor of the art museum.

Nancy walked into the gallery and found the glass case.

The cross was not empty.

A woman dressed in furs and wearing jewels was on the cross. She was drunk.

Investigators discovered that the woman was married to one of the richest and most famous men in the city.

He had given his wife all the money that she could desire, jewels, homes, servants, cars, and a yacht.

But he could never spare her his valuable time.

His wife had felt desperately alone in the midst of people who were paid to keep her company. Love was a mystery to her.

In the glass case a scroll was found and it said:

*You cannot serve God and mammon.*

When Manuel González walked inside a small rural church in Mexico, he sought a priest.

He found Joe English on the big wooden cross that had once held Jesus.

Joe lived in Cleveland, worked as an insurance salesman, supported his wife and five children, and told the Mexican authorities that he had lost the meaning of life. All that he did was work, pay higher prices and taxes, and grow increasingly isolated from his family. He could not communicate with his wife and children.

Lately he had come to hate his job but he knew no other way to earn a living. He was behind in payments. He spent two full hours each day on a noisy and smelly highway driving to and from his office.

Joe went to church for the sake of his family, but he no longer believed in anything. He drank and ate too much. Joe asked for psychiatric help when they got his body down from the cross.

A scroll found underneath Joe's cross contained these words:

*Consider the lilies of the field, how they grow; they
neither toil nor spin; yet I tell you, even Solomon in all
his glory was not arrayed like one of these. But if God
so clothes the grass of the field, which today is alive and
tomorrow is thrown into the oven, will he not much
more clothe you . . . ?*

Inside a jail in a country that had been seized by a military
regime, a political prisoner was subjected once again to torture.

He cried out helplessly, struggling to endure excruciating
pain.

His torturers were all loyal members of the church.

A cross hung on the wall of the room in which he was tortured.

A military chaplain knew that the prisoner was the victim of
men who acted under orders, for the chaplain served the same
command.

Afterward the prisoner lay on the floor of his cell. He felt that
he could bear no more of such savage pain. He fainted.

His torturers were now inside the room where the man had
suffered his agony.

One of them glanced at the cross and he screamed in panic. The
others recoiled in terror from what they saw.

The prisoner whom they had tortured hung upon the cross.

A scroll beneath the cross said:

*Blessed are the merciful, for they shall obtain mercy.*

Brenda Hayes drove to a suburban church for a benefit society
luncheon that would be followed by a fashion show. She would
meet most of her friends there.

Walking toward the parish house where the luncheon would
be served, she looked inside the church. Then Brenda noticed a
hole in the stained-glass window which had held Jesus on the
cross. Jesus was gone.

A tiny figure hung on a cross in the jagged, half-empty space.
She was an emaciated, starving child.

Near the stained-glass window Brenda saw a scroll. It contained these words:

> *Blessed are you poor, for yours is the Realm of God.*
> *Blessed are you that hunger now, for you shall be sat-*
> *isfied. Blessed are you that weep now, for you shall*
> *laugh.* "

In Toronto, Kate Longmans dropped into a church to light a candle and say a prayer.

She found Jacob Reuben, who lived in Chicago, on the cross. He told her that he was a practicing Jew, and had been harassed and persecuted because of his faith. Christians crucified him because he was a Jew.

A scroll found near Jacob Reuben's cross contained these words:

> *Who are my mother and my brothers?—Here are my*
> *mother and my brothers! Whoever does the will of God*
> *is my brother, and sister, and mother.*

The college chapel was empty when Brian Dobbs entered quietly.

He took a seat in one of the pews on the left side of the chapel. It was finals week, and this place would afford him privacy and a peaceful opportunity to study for his next day's exams.

But he was startled to hear someone softly crying.

Then he saw a figure hanging on the distant cross that stood upon the altar.

Brian drew close to the cross.

Eugene Moore hung on it. He explained that he was seventy-six years old. His three children were married and had families of their own, so they had no place for him.

Now he lived in a rotting hotel in a crime-ridden downtown section of Detroit. The elderly and sick people who occupied the rooms of the hotel were often mugged and robbed during the day, and were afraid to walk on the streets at night.

Eugene Moore did not have enough money to eat properly.

He had been rejected and felt very, very tired and without hope.

A scroll that lay on the college chapel altar contained these handwritten words:

*Foxes have holes, and birds of the air have nests; but the*
*Son of man has nowhere to lay his head.*


Certain crucifixions were more mysterious than others. Nurse Veronique de Saussune began her day at the Paris hospital by dropping into the chapel to meditate for a few moments.

When she pushed open the chapel door, immediately she saw a man upon the altar cross.

Tubes ran into his nostrils, arms, and legs.

He was from Rome and was dying of cancer.

The pain caused by his illness showed itself in the agony marked on his face.

The man on the cross told Nurse Veronique de Saussune that his suffering was redeemed and given meaning because Jesus had already suffered and died on the cross for him.

A scroll found in the hospital chapel read:

> *Enter by the narrow gate; for the gate is wide and the*
> *way is easy, that leads to destruction, and those who*
> *enter it are many. For the gate is narrow and the way*
> *is hard, that leads to life, and those who find it are*
> *few.*


### 4


People wanted very earnestly
to stop crucifying each other.
They honestly preferred loving to hating,
life instead of death,
and clearly perceived the harm
that they had brought to others as well as
to themselves.
It occurred to them
that they had apparently
paid lip-service to Christianity
without taking it very seriously
or even considering the possibility
of actually practicing it.

They saw how they had used
the cross as a symbol
in their churches' stained-glass windows
and on their altars, yet had not delved
at all deeply into its real meanings.
They had wanted to find out
what the crucifixion
of Jesus Christ really meant.

Now they wanted to know what the resurrection
of Jesus Christ really meant.
Jesus' seven last words from the cross
were universally examined.
"Father, forgive them;
for they know not what they do."

It was understood by an ever-increasing
number of people that sin
was not something
to be superficially equated
with sexuality,
as they had previously been taught.
More and more people were able to see
that the greatest sin
was probably an exaggerated form
of self-preoccupation
that simply shut out God
and everybody else.
The question was raised:
Could the very unawareness of such sin
be the gravest of sin?

"Truly, I say to you,
today you will be with me in paradise."

Acceptance now came to be offered
more freely to others.
For everybody
had to confront the question:

Who is worthy?
Who is unworthy?
Scrolls were found in subways,
bus terminals,
and supermarkets that contained
only these words:
*"Love your enemies."*

A deeper human relationship
came to be affirmed.
"Woman,
behold your son!—Behold your mother!"

People felt
a deeper belonging to one another.
Love came to be comprehended
as a responsibility, even a commandment,
and not just something
to make one feel better.

"I thirst."

Need was no longer perceived so selfishly
as it had been before.
Universal need was seen more clearly
in its many ramifications.
People asked:
"Who is my brother or sister?"
"Who is my neighbor?"

"My God, my God,
why hast thou forsaken me?"

People who had fallen into a sense of
being utterly abandoned
now gave voice to their feelings
and awareness of existence itself.

They cried to God:
for justice, for explanation.
They cried to other people for
sharing and love:
Brother, sister, where are you?

"It is finished."

A new sense of accomplishment and pride
came to the elderly and others
who had done their best,
run their course faithfully,
completed a hard but necessary task,
or stuck with a problem
that required infinite patience.
Countless people gained a new respect
for others as well as themselves.
In fact, they recognized Jesus
in members of their families, friends,
acquaintances, and strangers.
Too, they recognized Jesus in themselves
and so ceased to hate themselves
and be swallowed up in guilt and despair.

Jesus' last words from the cross,
"Into thy hands I commit my spirit,"
now provided a tremendous reassurance
to countless people.

This was seen as an affirmation of faith
in which they could share.
Soon people began to see that they
could make Jesus' resurrection a reality
in their own lives and those of others.
So, crucifixion and resurrection
were not abstractions
or events buried in the past.

Crucifixion happened now.

Resurrection happened now.

## 5

It was an excellent time in the lives of a great many people. Faith came to be actually practiced more and more in everyday life. Hope was genuine, rooted in an understanding of the resurrection.

Love abounded, as crucifixions became few and far between.

But now evil struck with relentless terror.

A sudden war left cities in waste, many thousands of lives destroyed, homes leveled, and unspeakable brutality practiced on the living.

A wave of persecution, imprisonment, torture, and utter regimentation of life swept the world. There was horror in the skies and on the earth.

Many could scarcely remember when there had been hope, beauty, and love.

An official pronouncement said that all expressions of faith must be rooted out without delay.

The state wanted pragmatism to exist in the place of mystery, grinding obedience where there had once been freedom of the spirit.

Faith? No place was allowed for it in the superstate. Indeed, faith, hope, and love were seen as subversive. People were now required to base their existence only on total submission to authority, disciplined action in the present, and the proper performance of prescribed roles.

All faiths represented in society were punished.

Followers of Jesus, however, were attacked with the utmost violence. This was because of Jesus' deep involvement in human life, culminating in his crucifixion and resurrection.

Jesus' action established the primacy of the Realm of God over the state, and offered eternal hope.

So, the memory of Jesus was to be eradicated from everyone's consciousness. It was commanded that all crosses should be destroyed.

Crosses were smashed, chopped up, thrown upon bonfires that also consumed Bibles, or melted in furnaces.

A few crosses were saved and hidden, but at the cost of terrible risk for the people who were involved.

The very idea of God as Lover, entering into human life and dying for the sake of people's salvation, then being resurrected from the dead and representing the Realm of God as an eternal homeland which had even greater power than the state, was anathema.

A scroll found in a public place said:

*In the world you have tribulation; but be of good cheer,*
*I have overcome the world.*


Followers of Jesus were publicly placed on trial, privately tortured.

But their faith persisted and grew stronger.

Earlier when the Jesuses had come down from all the crosses, and entered into the resurrection stream of life, they had set in motion a new force that could not be resisted by all the powers available to the state authorities.

For millions of people had learned how to see the reality of Jesus' presence in one another's lives.

Crosses were drawn with pencils on state posters that were publicly exhibited.

Chalk marks in the form of crosses were everywhere on pavements and walls of buildings.

"Emmanuel, God with us" was painted in red on a public utility building.

Scrolls were found. They said:

*Love your enemies.*

And also:

*Lo, I am with you always.*

People walking along the streets sometimes whispered to others, friends and strangers alike, "Hello, Jesus."

The idea of Jesus as a thirty-year-old man who had long hair and wore a long robe was no longer a part of people's consciousness.

For, of course, they saw Jesus in one another.

A stranger on a street passed a stout, white, middle-aged man wearing a double-breasted business suit and carrying a briefcase, and said, "Hello, Jesus."

A janitor walked past the desk of a black woman who was the manager of an office and said, "Hello, Jesus."

A lonely, solitary woman who had worked for thirty years in a building where no one had ever been her friend now found herself surrounded by friends.

An elderly man who had once been a religious leader, and suffered from spiritual pride although he looked humble, was quietly helped by new friends to free himself from the old shackles and be a new person in Jesus.

People shared food and clothing, conversation and books, transportation and hope.

More scrolls were found in public places. One said,

> *Truly, truly, I say to you, unless a grain of wheat falls*
> *into the earth and dies, it remains alone; but if it dies,*
> *it bears much fruit.*

Small groups gathered together for worship and meditation in rooms and apartments.

They took turns reading Scripture aloud to each other, prayed from their own hearts, hummed or very, very quietly sang beloved old hymns that were forbidden. They swung an incense pot if they liked, sometimes even went so far as to place lighted candles on a table or a mantel.

If one such group was arrested, a dozen new ones sprung up.

The followers of Jesus were listed as subversives because their ultimate allegiance was to the Realm of God and its tenets of belief rather than to the authoritarian state.

Enraged and baffled, authorities of the state announced that a public execution would take place in the great square at the center of the capital city.

A twenty-three-year-old follower of Jesus would be crucified.

While the authorities knew that they were conjuring up images highly dangerous to the state by utilizing the cross for this execution, their anger overrode wise counsel.

On the announced day of the execution, ten thousand people crowded into the city square.

Thousands more filled the nearby streets.

The authorities brought in their victim and prepared to place her on the cross.

"Crucify us!" the cry started from the crowd.

Within moments ten thousand people shouted in unison.

"Crucify us!" "Crucify us!"

Thousands more in the streets echoed their cry.

Soldiers now turned their guns upon the people.

"Crucify us!" the thousands chanted.

"Crucify us!"

"Crucify us!"

Some of the soldiers now wept openly. They began to throw their weapons on the ground.

Other soldiers embraced people in the chanting crowd.

The power of the state was broken.

A new order had come into being.

## 6

Everywhere people who had stopped trying to make needed changes in life, strive for God's justice on earth, and discern beauty before their eyes, decided to try once more.

And people who had never really given up, but often felt discouraged or even despairing, decided that they would try harder.

They would try harder to embrace faith, letting it open up closed rooms and ghettos of their lives.

They would try harder to nurture hope, letting it combat an ever-encroaching malaise of cynicism that threatened life.

They would try harder to accept and give love.

A scroll was found in a public place. Its handwritten message read:

*Alleluia!*

# Haunted House

There is a haunted house in my head
    I am so many different people
    have so many different ghosts
    have carried so much luggage into the house
    trunks, anxiety, joy, hurt
    victories, failures, boxes
    yearnings, hopes, packages
    attic filled, basement overflowing
    walls cluttered with pictures close to each other
    books stacked, old newspapers piled
    heavy pieces of furniture in the way
    why, you can't dance here anymore

Pieces that comprise
    what is known as life
    car keys
    office keys
    desk keys
    house keys
    social security number
    pills
    photographs
    telephone numbers
    credit cards
    a jigger of fear
    a dash of loneliness
    I have to hurry now

On a quiet rainy afternoon
    visit the attic
    look through a cardboard box
    filled with old letters and papers
    my grandmother's recipe for jelly roll
    3 eggs, 1/2 cup sugar
    2/3 cup flour, 3/4 tsp. baking powder
    butter a shallow pan
    bake in a quick oven
    postcards Jean sent from the Greek Islands
    the last letter from my father
    before he died, his writing wobbly,
    not so firm as before his illness
    "I love you dearly, son"

I talk to trees
    two baleful
    but secretly loving eyes
    peer at me from a sturdy trunk
    we have conversed in winter
    in snowdrifts
    I have walked beneath
    thick clusters of leaves,
    green turned to copper by strong sunlight,
    to sit by my friend in summer
    another tree is a prima donna
    her bewitching shape, bereft of lavish foliage
    amid winter ice, retains poised lines
    a bare hint of aristocratic madness
    I pay homage, remembering
    her costumed glory in August
    these friends never betrayed my trust
    engaged in idle gossip, cause me pain
    I respect their wisdom
    they forgive my youth

I look through a window
    at snow and ice on the ground

suddenly a rabbit darts in view
trembling, it pauses beside a frozen bush
the rabbit lives in the grip of the unknown
so do I
a nuclear war would destroy us both
its tiny gray body
and mine—larger, differently formed
vulnerable together
on the face of the earth
if people want to destroy themselves
let them take a vote
among the animals,
flowers and trees
any decision to die
should be a democratic one

When I was in high school
a friend and I
ate an eight-course Italian dinner
then went to see the movie *Stanley and Livingstone*
knew I was getting sick
hated to miss part of the film
the sickness was upon me
when Spencer Tracy said
"Dr. Livingstone, I presume"
spared no one within reach
in the row ahead
cries and the sound of rushing feet
drowned out Stanley and Livingstone
my friend and I made our way out
a hundred people stood in line
at the box office when
I violated the mosaic floor
of the movie holy of holies
consternation broke its bonds
my friend and I fled up the street
with the alacrity of pickpockets,
the zeal of converts

# Epilogue: Talking to Myself

I talk to Myself more than I used to.

I am aware time is running out.

These are the best times, *so live them,* I tell Myself.

"You know damned well they're not the best times," says Myself. "You're over the hill, a sad spectacle of prolonged mid-life crisis. Why don't you find a place in the sun, quit caring, shut up about controversies, give up your pose of meaning, and just enjoy the bones?"

At such a moment Myself tempts me. But I believe he is wrong.

"That would never work," I tell Myself. "Die in the saddle, that's the best way. I admit I feel a certain sadness about things lost. Present shock intrudes in my life. I strongly dislike indifference and cruelty. I prefer peace, but find war.

"However, that's not the whole story. I'm open to new ideas and people more than I ever was. I'm more sensitive and aware. I know what somebody else is thinking; I can listen. I *want* to listen, to understand, to become friends. You want me to put away these skills and give up just when I'm coming truly alive and appreciate what life's all about."

Myself looks at me, tips his coffee cup, and smiles sardonically.

"You're going to die, Malcolm."

Cup is placed on saucer for effect. The moment of silence expands in the room.

"Look, I don't know when," Myself continues. "But you've already started to read the orbits differently, looking for familiar names. You're no spring chicken even if you still get into those tight jeans and a lilliputian-size, undignified loincloth to swim.

When you don't see yourself as ridiculous, others do. You're not young anymore. The moment is coming, let's face it, when you're going to kick off."

"Damn it, so are you," I respond. "So is everybody. What has that to do with me? What's your point?"

Myself reaches out and gently touches my arm.

"Don't get so defensive and angry. I didn't mean to hurt you. I'm just trying to get you to look at reality."

"Reality?" I shout. "Dying is a part of living. I can live to ninety, to a hundred. Why make me carry the extra baggage about dying? Don't I have enough baggage now?"

We've squared off and aren't speaking again. I'm mad. Myself is a bastard to have around at moments like this one.

"Okay, don't get sore," says Myself. "You're a nice guy. You even stopped putting that stupid black dye on your hair. You've owned up to being gray. Good. I admire that."

"I'm gray because I want to be gray," I respond. "I think you conveniently forget that. Don't patronize me. But I still think it's sexist that an older woman is allowed her hair color and expected to fix her eyes and the rest of it, and an older man isn't. Sexist."

"Older. You said it yourself, Malcolm."

Myself laughs.

"You're still edgy, despite your protest that you've found idyllic peace. Do you remember where you lost your sense of humor, Malcolm?"

"I didn't. You know that."

But it's too late. I made the mistake of biting the bait.

"Come off it," Myself says. "If I hurt your feelings, I'm sorry."

"I get a little tired of being the strong one all the time," I tell him. "You forget the bad times. Why do you make me say this, tell you this? Can't you quietly accept and comfort me?"

"I know you've suffered, been lonely, tried and failed again. Feel better? If you want to talk about it, I won't go away. But can you at least keep it interesting? After all, I've got feelings, too."

# Index